Decade II:
An Anniversary Anthology

Edited by
Julián Olivares and Evangelina Vigil-Piñón

Arte Público Press
Houston
Texas
1993

This book is made possible through a grant from the National Endowment for the Arts, a federal agency, the Lila Wallace-Reader's Digest Fund and the Andrew W. Mellon Foundation.

Arte Público Press
University of Houston
Houston, Texas 77204-2090

Cover design by Mark Piñón

Decade II: an anniversary anthology / edited by Julián Olivares.
    p.   cm.
    ISBN 1-55885-062-7 : $12.00
    1. American literature—Hispanic American authors.   2. Hispanic Americans—Literary collections. 3. American literature—20th century. I. Olivares, Julián, 1941   . II. Title: Decade 2. III. Title: Decade two.
PS508.H57D43 1992
810.8'0868–dc20   92-35458

                                                                              CIP

The paper used in this publication meets the requirements of the American National Standard for Permanence of Paper for Printed Library Materials Z39.48-1984. ∞

Contents

Introduction   6

Prose

Helen María Viramontes *Miss Clairol*   9

Nicholasa Mohr   *An Awakening ... Summer 1956*   14

Alberto Ríos   *The Birthday of Mrs. Piñeda*   20

Alejandro Morales   *Cara de caballo*   29

Roberto Fernández   *Raining Backwards*   33

Nash Candelaria   *Affirmative Action*   39

Ed Vega   *Mayonesa Peralta*   47

Lionel García   *The Day They Took My Uncle*   57

Roberta Fernández   *Andrea*   66

Arturo Mantecón   *The Cardinal Virtues of Demetrio Huerta* 84

Judith Ortiz Cofer   *The Black Virgin*   94

Guillermo Reyes   *Miss Consuelo*   100

Rima de Vallbona   *La tejedora de palabras*   116

Pablo La Rosa   *Chronicle of the Argonaut Polypus*   124
Elías Miguel Muñoz   *Carta de Julio*   130

Rosaura Sánchez   *Tres generaciones*   137

Poetry

Sandra María Estevez   *Amor negro*   144
                        Portraits for Shamsul Alam   145
                        Transference   147

Ángela de Hoyos   *Ten Dry Summers Ago*   149
                         How to Eat Crow on a
                            Cold Sunday Morning   150
                         Ramillete para Elena Poniatowska   151
                         When Conventional Methods Fail   152

Judith Ortiz Cofer   *La fe*   153
                         El olvido   154
                         So Much for Mañana   155
                         The Latin Deli   156

Achy Obejas   *Kimberle*   158
                         Sugarcane   159

Evangelina Vigil-Piñón   *The Bridge People*   161
                         Dumb Broad!   163
                         Telephone Line   166

Yvonne Sapia   *Del medio del sueño*   169
                         La Mujer, Her Back to the Spectator   170
                         La desconocida   171
                         Defining the Grateful Gesture   172
                         Aquí   174

Pat Mora   *Bailando*   175
                         Elena   176

Martín Espada   *David Leaves the Saints for Paterson*   177
                         Colibrí   178
                         The Words of the Mute Are
                            Like Silver Dollars   180
                         Shaking Hands with Mongo   181

Alberto Ríos   *Five Indiscretions, or*   182
                         On January 5, 1984, El Santo
                            the Wrestler Died, Possibly   187

Jimmy-Santiago Baca   *Martín III*   189

Luis Omar Salinas   *What Is My Name?*   194
                         Nights in Fresno   195
                         When the Evening Is Quiet   196
                         Middle Age   197
                         Sweet Drama   198
                         Poem for Ernesto Trejo   199

Ray González	*Walk*	200
	Two Wolf Poems	201
Tato Laviera	*Latero Story*	203
	Viejo	205
	Melao	207
	Bochinche Bilingüe	208
Lucha Corpi	*Invernario*	209
	Fuga	210
	Canción de invierno	212
Ricardo Sánchez	*En-ojitos: canto a Piñero*	213
	Notas a Federico García Lorca	215
Caroline Hospital	*Dear Tía*	223
	Papa	224
Diana Rivera	*Learning to Speak*	225
Pablo Medina	*Madame America*	229
	The Apostate	232
Lorna Dee Cervantes	*The Poet Is Served Her Papers*	233
	Blue Full Moon in Witch	234
	From the Cables of Genocide	235
	On Love and Hunger	236
	The Captive's Verses	237
Leo Romero	*I Bring Twins Over to Meet Pito*	238
	How Did I Land Up in this City	240
	Pito Had a Dream That	241
	Diane's Knocking	244
	When Pito Tried to Kill	245
Rane Arroyo	*Blonde as a Bat*	248
	Columbus's Children	251
Gustavo Pérez Firmat	*Lime Cure*	253
	The Poet's Mother Gave Him a Birthday Present	254
Amalio Madueño	*Alambrista*	255
	The Bato Prepares for Winter	256

Decade II: An Anniversary Anthology is a select collection from *Revista Chicano-Riqueña/The Americas Review* during the decade 1983–1992, and a celebration of the Twentieth Anniversary of the founding of the most important U.S. Hispanic literary magazine. In 1973 Luis Dávila and Nicolás Kanellos, at Indiana University, began a quarterly literary magazine dedicated to Latino literary expression. It was called *Revista Chicano-Riqueña,* and counted among its first contributors Luis Leal, Tomás Rivera and Tino Villanueva. Through the determination of the founding editors and the talent displayed on its pages, *RCR* became the most important Latino magazine and, in 1986, became *The Americas Review.* Furthermore, out of *RCR* emerged, in 1979, Arte Público Press, whose inaugural publication was *La Carreta Made a U-Turn,* by Tato Laviera. Arte Público Press now publishes twenty five books yearly by major and emerging talent, and enjoys universal recognition.

In its early and struggling years, grants from the Coordinating Council of Literary Magazines made it possible for the magazine to survive; and since 1976 *RCR/TAR* has received continuous support from the National Endowment for the Arts, for which we are extremely grateful. Recognition of the magazine's success came in 1979 when Nicolás Kanellos received the Outstanding Editor Award from CCLM, and again in 1980 when he received similar accolades from MELUS, the Society for the Study of Multiethnic Literature of the Modern Language Association. Under the banner of *The Americas Review*, the present editors—who joined the staff in 1981, along with José D. Saldívar 1982–'87—received in 1986 the Citation of Achievement for Editorial Excellence and Vision from CCLM. Of three-hundred literary reviews, only ten received this distinction, which was repeated in 1987.

Revista Chicano-Riqueña left Indiana in December, 1979, when Nicolás Kanellos accepted a professorial appointment at the University of Houston, at which time Arte Público Press emerged and began to prosper. Considerable impetus and assistance for *RCR/* Arte Público Press came in 1984 from the NEA Advancement/Challenge Grant Program, not only in the form of financial assistance but also through the literary and marketing consultation provided by the NEA. It was at this time that we began to contemplate a name change for the magazine. *Revista Chicano-Riqueña* was a tongue-twister for librarians, upon whom many subscriptions depended. A decisive factor, however, was the ever increasing literary contributions of other Hispanic groups, primarily Cuban Americans. Thus, in order to embrace all under one banner, the magazine became, in 1986, *The Americas Review: A Review of Hispanic Literature and Art of the USA*, now a triquarterly publication, which included a special double issue.

For twenty years *RCR/TAR* has been a vanguard literary review. In its pages first appeared writers who would develop into the major U. S. Hispanic writers: Julia Álvarez, Jimmy Santiago Baca, Ana Castillo, Lorna Dee Cervantes, Denise Chávez, Sandra Cisneros, Roberta Fernández, Rolando Hinojosa-Smith, Ángela de Hoyos, Tato Laviera, Miguel Piñero, Alberto Ríos, Tomás Rivera, Luis Omar Salinas, Ricardo Sánchez, Ed Vega, Evangelina Vigil-Piñón, Tino Villanueva, María Helena Viramontes—and on and on. Writers whose contributions in the magazine received awards include Gary Soto, Pushcart Prize; and Luis Omar Salinas, General Electric Younger Writer Award. Numerous selections from the magazine have been reprinted in texts and anthologies; and with this Anniversary Anthology, we celebrate another milestone and pay special tribute to a select group of writers.

A feature that began in *RCR* and that has become a frequent format in the past decade is the simultaneous publication of a special issue and book revolving around a single theme. Under the masthead of *Revista Chicano Riqueña*, in 1979, appeared the stellar *Nuevos Pasos: Chicano and Puerto Rican Drama*—which featured the collaboration of Guest Editor Jorge Huerta, followed in 1982 by *A Decade of Hispanic Literature: An Anniversary Anthology,* featuring the best of *Revista Chicano-Riqueña* since its founding; and in 1983 appeared the ground-breaking *Woman of Her Word: Hispanic Women Write,* edited by Evangelina Vigil. The final special *RCR* issue/book was *International Studies in Honor of Tomás Rivera,* 1985, a *festschrift* for a major writer and a founding contributing editor who passed away in 1984.

A feature that appeared under the banner of *The Americas Review* was the increased advancement of critical appreciation of U.S. Hispanic literature, again in the form of simultaneous publications. Foremost among these are: *The Rolando Hinojosa Reader* (1986); *Charting New Frontiers in American Literature: Chicana Creativity and Expression* (1987/1988), guest-edited by María Herrera-Sobek and Helena María Viramontes; and, focusing on the literature of exile, *Paradise Lost or Gained?: The Literature of Hispanic Exile,* with Guest Editors Fernando Alegría and Jorge Ruffinelli.

Now at the end of our second decade, we celebrate the select writers of this period with *Decade II: An Anniversary Anthology.* From the first anniversary*Decade* there are fourteen writers who have repeated their literary accomplishment: Ed Vega, Rosaura Sánchez, Jimmy Santiago Baca, Lorna Dee Cervantes, Lucha Corpi, Sandra Esteves, Ángela de Hoyos, Tato Laviera, Leo Romero, Luis Omar Salinas, Ricardo Sánchez, Evangelina Vigil, Nash Candelaria, Roberta Fernández. The remaining selections in *Decade II: An Anniversary Anthology* are authored by twenty-seven new and younger voices which speak of new experiences and from fresh perspectives, enriching and enlarging the horizon of U.S. Hispanic Literature. As we look forward to our next decade and third anniversary, we hope there will be repeats from both groups, and aspire for a greater future of new voices.

Julián Olivares   *Evangelina Vigil-Piñón*

Miss Clairol

Arlene and Champ walk to K-Mart. The store is full of bins mounted with bargain buys from T-shirts to rubber sandals. They go to aisle 23, Cosmetics. Arlene, wearing bell bottom jeans two sizes too small, can't bend down to the Miss Clairol boxes.

"Which one amá" asks Champ, chewing her thumb nail.

"Shit, m'ija, I dunno." Arlene smacks her gum, contemplating the decision. "Maybe I need a change, tú sabes. What do you think?" She holds up a few blond strands with black roots. Arlene has burned the softness of her hair with peroxide; her hair is stiff, breaks at the ends and she needs plenty of Aqua Net hairspray to tease and tame her ratted hair, then folds it back into a high lump behind her head. For the last few months she has been a platinum "Light Ash" blond, before that a Miss Clairol "Flame" redhead, before that Champ couldn't even identify the color—somewhere between orange and brown, a "Sun Bronze." The only way Champ knows her mother's true hair color is by her roots which, like death, inevitably rise to the truth.

"I hate it, tú sabes, when I can't decide." Arlene is wearing a pink, strapless tube top. Her stomach spills over the hip hugger jeans. Spits the gum onto the floor. "Fuck it." And Champ follows her to the rows of nail polish, next to the Maybelline rack of make-up, across the false eyelashes that look like insects on display in clear, plastic boxes. Arlene pulls out a particular color of nailpolish, looks at the bottom of the bottle for the price, puts it back, gets another. She has a tattoo of purple XXX's on her left finger like a ring. She finally settles for a purple-blackish color, Ripe Plum, that Champ thinks looks like the color of Frankenstein's nails. She looks at her own stubby nails, chewed and gnawed.

Walking over to the eyeshadows, Arlene slowly slinks out another stick of gum from her back pocket, unwraps and crumbles the wrapper into a little ball, lets it drop on the floor. Smacks the gum.

"Grandpa Ham used to make chains with these gum wrappers" she says, toeing the wrapper on the floor with her rubber sandals, her toes dotted with old nailpolish. "He started one, tú sabes, that went from room to room. That was before he went nuts" she says, looking at the price of magenta eyeshadow. "¿Sabes qué? What do you think?" lifting the eye shadow to

9

Champ.

"I dunno know" responds Champ, shrugging her shoulders the way she always does when she is listening to something else, her own heartbeat, what Gregorio said on the phone yesterday, shrugs her shoulders when Miss Smith says OFELIA, answer my question. She is too busy thinking of things people otherwise dismiss like parentheses, but sticks to her like gum, like a hole on a shirt, like a tattoo, and sometimes she wishes she weren't born with such adhesiveness. The chain went from room to room, round and round like a web, she remembers. That was before he went nuts.

"Champ. You listening? Or in lala land again?" Arlene has her arms akimbo on a fold of flesh, pissed.

"I said, I dunno know." Champ whines back, still looking at the wrapper on the floor.

"Well you better learn, tú sabes, and fast too. Now think, will this color go good with Pancha's blue dress?" Pancha is Arlene's comadre. Since Arlene has a special date tonight, she lent Arlene her royal blue dress that she keeps in a plastic bag at the end of her closet. The dress is made of chiffon, with satin-like material underlining, so that when Arlene first tried it on and strutted about, it crinkled sounds of elegance. The dress fits too tight. Her plump arms squeeze through, her hips breathe in and hold their breath, the seams do all they can to keep the body contained. But Arlene doesn't care as long as it sounds right.

"I think it will" Champ says, and Arlene is very pleased.

"Think so? So do I m'ija."

They walk out the double doors and Champ never remembers her mother paying.

*   *   *

It is four in the afternoon, but already Arlene is preparing for the date. She scrubs the tub, Art Labo on the radio, drops crystals of Jean Naté into the running water, lemon scent rises with the steam. The bathroom door ajar, she removes her top and her breasts flop and sag, pushes her jeans down with some difficulty, kicks them off, and steps in the tub.

"M'ija. M'IJA" she yells. "M'ija, give me a few bobby pins." She is worried about her hair frizzing and so wants to pin it up.

Her mother's voice is faint because Champ is in the clóset. There are piles of clothes on the floor, hangers thrown askew and tangled, shoes all piled up or thrown on the top shelf. Champ is looking for her mother's special dress. Pancha says every girl has one at the end of her closet.

"Goddamn it, Champ."

Amidst the dirty laundry, the black hole of the closet, she finds nothing. "NOW"

"All right, ALL RIGHT. Cheeze amá, stop yelling" says Champ, and goes in the steamy bathroom, checks the drawers, hairbrushes jump out, rollers, strands of hair, rummages through bars of soap, combs, eyeshadows, finds nothing; pulls open another drawer, powder, empty bottles of oil, manicure scissors, Kotex, dye instructions crinkled and botched, finally, a few bobby pins.

After Arlene pins up her hair, she asks Champ, "¿Sabes qué? Should I wear my hair up? Do I look good with it up?" Champ is sitting on the toilet.

"Yea, amá, you look real pretty."

"Thanks m'ija" says Arlene, "¿Sabes qué? When you get older I'll show you how you can look just as pretty" and she puts her head back, relaxes, like the Calgon commercials.

*   *   *

Champ lays on her stomach, T.V. on to some variety show with pogo stick dancers dressed in outfits of stretchy material and glitter. She is wearing one of Gregorio's white T-shirts, the ones he washes and bleaches himself so that the whiteness is impeccable. It drapes over her deflated ten year old body like a dress. She is busy cutting out Miss Breck models from the stacks of old magazines Pancha found in the back of her mother's garage. Champ collects the array of honey colored haired women, puts them in a shoe box with all her other special things.

Arlene is in the bathroom, wrapped in a towel. She has painted her eyebrows so that the two are arched and even, penciled thin and high. The magenta shades her eyelids. The towel slips, reveals one nipple blind from a cigarette burn, a date to forget. She rewraps the towel, likes her reflection, turns to her profile for additional inspection. She feels good, turns up the radio to ... your love. For your loveeeee, I will do anything, I will do anything, forrr your love. For your kiss ...

Champ looks on. From the open bathroom door, she can see Arlene, anticipation burning like a cigarette from her lips, sliding her shoulders to the ahhhh ahhhhh, and pouting her lips until the song ends. And Champ likes her mother that way.

Arlene carefully stretches black eyeliner, like a fallen question mark, outlines each eye. The work is delicate, her hand trembles cautiously, stops the process to review the face with each line. Arlene the mirror is not Arlene the face who has worn too many relationships, gotten too little sleep. The last touch is the chalky, beige lipstick.

By the time she is finished, her ashtray is full of cigarette butts, Champ's variety show is over, and Jackie Gleason's dancing girls come on to make kaleidoscope patterns with their long legs and arms. Gregorio is still not home, and Champ goes over to the window, checks the houses, the streets, corners, roams the sky with her eyes.

Arlene sits on the toilet, stretches up her nylons, clips them to her girdle. She feels good thinking about the way he will unsnap her nylons, and she will unroll them slowly, point her toes when she does.

Champ opens a can of Campbell soup, finds a perfect pot in the middle of a stack of dishes, pulls it out to the threatening rumbling of the tower. She washes it out, pours the contents of the red can, turns the knob. After it boils, she puts the pot on the sink for it to cool down. She searches for a spoon.

Arlene is romantic. When Champ begins her period, she will tell her things that only women can know. She will tell her about the first time she made love with a boy, her awkwardness and shyness forcing them to go under the house, where the cool, refined soil made a soft mattress. How she closed her eyes and wondered what to expect, or how the penis was the softest skin she had ever felt against her, how it tickled her, searched for a place to connect. She was eleven and his name was Harry.

She will not tell Champ that her first fuck was guy named Puppet who ejaculated prematurely, at the sight of her apricot vagina, so plump and fuzzy. "Pendejo" she said "you got it all over me." She rubbed the gooey substance off her legs, her belly in disgust. Ran home to tell Rat and Pancha, her mouth open with laughter.

Arlene powder puffs under her arms, between her breasts, tilts a bottle of *Love Cries* perfume and dabs behind her ears, neck and breasts for those tight caressing songs which permit them to grind their bodies together until she can feel a bulge in his pants and she knows she's in for the night.

Jackie Gleason is a bartender in a saloon. He wears a black bow tie, a white apron, and is polishing a glass. Champ is watching him, sitting in the radius of the gray light, eating her soup from the pot.

Arlene is a romantic. She will dance until her dress turns a different color, dance until her hair becomes undone, her hips jiggering and quaking beneath a new pair of hosiery, her mascara shadowing under her eyes from the perspiration of the ritual, dance spinning herself into Miss Clairol, and stopping only when it is time to return to the sewing factory, time to wait out the next date, time to change hair color. Time to remember or to forget.

Champ sees Arlene from the window. She can almost hear Arlene's nylons rubbing against one another, hear the crinkling sound of satin when she gets in the blue and white shark-finned Dodge. Champ yells good bye.

It all sounds so right to Arlene who is too busy cranking up the window to hear her daughter.

Nicholasa Mohr

An Awakening ... Summer 1956

for Hilda Hidalgo

The young woman looked out of the window as the greyhound bus sped by the barren, hot, dry Texas landscape. She squinted, clearing her vision against the blazing white sunlight. Occasionally, she could discern small adobe houses clumped together like mushrooms, or a gas station and diner standing alone and remote in the flat terrain. People were not visible. They were hiding, she reasoned, seeking relief indoors in the shade. How different from her native Puerto Rico, where luscious plants, trees and flowers were abundant. Green was the color of that Island, soothing, cool, inviting. And people were seen everywhere, living, working, enjoying the outdoors. All of her life had been spent on her beloved land. For more than a decade she had been in service of the church. Now, this was a new beginning. After all, it had been her choice, her sole decision to leave. At the convent school where she had been safe and loved, they had reluctantly bid her farewell with an open invitation to return. Leaving there had been an essential part of working it all out, she thought, one had to start somewhere. Still, as she now looked out at all the barrenness before her, she felt a stranger in a foreign land and completely alone.

She was on her way to spend the summer with her good friend Ann. They were going to discuss the several directions in which she might continue to work. After all, she had skills; her degrees in elementary education and a master's in counselling. There was also the opportunity offered her of that scholarship toward a doctorate in Ohio. The need to experience the world independently, without the protection of the church, was far more compelling than her new apprehension of the "unknown."

The young woman checked her wristwatch.

"On time ... " she whispered, and settled back in her seat.

Her friend Ann was now a social worker with the working poor and the Mexican American community in a small town in rural Texas. The invitation to spend most of this summer with Ann and her family had appealed to the young woman, and she had accepted with gratitude.

"You know you are welcome to stay with us for just as long as you want," Ann had written. "You will be like another member of the family."

The knowledge that she would once more be with her good friend, discussing ideas and planning for the future, just as they had done as co-workers back home, delighted and excited her.

"Clines-Corners ... " the bus driver announced. The next stop would be hers.

"Now, please wait at the bus depot, don't wander off. Promise to stay put, in case of a change in schedule, and we will pick you up," Ann had cautioned in her last letter.

"Sentry!" the bus driver shouted as the bus came to a sudden halt. She jumped down and the bus sped off barely missing a sleeping dog that had placed itself comfortably under the shade of a large roadside billboard. The billboard picture promised a cool lakeside ride on a motorboat, if one smoked mentholated cigarettes.

She found herself alone and watched a cloud of dust settle into the landscape as the bus disappeared into the horizon. She approached the depot building where two older Mexican men and a young black man, laborers, sat shaded on a wooden porch, eating lunch. She smiled and waved as she passed them. They nodded in response.

Inside at the ticket booth, a tall man with very pink skin peered out at her from under a dark green sun visor.

"Good day," she cleared her throat. The man nodded and waited. "I was wondering ... eh, if there was some message for me?"

"What?" he asked.

Feeling self conscious and embarrassed, she repeated her question, adding "I'm sorry, but it is that my English is not too perfect. I am not used to speaking English very often."

"What's your name? I can't know if there's a message for you if I don't know your name." She told him, speaking clearly and spelling each letter with care.

"Nope," he shook his head, "ain't nothing here for nobody by that name." The man turned away and continued his work.

The young woman stood for a moment wondering if her friends had received her wire stating she would arrive several hours earlier than expected. Checking the time she realized it was only twelve thirty. They were not expecting her until five in the late afternoon. She walked to the pay phone and dialed Ann's number. She waited as it rang for almost two full minutes before she replaced the receiver. Disappointed, she approached the clerk again.

"Excuse me, sir ... can I please leave my luggage for a while? There is not an answer where my friends are living."

The man motioned her to a section of luggage racks.

"Cost you fifty cents for the first three hours, and fifteen cents for each hour after that. Pay when you come back." He handed her a soiled blue ticket.

"Thank you very much. Is there a place for me to get a cold drink? It is very hot ... and I was riding on the bus for a long time."

"There's a Coke machine by the garage, right up the street. Can't miss it."

"Well, I would like a place to sit down. I think I saw a small restaurant up on the main street when I got off the bus."

"Miss, you'd be better off at the Coke machine. Soda's nice and cold. You can come back and drink it in here if you like." He looked at the young woman for a moment, nodded, and returned once more to his work.

She watched him somewhat confused and shrugged, then walked out into the hot empty street. Two mangy, flea-bitten mutts streaked with oil spots walked up to her wagging their tails.

"Bueno ... " she smiled, "you must be my welcoming committee." They followed her as she continued up the main street. The barber shop and the hardware store were both closed. Out to lunch, she said to herself, and a nice siesta ... now that's sensible.

Playful shouts and shrieking laughter emanated from a group of Mexican children. They ran jumping and pushing a large metal hoop. She waved at them. Abruptly, they stopped, looking with curiosity and mild interest at this stranger. They glanced at each other and, giggling, quickly began once more to run and play their game. In a moment they were gone, heading into a shaded side street.

The red and white sign above the small store displayed in bold printed letters: NATHANS FOOD AND GROCERIES—EAT IN OR TAKE OUT. On the door a smaller sign read, OPEN. Thankful, she found herself inside, enjoying the coolness and serenity of the small cafe. Two tables set against the wall were empty and except for a man seated at the counter, all the stools were unoccupied. No one else was in sight. She took a counter seat a few stools away from the man. After a minute or two, when no one appeared, the young woman cleared her throat and spoke.

"Pardon me ... somebody. Please, is somebody here?" She waited and before she could speak again, she heard the man seated at the counter shout:

"ED! Hey Ed, somebody's out here. You got a customer!"

A middle-aged portly man appeared from the back. When he saw the young woman, he stopped short, hesitating. Slowly he walked up to her and silently stared.

"Good day," she said. "How are you?" The man now stood with his arms folded quite still without replying. "Can I please have a Pepsi-Cola."

Managing a smile, she continued, "It is very hot outside, but I am sure you know that ... "

He remained still, keeping his eyes on hers. The young woman glanced around her not quite sure what to do next. Then, she cleared her throat and tried again.

"A Pepsi-Cola, cold if you please ... "

"Don't have no Pepsi-Colas," he responded loudly.

She looked around and saw a full fountain service, and against the rear wall, boxes filled with Pepsi-Colas.

"What's that?" she asked, confused.

The man gestured at the wall directly behind her. "Can't you read English."

Turning, she saw the sign he had directed her to. In large black letters and posted right next to the door she read:

> NO COLOREDS
> NO MEXICANS
> NO DOGS
> WILL BE SERVED ON THESE
> PREMISES

All the blood in her body seemed to rush to her head. She felt her tongue thicken and her fingers turn as cold as ice cubes. Another white man's face appeared from the kitchen entrance and behind him stood a very black woman peering nervously over his shoulder.

The silence surrounding her stunned her as she realized at the moment all she was—a woman of dark olive complexion, with jet black hair; she spoke differently from these people. Therefore, she was all those things on that sign. She was also a woman alone before these white men. Jesus and the Virgin Mary ... what was she supposed to do? Colors flashed and danced before her embracing the angry faces and cold hateful eyes that stared at her daring her to say another word. Anger and fear welled up inside her, and she felt threatened even by the shadows set against the bright sun; they seemed like daggers menacing her very existence. She was going to fight, she was not going to let them cast her aside like an animal. Deeply she inhaled searching for her voice, for her composure, and without warning, she heard herself shouting.

"I WOULD LIKE A PEPSI-COLA, I SAID! AND, I WANT IT NOW ... RIGHT NOW!!" The words spilled out in loud rasps. She felt her heart lodged in her throat, and swallowed trying to push it back down so that she could breathe once more.

"Can't you read ... girl?" the man demanded.

"I WANT A PEPSI. DAMN IT ... NOW!" With more boldness, this time her voice resounded, striking the silence with an explosion. Taking out her change purse she slammed several coins on the counter. "NOW!" she demanded staring at the man. "I'm not leaving until I get my drink."

As the young woman and the middle-aged portly man stared, searching each other's eyes, that moment seemed an eternity to her. All she was, all she would ever be, was here right now at this point in time. And so she stood very still, barely blinking, and concentrated, so that not one muscle in her body moved.

He was the first to move. Shaking his head, he smiled and with slow deliberate steps walked over to the cases by the wall and brought back a bottle of Pepsi-Cola, placing it before her. As she picked up the bottle, she felt the heat of the liquid; it was almost too hot to hold.

"Very well," she said, surprised at the calmness in her voice. "May I please have an opener?"

"Girl ... we ain't got no openers here. Now you got your damned drink ... that's it. Get the hell out of here!" He turned, ignoring her, and began to work arranging cups behind the counter.

Her eyes watched him and just for an instant the young woman hesitated before she stood, grabbed the bottle and lifted if high above her bringing it down with tremendous force and smashing it against the counter edge. Like hailstones in a storm, pieces of glass flew in every direction, covering the counter and the space around her. The warm bubbling liquid drenched her. Her heavy breathing sucked in the sweetness of the cola.

"KEEP THE CHANGE!" she shouted. Quickly she slammed the door behind her and once again faced the heat and the empty street.

She walked with her back straight and her head held high.

"BITCH!" she could hear his voice. "YOU DAMNED MEXICAN COLORED BITCH! CAN'T TREAT YOU PEOPLE LIKE HUMAN BE-INGS ... you no good ... "

His voice faded as she walked past the main street, the bus depot and the small houses of the town. After what seemed a long enough time, she stopped, quite satisfied she was no longer in that town near that awful hateful man. The highway offered no real shade, and so she turned down a side road. There the countryside seemed gentler, a few trees and bushes offered some relief. A clump of bushes up on a mound of earth surrounded a maple tree that yielded an oasis of cool shade. She climbed up the mound and sat looking about her. She enjoyed the light breeze and the flight of large crows that dotted the sky in the distance. The image of the man and what had happened stirred in her a sense of humiliation and hurt. Tears clouded her view and she began to cry, quietly at first, and then her sobs got louder. Intense rage overtook her and her sobbing became screams that pieced the quiet countryside. After a while, her crying subsided and she felt a sharp pain in her hand. She looked down and realized she still clenched tightly the neck of the broken Pepsi-Cola bottle. The jagged edges of glass had penetrated in between her thumb and forefinger; she was still bleeding. Releasing her grip, the young woman found a handkerchief in her pocket. Carefully she pressed it to the wound and in moments the bleeding stopped. Exhausted, she closed her eyes, leaned against the tree, and fell asleep.

She dreamt of that cool lakeside and the motorboat on the billboard that might take her back home to safety and comfort. Friends would be there, waiting, protection hers just for the asking.

"Wake up ... it's all right. It's me, Ann." She felt a hand on her shoulder and opened her eyes. Ann was there, her eyes filled with kindness and concern. Again, the young woman cried, openly and without shame, as she embraced her friend.

"I know, we got your wire, but only after we got home. By then it was late, around three o'clock, and we went looking for you right away. This a very small town. You caused quite a stir. I should have warned you about things out here. But, I thought it would be best to tell you when we were together. I'm so sorry ... but don't worry ... you are safe and with us. We are proud of you ... the way you stood up ... but, never mind that now. Let's get you home where you can rest. But, you were wonderful ... "

In the weeks that followed, the young woman worked with Ann. She made lifetime friends in the small Texas community. There were others like her and like Ann, who would fight against those signs. Civil rights had to be won and the battles still had to be fought. She understood quite clearly in that summer of 1956, that no matter where she might settle, or in which direction life would take her, the work she would commit herself to, and indeed her existence itself, would be dedicated to the struggle and the fight against oppression. Consciously for the very first time in her life, the young woman was proud of all she was, her skin, her hair and the fact that she was a woman.

Riding back East on the bus, she looked at her hand and realized the wound she had suffered had healed. However, two tiny scars remained, quite visible.

"A reminder ... should I ever forget," she whispered softly.

Settling back, she let the rhythmic motion of the large bus lull her into a sweet sleep. The future with all its uncertainties was before her; now she was more than ready for this challenge.

Alberto Ríos

The Birthday of Mrs. Piñeda

Café Combate, ¡la gente toma!
Café Combate, ¡de rico aroma!

—a famous and old, commercial jingle ran on the radio in Mexico for many years, advertising a particular brand of coffee. It ran repeatedly, obsessively, and no one who heard it has been able to forget.

Café Combate, the people drink it!
Café Combate, such rich aroma!

The noise came through the mouth of his nose: "hummph."

Adolfo Piñeda had read the books on El Salvador, but they didn't matter. He understood them, all right—which is to say, he understood that he did not understand them. So he kept reading them, buying them, rereading them, shrugging his shoulders. He read them everywhere, all the time; the names were so familiar, so like his. He read them at dinner: a page turned, a mouthful of chilaquiles, a page, a napkin to his lips in a wipe of the sauce. At the part about the genitals in men's mouths, he thought twice before chewing, but only twice. Truly believing such a story would mean no dinner. Conscience is like that.

"Fito," his wife called at him. She was always young again when she called him like this, like the wind, which goes away but comes back again and is recognized easily. They had met at thirteen, when he was still Adolfito, and she was then his Mariquita.

"Fito!"

"Sí sí sí sí, what."

"Stop reading." She looked at the newest magazine. Dead children again on the cover. Dead and flat, the way magazine covers make them, so they cannot be touched, so that a hand cannot go under the head. "You said you would. So much blood and screaming, I can hear it all the way over in the kitchen. Close that story. You said you would, you promised. Read me about the Prince and la Diana *ésa*, read me about that baby. You said you would." She cleared his dishes away.

"Mari . . . "

"No. No coffee. Or Sanka. You want that, Sanka?"

"Ay, Mari. Give me coffee.

"Give me give me give me. If I had known . . . "

"What? If you had known what?"

"Give me give me. Thirty years ago, if I had known that would happen, what you . . . "

Adolfo Piñeda clicked his teeth to break her sentence in half. "Oh stop it. Come on, m'ija, it's just coffee, that's all I want. Chh. It's not going to keep me awake." María Piñeda looked at him. Inside, behind her eyes, she saw the old radio and hummed the jingle that took her back to all the lunch times of her growing up, to all the rice and ground beef meals she ate hearing it. She ate the music of the old coffee jingle with her ears, chewed it over and over: CAFÉ COMBATE, LA GENTE TOMA! CAFÉ COMBATE, DE RICO AROMA! All of it came back for the five seconds of humming that she took, then went back inside her. She wanted to give him coffee. Very strong, very black, *cariculillo, Tapachula*, or even the *Café Combate* of the song; for so many years they had kept it in their cups. They had taken it out of the thin, brown paper bags. He loved it, and she loved him to love it. Something about a man liking something passionately, anything, boxing even, something about it made her give in to anything.

"Ándale, m'ija, just this once, come on."

"But the doctor, you know . . . "

"It won't hurt, and I'm not going to tell him."

María Piñeda clicked her teeth at him and went to get the coffee. Humming. He got it three nights out of seven and sometimes twice in a night if he read to her about good things. He was a lion when he read. His roaring came from so many years of politics and smoke, of reading the smudged and crowded news prints of all the smallest newspapers from all the smallest countries *de abajo*, all the smallest countries down there with all the biggest names, the fat Indian names, and the names of saints.

But when he read to her about the good things, about Charles or about what her tía in San Luis Potosí wrote, he had to use his loud moments up on words like *kiss*, " . . . and he KISSED his wife," or bananas, so that the news was that her *tía* had gone to the market and bought BANANAS. He made it all sound so important, and María Piñeda would laugh at him invariably at some juncture of the night, and he would not understand. He would wrinkle his face up like paper and throw his fine mood into the waste basket. He would stop reading to her then and go back to his books, or his magazines, El Salvador, El Salvador, or his tiny and smudged letters in newsprint for which he would need the magnifying glass. And coffee. Slyly, he would add this. "And coffee," he would say, "and leave me alone."

"Here, m'ijo." She set down some new coffee next to him. Its steamy hands made him pay attention, pulling his head almost to its face.

"But this is only half, you didn't fill the cup ... " He frowned, till there was no room left on his face for more frowning. But he managed. It was a little something extra with the left half of the left eyebrow, perhaps an added twitch of the eyelid underneath.

"It was full when I started from the kitchen. *Ni modo.*"

Hummph. He said this more with his chest than with any sounds. He let his face relax a little as he took the flirting sip. Two and a half cups in one night was the best he had done this year. And anyway, he had seen half a cup disappear before, so he was not truly angry. Coffee disappearing was nothing new, he had seen it often, even before María. It was the uncles. His mother had told him, and it was true. Even dead uncles want coffee. Coffee is not a thing a man stops wanting. somewhere with his own hands Adolfo Piñeda could even remember picking coffee beans, could remember the smell even then, the wanting. Or it was a story somebody told him about his grandfather. The feeling went too far back to be clear, so he frowned again and tried to remember for a fact what had happened, what the story was ... "

"Anna came over today."

"Anna?" Adolfo Piñeda looked up from his reading, which was really thinking.

María Piñeda looked at him looking up from his reading and felt good. But now, because he looked up, this story of Anna was going to have to be a little better than what really happened. She had him, and had to take care.

*   *   *

He knew that, of course. He knew it the moment he lifted his head and was sorry for the little lie he was going to make her tell him. He should have remembered to look up earlier and say something casual, anything just so that his looking up now would seem less like a lion's or a bear's. But he could feel that she had him now like a tender fish. And she had better be careful or the fish would balloon-pop! into the lion they both thought of him as, into the bear he knew he sometimes was. The thing wasn't true, but he could tell it was there between them. After thirty years a feeling like that ... well, never mind, he told himself. He stopped thinking the thought. He knew it would get no clearer than the coffee beans.

Not in words, anyway. But a kind of heart that the mind has pulsed the thought through, regardless of his trying to stop it. This second heart always troubled him like that. It didn't pay attention. No attention to decorum—that was a word from the army, or from his grandfather—the decorum with which he now tried to live his life. It leaped so very quickly back and forth between times and events, this heart, that he didn't understand. And it scared him. Thirty years were nothing, and a minute sometimes was the entire lifetime of several men back to back.

Todasbodas. That's what it was saying to him now, in that language that was not words, and not the hummph intended for María. *Todasbodas.* It was reminding him of how he used to be an *all-weddings.* It skipped through the thirty years he was sitting down with now, back to the younger bones he used to have and the different shirts and the thin black moustaches of which he took such care in every mirror that he passed.

Adolfo Piñeda looked at his wife about to tell him the story of Anna's visit today, and his second heart remembered for him the time when his ambition was to swing from crystal chandeliers, to be expert in this, and to take his talent through the fanciest houses of the jungle countries, and then to Europe, to the continent, with final recognition and general applause in Paris, where they would in his old age offer him a pension in honor of his selfless and fine work in redefining wildness.

He looked at his wife and he smiled.

Today was her birthday. She was some age or other. She was nineteen when they married, and that was the only birthday that ever mattered to his second heart, and it only mattered because it was the first measure of her that he had. They had lived in Guaymas, the both of them then. He could remember that she was nineteen, but he could not remember the first time he had made love to her. That he could not remember is what he remembered now. Something was always indistinct to him there, about that. Like the coffee beans. What he knew now, what he remembered, was that he had known a number of girls and had told each one his story.

The story concerned a particular history of Guaymas, the *true history of Guaymas*, as he would say. It was a sham, but no more so than any other history—of Guaymas or of any other place. It was as true and as false as the things any people say to get each other's clothes off now and fast. The true history of Guaymas is told in eight separate volumes in the mayor's office, the back office, and he had read them by special permission before the fire. An intricate weave, he would say, and he hummed it like a song back to himself now, and intricate weave, the words were so familiar suddenly, not so far back, so ingrained, so like the lines on a wooden post; an intricate weave, he would say, about this traitor and that shopkeeper, some over of stray cats and three toothless women; but in truth there was no general who did *that*, not ever, not anywhere. Only in his words. Adolfo Piñeda told the story to impress some Mariquita, this Mariquita this time, and it worked, God, it worked, so it had to be real, this story, because it was the thing that got her print dress and thin shoes to come off, this story of himself as the youngest general with thin moustaches and a cape who, with his singleness of arm strength, pushed the difficult song of violence farther than the rest, but on the right side of things. At this the girl sighed with relief, sure that a man on the right side of things could not be wrong.

But it must have been the business of saving the six sisters of mercy against which this Catholic Mariquita could not win—none of them could win here; she could only melt like sugar into the arms of this particular history, the one that must be true even for hard Catholic girls from the desert north, melt like sugar into the arms, into the face of a man who talked through the seasons and the seasons of the night.

*   *   *

María Piñeda, about to tell the story of Anna's visit and wrestling around very quickly in her head for extra words to make the story better and so to keep his tender and old attention longer, saw Adolfo Piñeda smile at her.

Just smile at her.

He had not done that, not like that, since before, since the far before. He still smiled at her, but his smiles were embers now, not strong quick wood fires. They were warmer now, and more lasting, but his smiles no longer held a sense of danger, that they might burn, that they might reach off his face and stretch in some lightening bolt fist straight at her, down and through the electricity in the cells at the core of her inside self.

She had been María Elena then, daughter of the string vendor, strings for all occasions, and rough cotton threads, Don Miguel, and his wife, la señora Beltrán, who never smiled and so was never addressed by her first name.

But her Fito was smiling at her now, and she was standing in the time when he had called her by the names of various imported perfumes taken, he would say, from the wildest flowers of the wilted and perfect bouquets found in subtle crystal vases that sat on the absurd tables in one particular back street bistro in springtime Paris just the year before.

He said this, but it said nothing about what he would do. From that moment she could never disentwine her other memory of the time of perfumes, that time just after they had married when she had to go looking for him, had to step over a dried phlegm and dirt floor in a dark cock-fighting barn, had to step over this floor made of sputum from half-shaved, thick men and dying cocks, a floor bloodstained and scuffed into a kind of inexpert, misshapen setting of scab tiles. The sounds of the fight would not go away, the sounds of all those men huddled, nor the odor of that perfume, and she remembered how she had seen as she ran by the one soul-white cock splattered with blood like grease, hot, how it had an eye pulled clean out but continued to fight, and then, lost the other eye but continued to fight, stretching its head and neck up higher and higher, imagining that something must be blocking its view, trying to see, and trying higher to see, but never for a moment thinking that it was blind. The owners kept spraying the fighter birds with water from their mouths, spitting a mist, cooling and cooling, fooling them, until the winner, the not-white one, allowed itself to be cooled and soothed and rewarded, and the owner, who was laughing, took its head into his mouth, cooling him.

María Piñeda ran by them all, that perfume, into the rooms behind the barn, into one room of particular use, and she pulled Adolfo Piñeda physically out of another woman and dragged him drunk home.

*   *   *

"Why are you smiling at me?"

"It's your birthday. Did you think I had forgotten?"

María Piñeda clicked her teeth at him. "Don't you want to hear about Anna?"

"What about Anna, well. Tell me."

"She came over today."

"I know that."

"Fito! Stop it and let me tell you."

Again she called him by that name, and again she was young for him because of it. He liked the sound of the name as it came from her, even when she was angry. This was the second time at least tonight that she had called him that. Adolfo Piñeda knew that his wife was thinking about her birthday then. She felt young, too, he could tell. He smiled even more, and she turned around and said she wasn't going to tel him the story because he wasn't paying attention to her, not the right kind, that he was being silly. *Yes*, he thought, she was being young and he liked it. He could be young, too, for her birthday: he ignored her.

He went back to his coffee and this newest article on El Salvador. This is crazy, he thought, and this thought about the bodies with names like his took him away from his wife again. María Piñeda went to the kitchen to cry. This is crazy, he thought.

"This is crazy," he said to the kitchen. Adolfo Piñeda did not mean the killing and suffering, but that people would go there to see it and talk about it. Words. In a flat paper magazine. He put his hand over the picture of a line of shoeless bodies, piled in a half-hearted way. Nothing. He could feel nothing. Slick on his fingers.

He took a drink of coffee, long like a breath in the mountains. This, he thought, *this*. Coffee, from Colombia and Paraguay and there and there and there, from all the small placed *de abajo*. It comes from the dirt, straight up, from hell to heaven. I drink it, he thought, and it's a way of remembering something, it reminds me to remember. Black like the earth and all its shades. It is knowing what it is to be dead, to have disappeared, to have gone just gone. Knowing what being dead is—this keeps us alive. Coffee makes me jump, thought Adolfo Piñeda, makes me full with the spirit of wanting to do things, full with energy, with being young, full with the fear of being dead, of just lying there. Caffeine . . .

Hummph. He said this with his chest, again, bigger than with words, and rounder. No such thing exists, *caffeine*. The word is a failure, or its definition not yet finished. He could not find in any dictionary—after the doctor had told him about the word—anything about its being what it was: a power from the muscles of the dead, their backs and forearms, their dreams, and how they still want to do things, a kind of leftover need, yes, *seguro que sí*, the power of intentions never met, such strong intentions, and so many, that they could not go away. Coffee reminded him that he was alive, and would keep him alive, too, not make him one of those bodies, not like the doctor had said. These dead, they never speak in words, he thought, only whimpered, but the dead were out there. One could hear them in the wind, usually very quiet, a little irritating, but quiet, not real words. The dead have a humble streak a mile long, but not him, not Adolfo Piñeda. And not his wife, either—he would not let her.

"What are you doing in there, m'ija?" He called to her. This being young, this way, this way of ignoring her, but paying attention that she knew he was ignoring her, was maybe no good, but what could he do. This was the only way he knew. The dead, the energy, the slow electricity of caffeine, they gave him force, but no answers. She would stop crying.

He looked at the pictures again. This was his dessert, he guessed; he hadn't asked if she had made a cake. In a minute I'll ask her, he thought. When she stops crying.

The pictures. The whole thing of them, the way they were, so flat, so dimensionless, the way they were not really the dead people at all—was like doctors. If a person goes in bleeding, the doctors fix the cut but never ask the attacker what made him stab a man, never get the *vato* in, get him in with his knife and ask how his father could let him do such a thing to someone else. Then they should rough up that knifer a little. That's what's wrong with them: these new doctors see only blood. Even *ese* doctor, *¿cómo se* *llama?* el doctor Martínez. He at least should know better. At least him. He came from Guaymas, too, but maybe he's too young to know the world. At least he asks a question now and then about what the kitchen knife felt like, asks that of a husband, or about how many links and how heavy they were in the hoodlum's chain that did this or that to the face.

"Did you see these pictures, m'ija? Did you see them? El Salvador, *otra vez*. They can't get enough. Whatever happened, what about this boy that was shot, *¿cómo se llamaba* ... Casillas? Remember his face? Who ever talked about him, right here in Phoenix?

"Are you all right, m'ija?

"A gun and blood and by strangers and everything. Everything all wrapped up in one boy's body. A man. Remember him? But it doesn't count. Maybe with presidents it counts."

Adolfo Piñeda could still hear his wife, but a little less now, in the kitchen. She was feeling better. He knew she would.

Hummamph. "Let the Anglos go there. We've already been there, huh? Let the Anglos go there—they go like flies anyway, like flies on the blood of cows. They're crazy. One stays away from a place like that. It only makes sense. But it's like dinner or something to them. They must feel good or something. I don't get it, m'ija.

"So they're crazy I think. That's not where the answers are. Everybody knows that. What jokes, JOKES. Look at these PICTURES. Like a MAG-NET was pulling them. It STINKS. Like when the president was shot, or the POPE, or some other big guy. I don't know what will happen next."

María Piñeda came out of the kitchen and sat to listen—because she liked to, like always. When he was a lion like this, everything fell away. A lion.

Hummphh. "Look at them. A president gets shot and they spend three days on television trying to explain it. Of COURSE it takes three days. There's nothing to explain. And they couldn't DO it, the *pendejos*. They CAN'T explain what has no explanation." Humnnphj. "Next time somebody's SHOT they'll take two weeks and so WHAT. They STILL won't have an answer. So what."

"It's my birthday." María Piñeda looked at him. She was Mariquita, and he didn't know what to say.

* * *

"Well, tell the story then."
"What story?"
"*M'ija*, don't be *tan simple*. You know. About Anna."

"Anna?"

"*Sí-sí-sí-sí.* Come on, come on. Anna, you know, Anna?"

María Piñeda began her story then, about this Anna whoever she was, and it went on in its particulars, one thing bringing up another more important than the last, some things making her cry large, toad-size tears, some things not.

Mariquita Piñeda began her story on her birthday, and it went on, and on further, through the night and pushed a shoulder against lunch time of the next day.

Alejandro Morales

Cara de caballo

Nowhere in the recorded histories of California is there an explanation for why Doña Arcadia Bandini married Abel Stearns. Both were from prominent families, well known and respected in Southern California. But the match of these two people was considered truly a fairy tale.

Don Juan Bandini's daughters were famous for their beauty, and the most beautiful of them all was the eldest, Arcadia Bandini. Don Juan, one of the most powerful and wealthy men of his time, believed he was destined to become a great leader. When the United States took over the northern Mexican territories, Don Juan supported the new government. He believed that California would prosper once the people accepted the new leadership, and he thought his support would one day be rewarded.

A small and dapper man, Don Juan was also highly intelligent and given to sarcasm when matters did not go his way. He possessed one of the largest ranches in Southern California, lands which stretched from the Mexican frontier to the San Bernardino Mountains. At the height of his success, Don Juan was a ranchero whose holdings assured him a position of great respect.

Don Juan was married twice. His first wife was Doña Dolores, a lovely woman of the Estudillo family who bore him five children, three daughters, Arcadia, Isadora, and Josefa, and two sons, José María and Juanito. His second wife, Arcadia's stepmother, was Refugio, also of great beauty, from the Argüello family. Doña Refugio and Don Juan had five children, three sons, Juan de la Cruz, Alfredo and Arturo, and two daughters, Monica and Herma. Arcadia was the oldest of all his children, and don Juan carried for her a special flame in his heart. She was born at the zenith of his power, and she buried him in 1859 a disillusioned man.

Don Juan was respected as a man of education and of generosity, even during times of personal misfortune. He made two bad investments, the financing of a store in San Diego and a hotel in San Francisco, which forced him to seek loans to cover his family's living expenses. He went to a French gambler, poet and novelist, Leon Hennique, and asked for ten thousand dollars. Hennique gladly gave him the money, but tagged on a four percent monthly interest rate. Don Juan was confident he could repay the loan in a few months with revenue from cattle sales. But an unforeseen slump in cattle sales forced Bandini to ask Hennique for an extension on the loan. The Frenchman granted the extension but insisted on the deeds to Don Juan's homes as guarantees of payment. As the months passed, more bad luck plagued don Juan, until he found himself trapped in an economic labyrinth from which he could see no escape. In his panic he made more impulsive decisions, causing his business affairs to decline even further.

During this period of economic crisis, the Bandini family was constantly at odds. Doña Refugio continued to plan one expensive fiesta after another, and Don Juan's sons, acting as if the money in the Bandini coffers had no end, pursued their costly gambling activities. Another kind of friction also appeared. Don Juan's sons had married Mexican women, but three of his daughters had married Anglo American men. Don Juan became convinced that the reason for his bad luck and the disharmony in his family was due to the foreign element, the *gringo* influence that had entrenched itself in his family through his daughters. He was bitter that his daughters had chosen *gringos*, but what hurt most of all was the fact that he had encouraged those unions. He had supported the new government all the way, even delivering his virgin daughters to its men.

Now the Bandinis were on the verge of economic disaster. Charles R. Johnson, who had married the sixteen-year-old Monica, offered to advise his father-in-law. Don Juan resisted, but Johnson was finally able to convince him to sign over a temporary power of attorney. Johnson then sent Don Juan and Doña Refugio to Monterrey on vacation. Arcadia remained alone with the servants on the San Diego estate.

Johnson and his brother-in-law, J.C. Couts, who was married to Isadora, reflected the Anglo attitude towards Mexican men. They considered them incompetent and lazy. But J.C. Couts was, at least, a decent man and he finally convinced Johnson to speak with Abel Stearns about a loan for Don Juan Bandini. Johnson knew Don Juan disliked Stearns because of Stearns' hostility to Mexico and Mexicans. He also knew Don Juan and Stearns had often competed for the best *vaqueros* to work their respective ranchos. Nevertheless, Johnson decided to ignore Don Juan's feelings and he asked Stearns for a loan of four thousand dollars. Johnson described to Stearns the crisis the Bandini family was going through, and he told him that to save Don Juan's land was to save his life. Stearns agreed to inspect the Bandini holdings and consider the loan.

On the morning of April 28, 1851, Isadora and Monica arrived at the Bandini estate in San Diego to inform Arcadia that Abel Stearns was to visit that afternoon. The servants were ordered to prepare a grand feast. The two sisters then lectured Arcadia for not making herself available to men, and they advised her to make herself beautiful for Abel Stearns, who just happened to be one of the richest men in the state. Arcadia listened with half an ear. The two sisters broke off their complaints when Stearns arrived with Johnson and Couts. The three women waited on the porch of the large adobe ranch home. As Stearns approached, he kept his eyes on Arcadia, not even glancing at her sisters when they were introduced. With side long looks of satisfaction, the two couples left Arcadia and Stearns alone on the porch.

Abel Stearns was born in Mexico in 1799 and came to California in 1829. He was fifty-one years old when he met Arcadia. He was the largest landowner in Southern California, and certainly one of the wealthiest. He was also one of the ugliest men in Southern California. Born a homely man, he was severely wounded in a quarrel over some wine. A deep cut ran through his nose and both lips, giving him a distinct speech impediment. He was called *Cara de caballo*; some people found it difficult to look at his face. This was the man who stood before Arcadia Bandini, a woman so beautiful that he could only gaze at her and whisper *gracias*.

Arcadia stared at Stearns' grotesque face. His disfigurement forced him to breathe heavily and noisily through his deformed mouth. She noticed how large his hands were, his arms ridiculously long. But as she studied his face, she saw a kindness, a promise of a good man behind the physical distortion. Stearns asked her to marry him. He spoke of his wealth and of the things he could do for her family, for her beloved father. He promised to love her forever and to make her the happiest woman in California. Arcadia made her decision. "Abel Stearns, you are the ugliest man I have ever seen. I will marry you and I will be yours to the last moment of your life." Stearns' broken lips formed a smile. He kissed her hand and went off full of excitement to explore the Bandini estate. Arcadia called for her sisters and announced her engagement. "Send for our father and mother. Tell them I am to be married upon their return. Let the people know that Arcadia Bandini will wed Abel Stearns."

And so she did. Two days after the Bandinis returned from Monterrey, their most beautiful daughter was wed to the ugliest man in Southern California. At Arcadia's request, the private ceremony was held in the open plains of the Rancho Alamitos. The newlyweds spent their wedding night in a simple cabin atop a hill on Stearns' Rancho Laguna. The cabin was to become their favorite place, their escape from everyday life.

The years passed and the Stearns became even more prominent members of Southern California society. To Abel's extreme disappointment, they had no children. Arcadia was relived, because she did not want to take the chance of passing on her husband's ugly traits to innocent children. To insure her infertility, she took special baths, ate particular herbs, and drank potions prepared for her by Indians and Mexican women. To compensate for her deliberate lack of fertility, Arcadia made love to her husband as if he were Apollo himself. Abel could hardly believe his good fortune, and he lavished the same affection on his beautiful wife. They made love with such passion and so often that Abel could not understand why they did not conceive a child. There were times when he thought he had committed a grave sin by marrying such a beautiful woman, and that God was punishing him by denying him children. Arcadia's infertility preoccupied him on his business trips, but when he was with her he forgot all their problems and let himself become engulfed by the love of this beautiful woman.

Only once did Arcadia actually tell Abel she loved him. They were in their cabin on the Rancho Laguna, and she began to think about her popularity with so many men and women. She realized it was because she was married to *Cara de caballo*, because whenever she appeared on his arm at fiestas, balls or even on the sidewalks of Los Angeles or San Francisco, her beauty was instantly exaggerated. For all that attention, for the wonderful life he had given her, Arcadia loved him very much. He was seventy years old at that time, and Arcadia was as lovely as when they had married. They made love on the braided rug in front of the fireplace, and their passion was as strong as it was twenty years before.

Abel Stearns died in San Francisco in 1871. He was seventy-two. His body was returned to Arcadia in Southern California. He of course left his entire estate to her, making her the wealthiest woman in California. When she was fifty, Arcadia Bandini de Stearns married a handsome and prosperous young man from Rhode Island, Jonathan Hawthorn Blake. Blake never asked Arcadia her age; to his eyes she was always young and beautiful. The two of them lived contentedly in their homes in Los Angeles and San Diego. They travelled extensively to the Orient and to Europe. At the turn of the century, Arcadia was as beautiful as when she was twenty. Legend has it that she was consulting a *brujo* who prescribed a potion made from ground up brown insects. She had to drink the potion every day to conserve her beauty and her youth. Legend also has it that one day Arcadia failed to drink her potion, and the next morning her face was transformed into a *cara de caballo*. The few servants who witnessed her transformation lived only long enough to tell the story.

Roberto Fernández

Raining Backwards

—Keith, Kicito. Ven acá. Come here!

—Yes, abuela.

—You abuela no va a esperar a que llegue la ambulancia del rescue. Oíste esa sirena. La próxima es pa' mí. ¡Qué va! ¡A mí sí que no me agarran!

—Slowly, abuela. Más des-pa-ci-o.

—Necesito que me ayudes. You help you abuela, ¿okay? You love you abuela, ¿right?

—Yes, I do.

—Bueno, listen. No voy a esperar a que llegue la ambulancia del rescue; me conectan a una máquina y no me dejan morir en paz. Además no quiero que me entierren aquí. Sería la primera y Dios sabe dónde enterrarán al próximo. ¡Muerta y sola! Además, quién se entiende con los muertos de este país. Kicito, aquí todo se desparrama, hasta los muertos. Quiero que me entierren en La Habana. Mi bury Havana, ¿okay? No here.

—But you aren't dying abuela. No mo-rir!

—Pronto. Anytime! Ya tengo . . . déjame pensar cuántos tengo. Mari, Mari, Mari-Clara m'ija, ¿tú te acuerdas cuántos tengo?

—(Please mother! I'm trying to concentrate on this last posture. No me molestes ahora.)

—Bueno anytime. Ya tengo muchos y ayer estaba lloviendo al revés. Dos meses antes de la muerte de papá también llovió al revés. Any minute now, any minute!

—Llo-ver al revés. No com-pren-do, abuela.

—Yes, Kicito rain backwards.

—It can't rain backwards! What a silly idea. No po-der llu-vi-a backwards.

—No seas incrédulo. Crees que tu abuela te engañaría.

—You had too much coffee, abuela. Coffee makes you high. You mucho ca-fe. Ca-fe te po-ni-o un po-co lo-ca en la ca-be-za.

—Uds. siempre lo remedian todo con la locura. No me explico por qué no me quieres creer. Acaso yo no te creí cuando hace años me dijiste que había un leñador gigante y que los conojos ponían huevos y que un hombre

33

había dormido durante veinte años sin despertarse y cuando despertó la barba le llegaba a los pies. Recuerdo que se lo conté a todas mis amigas del barrio. Mira Keith, abuela no estay here, ¿okay? Sylvia está sola. Sylvia alone. I go accompany her.

—But Sylvia is dead. Es mu-er-ta. You told me so.

—(Tiene ochenta y tres mamá, eighty three. Naciste en el tres.)

—¡Y qué te crees tú! Los muertos también se sienten solos. Tienen sentimientos. Necesitan otros para que los acompañen. Pero otros muertos de su edad, si no, no tienen nada de qué hablarse. Además, me quiero ir. Desde que llegué aquí nada más que he trabajado y trabajado. Sí, sé que tenemos esta casona con piscina olímpica y que la puerta del garaje se abre sola, y sé que tengo doce televisores a color en mi cuarto, y diez y seis radios despertadores, y un closet atestado de ropa y me van a regalar un VCR, pero ¿quién le habla a esta vieja? Tu madre en las clases de meditación trascendental y en las de aerobics, y tu padre en su taller de impotencia, y cuando hay fiesta me visten como un maniquí de vidriera y los invitados siempre dicen: "Granma, very nice," y de tus hermanos eres el único que hace por entenderme. Aquí me estoy volviendo un fantasma anémico por falta a quién espantar. Y cuando venga la ambulancia dirán todos: "Do everything you can to keep her with us. Hagan todo lo que puedan." Entonces me conectarán a una máquina y así estaré como uno de esos vegetales que no necesitan tierra para vivir. No is the coffee! You help you abuela ¿yes or no?

—Okay, okay. What do you want? But make it quick. I've got to go to the tryouts. Rá-pi-do. Yo ir prác-ti-ca football.

A la mañana siguiente, abuela me explicó los detalles de su fuga mientras me hacía jurar que no se lo revelaría a nadie. Tan pronto como terminó mi jura, le di la mano y nos encaminamos hacia los matorrales que crecían cerca de la casa. Íbamos en búsqueda de un árbol fuerte. En el medio de aquel pequeño bosque, abuela se detuvo, miró a su alrededor y seleccionó uno de tronco robusto. "Vamos, ¿qué esperas?, dijo al mismo tiempo que me ponía hacha en mano y como una enloquecida cheerleader gritaba: "Túmbalo, túmbalo, rarará! Fue entonces cuando divisé, en la copa del árbol, un nido de gaviotas negras. Bien sabía que el cedro sería el árbol más indicado para los propósitos de abuela, pero las gaviotas negras eran una especie en peligro. Después de pensar por varios minutos, le dije que el cedro estaba enfermo y seleccioné un carcomido roble. Ella sonrió al ver que de un hachazo lo había derribado, mientras gritaba: "You cut Kicito, you cut good." Yo sólo atinaba a sonreírle con cierto aire de superioridad ya que de seguro había salvado una especie al borde de la extinción.

Abuela me instruía cómo y dónde tallar. Seguí sus órdenes al pie de la letra, abriendo un hueco en medio del tronco. Mientras más entusiasmado estaba abriendo el hoyo, la capataz volvió a gritar:

—¡Quítale las ramas, quítale las ramas! Take the arms off the tree, take the arms off the tree! No la entendí y abuela, perdiendo la paciencia, me arrebató el hacha desmembrando el vegetal. Esa misma tarde el roble había quedado convertido en tabla agujereada por termitas humanas. Abuela contempló la obra satisfecha, al mismo tiempo que me daba una leve palmada en la espalda. Le sonreí una vez más mientras me deleitaba discurriendo que había salvado a las gaviotas negras de los caprichos de aquella viejecita impetuosa que aún no acababa de comprender.

Durante aquel mes fuimos religiosamente a los matorrales, donde camuflageada, se desarrollaba nuestra empresa que cada día tomaba más y más aspecto de viejo bajel. Tenía la embarcación dos compartimientos, uno para mantenerse sentado y el otro para provisiones. No poseía ningún tipo de propulsión, aunque sí tenía un falso timón. Hacia la improvisada proa, había un agujero donde colocar una pequeña asta para una bandera blanca. El exterior lo había cubierto de piedras del rin, que había sacado pacientemente de viejos vestidos testigos de antiguas glorias, y retratos de Julio Iglesias. Todo encolado a la superficie con superglue. Esa misma tarde, la almirante inspeccionó la obra al mismo tiempo que me hacía varias preguntas claves para asesorarse de mis conocimientos náuticos. Finalmente, le respondí algo apenado que ni siquiera sabía nadar bien. Con mucha calma, abuela me dijo que fuera a la biblioteca y me agenciara una carta de navegación.

—Kicito cuando te aprendas la carta vamos a tomar la camioneta de tu padre y colocar la embarcación allí, luego nos vamos hasta la Marina de Key Biscayne para alquilar un bote de motor. We take pick-up. We put embarkation and rent motor boat, ¿understand you?

—I guess so ma'm.

—Entonces vamos a remolcar mi barca hasta donde comienza la corriente del golfo. Allí hacemos mi trasbordo y tu cortas la soga. ¿Understand you?

—But why? Por-qué?

—Me voy pal sur. Me voy pa' La Habana. Sí Kicito, me voy pa' La Habana y no vuelvo más. I go to Havana no come back no more.

—But can't you take a plane? To-mar a-vi-on?

—Cuántas veces te he explicado que no hay otra forma de llegar.

—But you'll die on the way! Mo-rir en bo-te, abuela.

—No morir en bote. Morir aquí en tierra. No te preocupes. Llegaré en un par de días. Y cuando llegue les enseño mi bandera blanca, salgo de la barca, me tomo una taza de café, cojo un taxi y sigo rumbo al panteón donde está Sylvia y ...

Al otro día, después de aquella conversación, me encontraba en la biblioteca robándome una carta náutica que venía dentro de un deshojado *National Geographic*. Recuerdo que me la metí dentro de los calzoncillos evadiendo así el detector electrónico. Llegué a casa con mi botín. La abrí y asustado por su contenido la volví a doblar, escondiéndola en mi escritorio. El aprendizaje de la carta me habría de tomar casi tres semanas. Cuando le dije a abuela que me la sabía al dedillo, fue a su cuarto y rápidamente se puso su vestido de gala. Iba en dirección al mall, donde compró dos vestidos de noche, un parasol floreado y siete grabadoras, estilo "ghetto blasters." Me mostró los vestidos explicándome que el morado era para Sylvia, que no podía llegar con las manos vacías.

Cuando llegó el día señalado para la botadura, abuela vestía de luces y portaba su parasol como una auténtica torera primaveral. Le señalé hacia el camión. Le abrí la puerta con gran reverencia, a lo Sir Walter Raleigh, al mismo tiempo que la tomaba de la mano para ayudarla a subir al vehículo. Estaba contentísimo. Era la primera vez que manejaba la camioneta de mi padre. El ignoraba lo que estaba ocurriendo, pues él y mamá andaban de fiesta. Durante la noche, abuela había robado las llaves que colgaban de la puerta del armario. Arrancamos y salimos en dirección a los matorrales. al llegar, nos bajamos y con gran esfuerzo y tres poleas nos arreglamos para colocar la canoa dentro del pick-up. Serían como las tres de la madrugada y ambos íbamos eufóricos. Yo porque por primera vez conduciría por toda la U.S.1, y ella por el gusto de ver que su empresa tocaba a su fin.

Estacioné de un sólo corte la camioneta y nos dirigimos a alquilar nuestro remolcador. Nos montamos en el barco y abuela destapó una botella de coñac que llevaba debajo de la falda. Luego de atragantarme con el primer sorbo, abuela me pidió que cuando regresara a puerto me bebiera el resto. Ella bebió el suyo de un solo golpe.

Ibamos en dirección al Sureste, en búsqueda del Gulf Stream. Marchábamos despacio. No era tarea fácil remolcar aquel tronco acondicionado. Abuela hablaba incansablemente, contándome desde el día que se le trabó el dedo en la moledora de café hata el primer beso que le diera Nelson, mi abuelo, a través de las rejas de la ventana. Nos estábamos acercando al punto donde la corriente la llevaría a su destino. Aminoré la marcha del motor y abuela, dándose cuenta que nos aproximábamos, perdió la esfervescencia; volviendose algo pensativo, agregó:

—¿Sabes por qué tengo que hacerle compañia a Sylvia? El beso que me dio tu abuelo era para ella. Yo sabía que esa tarde pasaría a verla. Hacía tiempo que la andaba rondando. Me cubrí la cara con un velo de tul y me besó a través de la tela creyéndose que era Sylvia. Me descubrí el rostro y quedó prendado de mí. Sylvia murió soltera y sola. Nunca me lo perdonó. Dicen que mi pobre hermana murió vomitando estrellas.

—Es-tre-llas? Stars?, dije.

—Sí, estrellas. Creo Dios le recompensó su sufrimiento de esa manera. ¿No believe me?

—You can't throw up stars. No vo-mi-tar es-tre-llas!

—Okay y si te digo que se había tomado antes de morir una sopa de pollo y estrellas, chicken and estars soup, you believe me?

—Well, it makes more sense. Not a whole lot, but it makes more sense that she had soup. Cre-o una po-qu-i-ta más chicken and stars so-pa.

—Pero tengo algo más que contarte, Kicito. I have something more to tell to you. It is no all. Le fui infiel a tu abuelo dos veces. Solamente dos veces y nada más. I was infidel to your grandfather two time in my life. You abuela was one of the girls that Julio Iglesias loved before. Yo fui una de las que él amó, y también fui amada por Kirby. Fui la Sara Bernhardt de su poesía.

—Kirby, the black bean soup maker? El ja-ce-dor de so-pa fri-jo-les ne-gros?

—No, no, el poeta. The poet. Pero lo dejé porque era muy ordinario. I left him because he very ordinary. Trabajábamos en la fábrica Libby y él era el foreman. Pero después me di cuenta que era muy chusma y me desilusionó. Figúrate que todos los días al final del trabajo cuando sonaba el pito de las cinco me decía: "Nelia, cojón." !Qué ordinario! Por eso lo dejé. He say bad word in the fabric at five everyday when the whistle sounded. That is the why I left him.

—Still you don't make much sense abuela. No en-ten-der-te mu-cho.

—Es okay. But I loved your grandpa more. Remember that.

Después de nuestro último diálogo, abuela abordó la embarcación mientras yo cortaba la soga que había servido para remolcarla. La rústica canoa se iba alejando poco a poco, mientras ella sonriendo me tiraba un último beso.

—You good, ¿okay? Good bye honey. No worry you me. Si tengo problemas al llegar es easy, los compro con las grabadoras que pa' eso traigo. I buy them with the players.

No volví a mirar en su dirección. Arranqué el motor y mantuve la vista fija sin voltearme hasta llegar a puerto. Quizás iba algo triste ya que nunca había creído todos aquellos cuentos de estrellas y lluvias al revés o tal vez porque temía que se comenzara a hundir el carcomido roble que había seleccionado para salvar a las gaviotas negras.

*   *   *

El tiempo ha pasado con fugacidad, y la marea ha subido y bajado miles de veces desde aquel día en que abuela se marchó. Miles también han sido las veces que me he acercado a la marina para tan sólo mirar hacia el sur y beber un trago de coñac.

Hace una semana, por primera vez, vi que llovía al revés, y sorprendido llegué a comprender que los conejos, en realidad, no ponen huevos. Pensé en ella y comprendí que mi hora ya se avecinaba. Se lo dije a mi nieto y me respondió que seguramente había bebido demasiado café. Instintivamente, fui al viejo baúl y allí encontré la ya amarillenta carta de navegación que años atrás había utilizado para trazar la ruta que había seguido. La comencé a estudiar afanosamente. Quería desembarcar en el mismo sitio donde ella lo había hecho. De pronto, comprendí que las flechas qe indicaban la dirección de la corriente apuntaban hacia el noreste y no hacia el sur, como había creído. La había leído al reves. Un hondo pesar me recorió el cuerpo. Entonces, me la imaginé congelada con su vestido de luces en harapos y el parasol destelado, muriendo sola como una vieja vikinga tropical, envuelta en un témpano de hielo frente a las costas noruegas.

La sirena me sacó de lo que creía era un oscuro letargo, mientras alguien gritaba:

—Mouth to mouth. Give him mouth to mouth. Get some air in his lungs. Hook him up to the machine!

Para Rosalinda Wright

Nash Candelaria

Affirmative Action

Next to having her husband, Antonio, alive again, what Rosalía Soto wanted most of all was a place of her own. She had been forced to sell their little house in the Los Angeles barrio of Boyle heights when Antonio's insurance failed to cover the hospital bill for his fatal bout with cancer. Now she was a permanent guest—she could not really call it home—in her youngest daughter's house.

Not only did she lack a sense of control over her own life, she also lacked privacy which had become a necessity rather than a luxury as she grew older. Finally, there was her grandson Pancho's new wife, a gringa who brought an alien intrusion into the already crowded house. It was enough to weigh down the sturdiest soul.

This afternoon, like most afternoons at three o'clock, she retreated to her room that contained the remnants of her earlier, independent life. The large, round mirror on the 1930's Hollywood-style dresser reflected her short, stout body sacked in a black widow's dress. She did not give her reflection a thought; she did not care what she looked like. The bureau, a companion piece to the mahogany veneer dresser, was cracked in the upper right corner where her sons-in-law dropped it while moving.

Rosalía stretched out on the bed with matching headboard, the bed which she once shared with Antonio and now shared with her youngest granddaughter. She dared not look at Antonio's framed photograph on the bureau. She knew it would make her cry. She would just close her eyes for a few minutes until the younger children came home from school and the older members of the household came home from work.

Enjoy the quiet while you can, she thought. Soon the TV set in the living room will go on; one of the back rooms will turn into urban cowboy with that honky-tonk Texas music; another room will vibrate to cha-cha-cha, ranchero, mariachi boom-boom; while out front some high school boy will park his auto stereo with wheels, playing that electric rock music that makes my hair stand on end. No wonder nobody talks anymore, she thought. They can't get a word in edgewise. The noise machines have taken over.

She had barely closed her eyes when the too-polite, bootlicking voice called through the closed door. "Mama? Are you in there, mama?"

"Yes. What is it this time?"

The door opened a crack, and her daughter, María, poked only her face into private territory. An envelope extended tentatively, like an immigrant waiting for permission from the Border Patrol to cross the line. "Your Social Security check came," María said. But her voice told Rosalía that there was more, that the check was not the real reason she was here.

"Put it on the dresser."

As María put the envelope down, an expression of pain crossed her face. "Oh, mama. You look so sad."

Tears of rage welled up in Rosalía's eyes, but she willed them away. I don't know which is worse, she thought. To be pitied by María or to fight with my other daughter, Stella, who is so stubborn, malicious, and selfish. "What is it you want?" she snapped.

María's face paled, the look from her childhood when she had bad news: a poor grade on her report card or being late to mass. "Pancho and Maureen are bringing her father over for dinner tonight."

María stood with her elbows against her side, forearms out horizontally, hands hanging limply, like a dog on its hind legs begging for a bone. Rosalía groaned.

"They're moving out this weekend," María explained hurriedly. Rosalía already knew that. "They have their own little apartment near the aircraft plant," she added brightly. Rosalía already knew that too. "As long as Panchito doesn't get laid off—" Her voice trailed into silence as if she hoped that her mother would not hear this last.

"I'll be there," Rosalía said, meaning dinner.

"Do you think . . . " Here it comes, Rosalía thought. Oh, Lord, save me from timid hearts. " . . . you could make a nice batch of flour tortillas for dinner? You know how Mr. Fitzpatrick loves them."

Rosalía sat upright and nodded angrily, thinking: Yes. I'll put ground glass and rat poison in the batch for that old fart.

María left, but there was no use resting now. Rosalía looked up at the photograph on the dresser and felt the immense emptiness in her life.

She was back in Boyle Hights again, where she and Antonio moved when they first married and left Arizona. Where they had raised their family the way they were supposed to be raised. Where one could walk the streets and be in Mexico, surrounded by happy brown faces. Inhaling the fragance of posole and oregano from the cafes and delicatessens. Hearing the soft, beautiful sounds of their own Spanish language.

But then children grew up and did not appreciate what their parents had done for them. Boyle Hights wasn't good enough any more. "Oh, mama.

Who wants to live in this old dump? There are beautiful new houses in Rosemead and Pico Rivera."

Rosemead? What was Rosemead? A strip of wasteland along a freeway that some rich gringo developer plastered and painted and gave a fancy name to tempt dummies like María and Stella. Now they were over their heads in debt, their simple husbands chained to their jobs like monkeys tied to organ grinders. She even had to lend María and Ernesto the down payment, which was one of the many reasons she was here instead of with one of her sons.

Then, of course, moving out of Boyle Heights had been more than children rejecting what their parents taught them. It was rejecting their heritage. There, the clerks in the supermarket spoke Spanish. Here English—in the drugstore, the department store, at the movies. Even the priest here was a gringo. And with all that revolution of Pope John's, they didn't even say mass in Latin anymore. Turning to the left and turning to the right to greet your pew mates in church was silly. Just silly. What was the world coming to?

Like my simple grandson, Pancho, she thought. What would he expect? When María told me he was getting married, I was thrilled. Until I heard he was marrying this Irish girl. María santísima! It just goes to show you what happens when you don't stay with your own kind. Irish. I didn't know there were other people as dumb as us Mexicans. Otherwise how could you figure it?

Rosalía wiped her eyes and straightened her dress before going to the kitchen. The flour, lard, and rolling pin were already laid out, as if María wanted her to know what a good daughter she was.

Later the doorbell rang. It was too early for Pancho and Maureen. As the door opened, Rosalía heard the hated voice that almost at once broke into song. "Mexi ... cali Ro ... se," carried from the living room to the kitchen, warning her to stay put.

"Mama," María called. "Mr. Fitzpatrick is here."

For a moment Rosalía's eyes took on a life of their own, beaming at the cupboard door beneath the sink. What would a sprinkle of Drano do to the tortillas and that old lecher's stomach?"

Shortly after the young people arrived. Pancho and Maureen worked at the same aircraft plant. That's where they met. Pancho was a draftsman, and Maureen was a messenger girl who carried blueprints from place to place on roller skates.

Now that there were chaperones, Rosalía could go safely in the presence of old Fitzpatrick. At dinner she purposely sat across the table from him out of foot and arm range. You know what they used to say, she thought: He's not pure Irish. He's got Russian hands and Roman fingers.

At the wedding reception he had trapped her in the kitchen when no one was looking. That's when he had let it slip that he wasn't a widower at all, but had a wife in a convalescent home who was senile and needed constant looking after.

"Well," old Fitzpatrick said to Ernesto. "The boogies are moving in everywhere. Why just this week down at work—"

Rosalía remembered when she and Antonio were foolish enough to look for a place outside of Boyle Heights and had even rented one for a short time, until they learned about the petition going around the neighborhood. "No Mexicans wanted," it had said, with all those signatures on it. She had been heartbroken and insisted that they move back to Boyle Heights even if they lost a month's rent.

"I was taking the jack hammer out to the city truck when this big boogie comes up all smiles and white teeth," Fitzpatrick said as Ernesto nodded solemnly. " 'Well,' I think. 'New muscle to help out this old man.' But good God no. Not even a truck driver. He's our foreman. Can you beat that?"

She tuned out and looked the other way at Pancho and Maureen who were playing kissy-kissy right there at the table. Soon dinner was over and old Fitzpatrick started to coo at her like that old Irish actor in one of those movies that were so popular in the 1940's. When they left the table for the living room, he got her alone long enough to whisper in her ear.

"How about it?" he said. "You've been a widow almost two years, and I've been a widower even longer. There are some things that aren't natural for humans to do without."

Her face flamed like the head of a match scraped across sandpaper. She turned and rushed into the kitchen, furious. "Mexi ... cali Ro ... se" pursued her like an evil spirit, out-of-tune, not even the right lyrics.

María, Pancho, and Maureen stopped their huddled conversation in mid-word and looked up, but Rosalía could not be bothered about their secrets. "Coffee," she said and poured a cup.

When she carried it into the front room, old Fitzpatrick was sitting on the adjustable lounger giving Ernesto the business. "You Spanish people are the salt of the earth." Spanish indeed, Rosalía thought. Mexican! And proud of it. Then Fitzpatrick saw her and his old goat eyes lit up. "Coffee? You must have been reading my mind."

While he sat beaming, she took careful aim. She planned it so it would spill onto his lap in just the right place. If his thing hadn't shriveled up already, it would soon be scalded. Then he wouldn't go around molesting sweet old ladies.

His scream brought everyone running from the kitchen. Rosalía was all horrors and apologies. Then, after Maureen brought a dish towel to wipe her father's lap Rosalía worked up a few tears. On the pretext of being upset, she excused herself to go to her room ... for a little peace and quiet. No more "Mexicali Rose." Hopefully never again.

On Saturday, moving day, Pancho and Maureen slept in. There was a listless sense of disappointment in the air, and María avoided her mother. Finally, when no one else got up for breakfast and there were only the two of them across the table, María wiped at her dry, red eyes and spoke in a trembling voice.

"Pancho is being laid off," she said. "The government is not renewing some contract, and the people without seniority are being let go first."

"What about Maureen? If they don't need draftsmen, they surely don't need roller derby."

María shook her head with fast, tiny little movements that resembled trembling more than saying no. Then the tears started.

"What do you mean?" Rosalía's voice rose. "It's prejudice! They're doing it to us again, and it's against the law!"

María dripped tears onto her toast, and little pip-squeak sounds came from deep in her throat. She stood abruptly, almost knocking over the table, and rushed out of the kitchen. Rosalía was left with spilled coffee, tear-sogged toast and egg yolks congealing on a cold plastic plate.

She cleared the table and sat down alone for another cup of coffee. It was so quiet for a change. Ernesto had long since gone to work. The young people were making up for the sleep they had traded for playtime last night. María must be crying in her room, although it was such a timid cry that it couldn't be heard in the kitchen. If circumstances had been better, the rare early morning quiet would have been enjoyable.

A sound of footsteps. Not María's pussyfooting but the slap of bare feet on linoleum. Then *she* appeared in some kind of wrap that you could almost see through.

"Morning, Grandma Rosalía."

Maureen went to the stove and poured herself a cup of coffee, then plopped down at the table. Rosalía felt a strange apprehension. It was not fear, but an uncertainty that she felt with so many of these young creatures today. They weren't like she was when she was young. She didn't understand them. Then, too, she and Maureen had seldom been alone together in the three months the young bride had lived there. This thought surprised the old lady.

Maureen sighed and took a sip from her cup. "Did María tell you about Ricky?" Rosalía nodded. Then the girl's face turned red, and she glared intently with beady green eyes, thrusting her head forward aggressively. "I told him he was a fool to let them do that to him. I wouldn't put up with it. In fact, I didn't."

"You're not getting laid off?" Rosalía remembered María's trembling head that had already answered that question, but sometimes María got things wrong.

"They tried to." The girl flashed an impish smile. "When my supervisor told me, I went right to the Personnel Department and set them straight." Then her mood shifted. Rosalía could almost see the change on her face, like watching a TV screen when the channel selector was turned.

"I want my own place," she said adamantly. "Ricky and I need some privacy. I'm twenty years old, and I've never had a place of my own. There's always been papa. And mama when she was well."

"Do you need money?"

Maureen's expression answered: What a silly question. "We had the cutest little apartment picked out. With a swimming pool and sauna and everything." Then she blinked, lips compressed. "But we both have to work. Now this."

Rosalía looked at the blond young creature, at her freckles and her youth. In her wildest dreams she would never have believed that she had anything as important as a place of one's own in common with this daughter of that wretched old Irishman.

"I know how you feel," Rosalía said. The girl looked up in surprise that *anyone* would know that. When you're young, no one else in the world has your problems. Only you were chosen by God to suffer. And strangely, when you got older, it was the exact same thing.

Rosalía reached out and patted the girl's arm. "I could let you have a little money," she said. She was surprised to hear the words coming from her own mouth.

Maureen returned the pat. "Oh, Grandma. No. I wasn't asking for money." A look of stubborn determination crossed her face. "I told Ricky he'd better do what I did. Go to Personnel. With the two of us working we can manage it. We don't plan to have any children for a long time." Her eyes riveted on Rosalía, watching for any reaction. "I'm on the pill."

Ay, Dios, Rosalía thought. May the Pope have his fingers in his ears when she talks like that. Does María know? Of course not. She'd have eight kinds of fits, and ask old Father O'-what's-his-name to come over and threaten the young people with everlasting damnation.

"What could Pancho do about work?" Rosalía asked, sidestepping the pill.

"Exactly what I did. They have this Affirmative Action Officer at the plant, see. He's there to make sure the company carries out the government's rules. If they don't—trouble. No more contracts."

Rosalía did not understand. If the company broke a government rule and laid Pancho off, they'd lose their contracts. If they lost their contracts, Pancho wouldn't have a job anyway. It didn't make sense.

"So when my supervisor gave me two week's notice, I marched right over to Personnel to the Affirmative Action Officer.

" 'Look,' I said. 'I just got my notice, and I don't like it one bit.' "

"He smiled a tight little smile like he's sympathizing with me. All those Personnel finks practice that smile when what they're really smiling about is that it's you and not them getting laid off."

" 'One of our major contracts wasn't renewed,' he said. 'We have to reduce staff by five percent. We start by seniority, and unfortunately our younger workers are affected first. There'll be another job for ... ' "

"But I didn't want to hear this. Five percent bullshit! A hundred percent as far as I'm concerned. 'Look,' I interrupted him. 'My last name is Mendoza, and I'm an endangered species. If I get laid off it's because my supervisor is prejudiced, and I'm going over to the Federal Office in L.A. and not only report this, but sue your ass off.' "

"Well, he couldn't swallow that smile fast enough. 'Mendoza?' he said. 'You don't look ... ' "

"That made me mad, and I interrupted him again. 'Don't give that I-don't-look crap,' I said. 'You're just proving to me your own prejudice.' Which really drove him up the wall because he's Black, see." She smiled a wicked smile, her father's smile.

"But how can you do that?" Rosalía asked. "Your name's really not Mendoza."

Maureen rolled her eyes up at the ceiling, and there was a glint of anger in them when she glared at the old lady. "It is so," she insisted. "Sanctified by the priest and God and the state of California. My children, when I have them, will be Mendozas. Mexicans by name and half-Mexican by blood. Who has a better claim?"

Rosalía was taken aback by her audacity, but she could not disagree with her logic. "So they gave you your job back?"

Maureen shook her head impatiently. "Better." She started to laugh. "They want me to be a clerk in the Affirmative Action office. They think I'll be a good 'advocate,' whatever that is. I told them I'd think about it. Actually I'd rather work on roller skates; it's much more fun. But whatever, they'll find me a job."

Rosalía marvelled at this young thing who she thought was as dumb as Pancho. Her grandson got lucky when he found her. "Good for you," she said. "Stand up for your rights."

The girl smiled. Open, warm, friendly. "I wanted to tell you. Ricky thinks the world of you. You're the only one around here who would understand and not go around wringing your hands and worrying."

Rosalía was shocked that such a daughter could come from that old fossil, Fitzpatrick, while what she had to show for a daughter was María. She watched the girl pop a frozen strawberry tart into the toaster and pour them both another cup of coffee. What would happen, Rosalía wondered, if someone brought Maureen a signed petition that said she couldn't live here? She'd tear it up and throw it in their faces, then rent the place next door and bring in her old father and some of his disreputable cronies to liven up the neighborhood. She could just see it.

There was a pussyfoot pitter-pat from the hall, and María stole in with a timid smile. "I see you girls are having a chin feast," she said, waiting by the door to be invited into her own kitchen. "Is there half a cup of lukewarm coffee left for me?"

Maureen flashed Rosalía a warning look, while María went to the stove and poured her own coffee.

"Actually," Maureen said, "we were talking about what Ricky is going to do on Monday to get his job back. Grandma agrees that it's the right thing."

The girl's smile was angelic as she pulled the hot tart from the toaster with the tips of thumb and forefinger and dropped it onto a paper towel on the table. Rosalía smiled too. María sat with a worried look on her face. Then finally she smiled, though as usual she probably did not know why.

This young creature is not really so different from me, Rosalía thought. I wish that I could help her more. I pray that Pancho gets his job back. That soon they'll move into their little apartment with swimming pool and sauna. She is, after all, my granddaughter. And I have had my own place, while she never has.

Ed Vega

Mayonesa Peralta

Apparently, whoever had tagged Nemecio Peralta with the incongruous nickname of Mayonesa had long ago left the neighborhood. Peralta did not seem bothered by the name and, in fact, during those rare moments when he stopped his mad race with time and hovered around the edges of normal sociability, he appeared pleased by the familiarity of the name and the glee it produced in other people.

Well past sixty years of age, Peralta was still spry and energetic, a barrel-chested, powerful little man, who was forever on the move, his tree-stump limbs pushing at the air in front of him as if it offered unconquerable resistance when he walked. Driven by private demons, he appeared at war with life. On the infrequent occasions when I spoke with him I was surprised by his keen intelligence and sensitivity.

As for all people who dedicate their lives to creative endeavors there were apparent disappointments in his life. But of all the vicissitudes to which men of art are subjected when they insist on living life on their own terms, Peralta's greatest struggle was the manner in which he earned his living.

Each weekday he rose early and traveled by subway to the depths of Brooklyn, a trip of nearly two hours. Once there, he labored eight to ten hours, some days twelve hours, at turning bed posts for the Isadore Kaplan Furniture Company, Inc.

As Sisyphus, he began his upward struggle each day only to have it culminate in wasted effort. And yet he had to eat, had to clothe himself and continue working at his art. More importantly, I truly believe his powerful, scarred and knotted hands had a life of their own and would have withered and died without the feel of wood, of suffering cuts and bruises and painful splinters.

The first time I had the privilege of visiting his apartment I was moved deeply by the austerity and orderliness of his life. In a railroad apartment on top of the hill near Lexington Avenue he had fashioned a world so wondrous that I was spellbound for days afterwards. I also felt understandably ashamed that I had chosen to fashion images out of words when there was an existing physical reality around me which was more concrete and Peralta had captured

47

it in his work. It is rare to be awed by a contemporary, but on that occasion awe is what I felt.

The front room, which faced the street, was his living quarters: a single bed, neatly made; a bureau, singular in its beauty and crafted by him; a small table with two matching chairs; a refrigerator; cabinets filled with cans and boxes of food; a double hot plate and some pots and pans. The rest of the apartment had been given over to his art.

One room held his wood, mostly chunks and pieces which he found or asked for at lumber yards, never from Kaplan Furniture; the pieces were arranged by size and type of wood. The next room had floor to ceiling shelves along three walls and on these he had placed finished pieces, polished but as yet unpainted. The next room was the painting and drying room. Although well ventilated, there was a strong aroma of paints, shellacs, varnishes, turpentine, benzene and other spirits. My first reaction upon entering the room was to deduce that Peralta's odd reactions to the world around him had been caused by constant exposure to these toxic materials. Such was not the case, as I was subsequently able to learn.

The one fact which struck me about Peralta was his lack of pride in the fine wood carvings which stood on shelves and drying racks: saints, The Three Kings (in different sizes), nativity figures, doves, roosters. The pieces were articulated in odd cuts from his carving knives, but possessed that quality which a fine artisan gives a medium so that one has to stop and wonder why man, consciously or unconsciously, must seek to immortalize himself, to infuse his lifeblood into dormant, insentient material, marry it with nature and animate it after it has died.

Peralta believed odd things, gathered from conversations and snatches of philosophy which he had read, but they formed a clear view of life which drove him to suffer the indignity of working at Kaplan's so that after work and on weekends he could coax from the wood images of life. As some Buddhists, he believed all things possess life. Even when organisms die they do not entirely disappear but enter into a dormant stage to be awakened into future incarnations. So his job at Kaplan's was at once a way of keeping his passion alive by earning a living and a consternation, since the metaphor of turning bed posts lent itself to making inanimate matter more inanimate, dormant and in this case a vehicle for helping human beings themselves become dormant.

He seldom spoke to anyone and was rarely seen in the street, except when he went to and came back from work or when he shopped for necessities. The rest of the time, he carved. People came from all over the city to buy his carvings, which sold for paltry sums; often, he simply gave them away as if to cement a secret pact that he had made with himself. I liked to think that he deemed it more important to send his work out into the world than to be paid for it. I so much admired his altruism. It was as if the primary consideration was to set his work free. People in the street mocked him. They greeted him with the name Mayonesa and laughed as he strode past them, his gait simian and short, his eyes blazing with a fire seen only in madmen or the holy. Once a year, during his vacation from Kaplan's, Peralta would disappear from the neighborhood. Some people said he returned to Cacimar to visit his family, but no one was sure of this, because those times when he was seen leaving the block he had no suitcase and upon returning he looked as if he had spent his time with derelicts in the Bowery. This I found out is exactly what Peralta did. Why he chose this course of action for two weeks out of the year became a mystery to me.

One year, in the middle of writing the final draft of *The Tragedy of Cacimar*, the story of the great chieftain of the Taíno Indians, who slaughtered his children and flung them from a cliff into the sea rather than see them become slaves of the Spaniards, I was suddenly seized by a passionate urge to uncover the mystery of Mayonesa Peralta.

Driven by my own madness I began asking questions. Why was he called Mayonesa? No one knew, but old timers, like Sinforoso Figueroa, who owned *Bodega Cacimar* on the block where I lived, swore the name dated back to the end of World War II and that Peralta was already in the neighborhood. This was established early on. Peralta spoke English with only the slightest trace of an accent. He had served in the infantry during the war and was wounded slightly. As I researched further, I learned that he had been married to an American woman from New Bedford, Massachusetts, an heiress of considerable beauty, whom he had met while they were both in Italy, he as an infantryman and she as a Red Cross nurse.

Had anyone ever seen her? Ramón Aguirre, the old baker, had.

"She was blonde and had very good manners," he told me. "Very good looking, even though she had hardly any lips. They lived on 116th Street in a brownstone which she bought. They had a Hudson with whitewalls and Mayonesa always dressed in a suit. Everyone thought he was a gangster, but he wasn't."

In talking with the old timers I learned that her name was Constance Bickford and that she knew pupils of Rodin and had introduced Peralta to them; that Peralta had studied sculpting in Europe after the war and that the back yard of the brownstone was filled with large pieces of stone at which Peralta worked.

And what had gone wrong? This no one knew. One year the two of them disappeared and eight or ten months later Peralta returned to the neighborhood, disheveled and bearded, his eyes wearing that look of fury which he still retained nearly forty years later. But why the name? Everyone I asked laughed and shrugged his shoulders. It isn't uncommon for our people to give each other odd names, but if one looked deep enough it was possible to find a logical answer to why the person had been rechristened: a predilection for a food, an idiosyncrasy of behavior, a word spoken incorrectly or at the wrong time, a certain look. In Peralta's case, each time I turned in a different direction I met a dead end.

I struggled on with my work until finally one day in late spring, I finished the final revision and shipped it off to be read or not read, but most likely to be rejected, for it was a work filled with anger that we, as a people, must still undergo ritual suicide in order not to be enslaved by our present "masters."

It was then that I made a conscious effort to befriend Peralta and find out directly from him why he had been tagged with such an odd name. A week of timing his arrival from work with a walk in his area of the neighborhood proved useless. I inquired as to his whereabouts and was told that he had disappeared. "Probably on vacation," said Manrique, the superintendent of his building.

It was useless and I nearly gave up trying to find him. I imagined all sorts of incredible romances. She had passed away and each year Peralta would travel to Massachusetts to place flowers on her grave and pray for her eternal repose. Or else they had produced a beautiful mentally deficient child which they both loved but had to institutionalize and each year they journeyed to some secret hospital and visited their thirty year old infant. As in all chimeric matters I was absolutely wrong. Somehow in nearly giving up I found myself mystically encountering Peralta in the most unusual and tragic of circumstances.

One day, after meeting with my good friend, Bertrand Saddler, the internationally known law scholar, in order to check a fine point of law concerning the Spanish Courts of the time of the conquest of the island, I came out of his apartment house on Park Avenue near 70th Street when I heard an overwhelming torrent of the foulest language I had ever heard, all of it in Spanish. I turned and, across the street, through the shrubbery and tulip gardens of the center dividers which adorn Park Avenue in this section of the city, I saw Peralta, his winter coat on and a purple woolen hat on his head. He was gesticulating wildly and shaking his fist while spewing forth a continuous stream of obscene epithets wholly directed at women for the ease with which they could lie back and give themselves freely without having to concern themselves that they were not fully aroused. Peralta was drunk beyond redemption and totally unbalanced as to his mental state. Of the latter there was little doubt in my mind.

I crossed the street and saw that Peralta was carrying a large white jar. As I drew closer I saw that it was a restaurant-size jar of Hellman's mayonnaise and that every once in a while he would dip his hand in the jar and attempt to fling the contents at a window on the second or third floor, all the while screaming at the top of his lungs that American women were frigid and dry and what they needed was lubrication in the form of mayonnaise. More obscene yet, he proclaimed that the reason they had developed this condition was that mayonnaise was made from the collected vaginal fluids of American females in order to please American males, who were more interested in a well-made sandwich than they were in satisfying their women and that he didn't care how many books the son of a bitch had written or how many bulls he had fought or fish he had caught, it didn't give him the right to impose himself on his woman and that he would go on challenging him to a fist fight even in death and how come, since he thought he was such a great boxer and such a brave macho, he had to go and blow his brains out without first giving him satisfaction in the field of honor.

All of this in Spanish so that the Cuban doormen in front of the buildings ducked back inside in order not to be identified with this madman, who, they explained to the affluent tenants, was not Cuban or even Dominican, or any other Latin type, because no one would behave this way except Puerto Ricans. This attitude on the part of the doormen I learned about from my friend Bertrand Saddler a few days later.

But at that point I could no longer endure the pain of watching this great man, who worked so well with wood, demean himself in such a fashion. I thought of walking up to him and suggesting that he come with me back to the neighborhood, but I knew that he would feel doubly ashamed to be found under such conditions now that he knew we shared common ground as artists.

Instead, I walked sadly away and returned to my apartment troubled by what I had seen. I had learned why he was called Mayonesa, but now a bigger puzzle was confronting me. There was no doubt that Peralta was referring to the great Ernest Hemingway in his attack. What was the connection between Peralta and Hemingway?

When I reached my apartment I immediately called Saddler back and, without going into elaborate detail asked, if he knew anyone nearby who would have known Hemingway. He wanted to know what I meant by nearby and I said within a block or two of where he lived on Park Avenue. He said he did not but that he would inquire and get back to me if he found anyone.

A few days later Peralta returned to the neighborhood, again disheveled, dirty, haggard, his beard matted and more pained than ever. He remained in his apartment several days and then emerged sober and returned to his routine of traveling to Brooklyn to work and then come home to devote his spare time to his carvings.

A month or so later I received notification from Houston that my novel *The Tragedy of Cacimar* had been accepted and that upon publication I would fly there for a book party and several public readings. I was overjoyed and forgot about Peralta. Sometime in late June Bertrand Saddler called me and said he had found a widow who had known Hemingway and would I be interested in meeting her. At first I didn't make the connection between my interest in Peralta and the phone call, but as soon as I realized what Saddler was referring to I felt the same urgency that I had felt several months before.

"At your earliest convenience, Bertrand," I said.

"Very well, Ernesto," he said. "I shall get back to you within the hour."

An hour later Saddler called back and asked if it was possible for me to come to his home the following Friday evening. I said it would be no problem at all. That entire week I could do no work. When Friday came I dressed in my old summer suit of white linen, my white shoes and Panama hat and went to Saddler's home, a large, elegant apartment befitting my friend's stature.

I was shown to the library by his butler. Seated there was a woman of some sixty years of age, quite delicate and still very beautiful.

"Ernesto, may I present Mrs. Constance Bickford Clay," Saddler said. "Constance, this is my dear friend, Ernesto Mendoza, novelist and raconteur par excellence."

I bowed solemnly and kissed her hand, barely brushing the skin with my lips.

"How do you do, Mrs. Clay," I said.

"Very well, thank you, Mr. Mendoza," she said. "It is a pleasure to meet you. Bertrand has told me many wonderful things about you."

We had drinks before dinner and then we went into the dining room and had a light seafood meal with superb wines. All through dinner we talked about literature and painting and the world situation but never once was the subject of Hemingway broached by the three of us. When dinner was over we returned to the library and then Mrs. Clay asked me directly, while she was stirring her coffee, about my interest in Hemingway, that yes, she had known him briefly in Paris *and* Spain after the end of the Second World War, while she was a correspondent for a Boston newspaper, but that after that time she had lost contact with him.

"Are you doing some type of research on him?" she said.

"No, not really," I said.

I went on to explain my concern and said that I had a friend who was very troubled and perhaps it was possible that she might have known him.

She asked me his name and when I told her she readily admitted that she had been married to him. I thought I detected a slight pained expression cross her face, but she quickly regained her composure and went on to say that what had happened between them had been unfortunate but in many ways made her realize how foolishly romantic she had been.

"Please, don't misunderstand me," she said. "Nemecio was an extremely talented man. A man of boundless energy and an enormous appetite for life."

Candidly, she went on to explain that she had been head over heels in love with him, would have given the world to remain with him, but that she could not endure his obsession with Hemingway and his insistence that she and the famous author had had an affair. She laughed heartily and wiped her delicate mouth with her napkin.

"In truth," she said, "I despised the man. He was a braggart and a bully. If you did not worship at his shrine, you became his mortal enemy. I—she added, haughtily—do not worship anything but life itself. Certainly not a man like the late Mr. Hemingway, in spite of his literary success. He was a troubled man, driven and without spiritual substance. Much weaker than Nemecio. And yet poor Nemecio could not see that. He was driving himself mad with jealousy."

She explained how they had moved from New York to Martha's Vineyard and attempted to live there. She had tried everything in order to restore Peralta's self-esteem but nothing had worked. In time her love for him withered away when he became abusive and began using foul language against her, which she could not tolerate.

"To the end he insisted that I had been Hemingway's lover," she said.

"Are you aware that he often comes to this neighborhood and behaves quite abnormally?" I asked.

"For a number of years," she replied. "At first I thought of calling the police, but then I realized that he was quite harmless."

"Yes," I said.

We were silent for a long while and then she spoke, but her tone was not as formal.

"You care for him a great deal," she said.

"He's a fine artist," I said.

"Does he still work in stone?" she asked, her voice quivering slightly and her eyes suddenly misting.

"Wood," I said.

"Yes, he always spoke about wood with great longing."

Her words trailed off and we were once again silent. Bertrand Saddler excused himself from the room and then Constance Bickford asked me if I thought he was well. I explained all that I could about his life and his work and how each year about the same time he went on a drinking binge, but that the rest of the time he simply went from his job to his apartment and his carvings.

"Is he married?" she said.

"Not that I know of," I said.

Silence once more. This time much longer than previously. I became uncomfortable and finally said that he was in good health and remarkably strong for his age.

"Yes, he always had a strong constitution," she said, and laughed for the first time. "Please answer me truthfully."

"If I'm able," I said.

"Do you think I could see him sometime?" she said. "What I mean is, do you think it would upset him to see me?"

"I truthfully don't know, Mrs. Clay."

"Please find out."

"Very well."

We said good night and I returned to my apartment more troubled yet. How was I to approach Peralta? I thought it over for nearly two weeks before I decided on a direct approach. One Thursday in July I went to his building and sat on the front steps until he arrived. When he saw me he frowned and then greeted me. We spoke in Spanish.

"You made a mistake, Peralta," I said.

"What are you talking about?" he snapped at me.

"That Hemingway business," I said, sternly, but quaking inside since I was no match for his physical strength.

"Come upstairs and have a cup of coffee," he said.

I followed him up the stairs and watched him as he made coffee. We didn't speak until he had set the cups on the table and we were sipping from the strong, sweet *café con leche*.

"What's this about Hemingway, that son of a bitch," he said. "What in the hell do you know about it?"

"Constance told me," I said.

"Where do you know the whore from?" he said.

"Quiet, you old fool," I said.

"Watch your mouth, Mendoza," he said, menacingly, his eyes on fire, his huge hands opening and closing. "I could kill you with one blow."

"I know you could, but you still made a mistake and that's all there is to it. She never had anything to do with Hemingway. She loved you and you were too blind to see it. She probably still does."

He was stunned and sat there looking beyond me at the street outside his window, his eyes growing cloudy and his powerful body visibly shrinking with shame.

"I thought she was sleeping with him," he said. "I wanted to kill him. Not her, though. We came back to New York and things got worse and worse. Did you see me outside her building?"

"Yes, I did," I said, feeling all of his shame and all of his pain. "It's all right. I understand."

"You understand about the name, then?"

"Yes, I understand." I said.

"I haven't cared about my life," he said.

"I know, but you should. You're a fine artist."

"Thank you," he said, and nodded several times. "Thank you very much. You are a man of great courage."

"A man of great stupidity," I said. "You could have destroyed me."

He laughed and shook his head.

"No, I'm all bluff," he said. "All I care about is making things, not destroying them."

He then asked about Constance and I told him what I knew. When I told him she was a widow, he seemed relieved and when I said she wanted to see him, he became embarrassed and said it would be impossible for him to face her.

"It's never too late," I said.

"Perhaps you're right," he said. "But I must have time. Tell her that for me."

I said I would and we said good bye. We became good friends after that and I began urging him to get out more. Although I am somewhat of a recluse myself, I found that for his sake I would spend time walking around New York City with him, stopping off at sidewalk cafes and discussing life. Each time I asked him if he was ready to see Constance, he said he wasn't. And then one day in late fall when the trees had shed all of their foliage and the days had grown shorter, he announced without my broaching the subject that he was ready to see Constance.

"At my place," he said. "Next Saturday."

I immediately conveyed the message and the following Saturday, Constance Bickford Clay emerged from her limousine, climbed the steps of the tenement building where Nemecio Peralta lived and I escorted her upstairs to his apartment. They greeted each other cordially, a certain familiar warmth apparent but held in reserve.

In the middle of the front room draped with a sheet there stood what I surmised was a sculpture. After she was seated at the table and he had made coffee for the three of us, Nemecio stood up and pulled the sheet away from the sculpture. It was a beautiful polished wooden carving of Constance as a young woman, her naked body so sensuous and inviting that I turned away quite embarrassed by the life-like quality of the piece. When I turned Constance was blushing. Her reaction made me even more uncomfortable. Peralta was smiling.

"Do you like it?" he said to her.

She nodded ever so demurely and I announced that I had several matters to which I had to attend. They did not hear me so I let myself out of the apartment and immediately decided to contact Esperanza on the island. Wherever she was I had to find her and convince her that it was not too late, that she need not feel she was too old to share her life with me. I felt lighter and happier than I had felt in years and knew then that no matter what happened to my life from that moment on, I had lived fully and with a certain measure of courage and, ultimately, that is what counted.

Lionel G. García

The Day They Took My Uncle

The day they took my uncle I had been under the house playing all morning long with a little girlfriend older than me and she had shown me her female part. I was amazed, seeing it for the first time, at how simple it was. At that age I could never have imagined it as I had seen it that morning. Afterwards, I could never get her, teaser that she was, to show it to me again. So the memory of it faded from me and I was left with a blur, a blur much like the pictures of female pubes in nudist colony magazines that I had a peek at as a child. I imagined that these magazine pictures had been true and that these female parts were constantly moving at a great rate of speed. Why else would they create a blur on a photograph? But that was not what I had seen that morning. What I had seen was standing still. I had been educated. But that in itself is another story.

My uncle was insane, crazy. He was also missing, but I knew where he was. His insanity was well known throughout town. He had been insane for many years. His problem was that, at a spur of the moment and without forewarning, this lean and sallow man would rise to his feet, if he was sitting or squatting on his haunches, and start walking desperately. Then he would grab his ears, the lobes, and start yanking them down violently, as if trying to shake some diabolical voices from his ears. Then he would begin to curse violently. He cursed at people, naming names. He had the indelicate habit also of bringing up pasts that were better left behind and he would talk about the people and about what they had done. I don't know where he got his information, but a lot of it was not true. It was all right as long as he stayed within the family and in our yard or in the immediate neighborhood. But, for no apparent reason, he began to set off in his tirade to the mayor's house: cursing, yanking at his ears, impugning the mayor's ancestry, calling him a sonofabitch and a son of a whore, plus a bastard. The mayor's wife was not spared. My uncle stoutly proclaimed that she was fucking the mayor's cousin. The poor mayor's wife was a frail little dried up person of a woman who probably didn't even do *it* with the mayor. He also called her a whore and a bitch. I knew he had done this for sure. I was with him that day.

I was, for some reason, his favorite and he tried to do things for me. He would whittle away with his knife, occasionally having these fits, the knife in his yanking hand, until he would finish some little wood carving for me. He made a great fuss over giving me these carvings as if he were really giving me something of great value. He was not a good whittler. In fact, he was not good for anything except for drinking and causing the family trouble.

He was an alcoholic. Which brings me to the supposed cause of his bedevilment. He had been possessed, my grandmother told us, when he accidentally drank the dregs of a bottle of beer that had been laced with a special potion, a potion so powerful it would cause insanity. It was, she said, a potion meant for someone else. I cringed at the thought that some day I would encounter the potion accidentally as my uncle had done and that I would be rendered into that same state. Therefore, I resolved at an early age never to drink left-over beer.

His life consisted of whittling or drinking from early on in the day and coming home, but there was always someone who would buy him a beer. He was a source of entertainment in these taverns, for no one knew when he would get these cursing attacks. No one knew when he would explode. When he did, inside the tavern, he would walk round and round among the men pulling violently at his ears and cursing. The fun was that no one knew who he was going to curse. In this small town it was usually someone everyone knew and the men would hoot and holler, as my uncle went round and round screaming his insults. Soon, after a few minutes, he would come to and stare blankly for a while, gather his thoughts and sit down and mumble to himself. The men would laugh and then my uncle would start laughing with them. Sometimes, when he had a fit in town, the children would run behind, taunting him.

Whether he remembered what he did or not I never knew. I never asked him. In fact, after he was through with his maniacal episodes, I would try to change the subject—talk of something else, something more cheerful. And it seemed as if he preferred it.

But he loved me most of all and that was my problem. He involved me, at a very early age, in things that I never should have been involved in. I can't believe to this day that my parents allowed me to walk the streets with him.

One day, drunk as usual, he took me by the hand and we went to get the milk cow which he had tied across from the mayor's house. As we came by the house, I could feel a slight trembling starting in his hand. And suddenly, as if a demon had possessed him, he started cursing and running toward the mayor's house, towing me along with him. This time he jerked only at one ear at a time. His other hand was holding mine. I was barely touching the ground as he swung me around on his rampage. He started with the mayor and cursed him, and then he continued with the mayor's wife. I could see the poor lady, worried as she was and scared, peeping through a crack in the curtain, watching all this: a deranged man yanking at his ears holding a little boy by the hand and running, menacingly, toward her house.

It was embarrassing to have an uncle like this one around the family. Your friends needed to be very tolerant. My sister didn't like him too much. She could never invite anyone over.

One time a young man came uninvited to call on my sister, and, as he was walking to the front door, my uncle started having a fit inside the house and ran out, bursting through the front door, screaming, just as the man was coming up the stairs, and my uncle ran right through him and knocked him down. The man got up fast and started running away, but everywhere he tried to run it seemed he'd run into my zig-zagging uncle. He never came back to call on my sister. He was known to have said that he would never call on a girl who had heard so many curse words in her young life.

He didn't stay with us at night. I guess he realized the inconvenience it would have caused. He lived next door in a small house with no electricity, no heat and no water. Later on when he became sick and right before he died my grandmother moved him into the dining room that we never used and set up a small cot for him. It was interesting, as I was told, that in his last days the doctor told him he couldn't drink anymore unless he wanted to die. So he quit drinking and died within the week. What he died of no one knew and no one cared. That was the beauty of life in a small town. People died and that was that. There was no need for heavy medical expenses or lengthy hospital stays or exotic diagnostics. If a person got sick and then got well that was a cause for joy. If a person got sick and died, well, they buried the person and everyone kept on living. So when he died, he just died. Even the doctor was not particularly interested as to why a person had died. He was there to treat well people.

The mayor was not home when we were trampling his front yard, but his wife told him about it and, rightfully so, the mayor became very angry. He had already been angry before, since that was not the first time my uncle had gone on a rampage against him and his wife.

That night the mayor came over and talked to my grandmother, my mother and my father, and they had assured the mayor that they would scold my uncle. My uncle, in the meantime, was at the tavern begging for beer and getting drunk and forgetting to bring the cow home.

You see, my uncle had only one job to do. He was to take the cow to a pasture in the morning after milking her and then he was supposed to bring the cow back before sunset, milk her, and put her up for the night. He was able to do the morning part of the job well and with consistency, but bringing the cow back presented a problem to him. If he was in the middle of a fit, he would forget what time it was or whether he had already taken the cow home or, if he were drinking steadily, if someone was buying him beer, he didn't want to quit just to bring a cow home.

So frequently, as we did that night, my father and I went to look for the patiently waiting and confused cow to bring her home. I say we had to look for the cow because we never knew for sure where my uncle had tied her that morning. The tethering of the cow and it's location was left entirely up to him. If he found a lush grassy place by the cemetery, he would tie her there. The next day he would tie here somewhere else. Usually the cow was never at the same place on two successive days.

My father and I would go looking for the cow and I would hold the lantern as we walked the dusty streets and, when we thought we saw the huge bulk of the animal in the darkened field, he would take the lantern from me and raise it above his head to see if we had located the cow.

My father never got angry with my uncle. He would scold him lightly and in a very gentle way. My uncle would look at him with his large sorrowful eyes and would promise to do anything that my father wanted him to do. Then he would walk away, the halter rope in his hand, the cow walking slowly behind him and sometimes he would start his fit at this time and let go of the cow and he would walk hurriedly away, tugging at his ears and cursing at the sky. The cow would stop, look at him stoically, as if she knew this was the cross she had been given to bear, and wait patiently for him to complete the fit.

He had another one of his fits while he was walking through downtown main street and this time everyone there heard him curse the mayor and his wife.

The sheriff's car came slowly by the house, went slightly past it and I could see from under the house the sheriff straining to see if he could spot my uncle. He stopped the car and backed up and parked in front. He got out. He was a formidable man, over six feet with a large belly, his gun belt hidden by the bulge in front. He carried a large long-barreled revolver and a pair of hand-cuffs were tucked under the belt at one side.

My girlfriend and I looked at each other. I suspected why he was here. You see, a week before, the doctor and the sheriff had come by the house and I overheard them telling my parents about what my uncle had done and that my uncle had to be placed in an insane asylum. My parents were law-abiding people and they agreed that, if that was what was best for my uncle, then that's the way it had to be. The sheriff said it was the legal and proper thing to do. He said that my uncle was a menace and a constant source of embarrassment to the community. Even the Sister's of Charity, the three nuns that were left behind after the parochial school closed, were demanding that something be done. The priest, of course, was in complete agreement. Since the school and the rectory and the church were across the street, they, the priest and the nuns, could hear my uncle shouting obscenities. The priest said he had condoned it for some time, but he figured it was time to do something now that the mayor and the sheriff and the doctor were in agreement. He hadn't wanted to be the first one to complain, being a priest and all. The solution, of course, was to get my uncle into an insane asylum in Galveston.

We could see the sheriff come up the dirt path, the path bordered by lime-covered rocks. He came up the stairs and walked above us onto the little porch and he knocked heavily. The whole house seemed to shake under his heavy fist.

We could hear the footsteps above us as my mother came to answer the door. "Coming, coming," my mother said.

"María," the sheriff said in his gruff voice. "I've come for Mercé. It's time. This is the day we agreed on."

"Come in, come in," my mother was saying to him and, to us eavesdroppers under the house, it seemed that everything that was said had some humor in it. My girlfriend placed her small dirty little hand over her mouth to cover up a giggle. I was smiling at the thought that no one knew we were there.

"Sit down," my mother said, "sit down." She had the habit of repeating everything when she was nervous.

"I don't have time to sit," the sheriff informed my mother. I could tell he was angry. "We need to get him out of town and put him up somewhere, like Galveston, where someone who knows about these things can help him."

"My husband and I agree," my mother replied, "We'll cooperate in whatever way we can."

"Well it's been a long time. I mean he's been hanging around town cursing at everybody for a long time. It's just come to a head recently, that's all. Maybe we should've done it sooner. It's just that we all treated it as a joke."

"He's always been harmless," my mother said. "He wouldn't hurt a fly."

My uncle and I often went hunting but we never killed anything. He carried the rifle and I walked by his side. Once in a while he would hold me up as I stopped to pick a burr out of my foot. He would wait patiently, much like the cow had done for him, as I balanced on one leg and dug out a goat-head from the sole of my foot. When we came upon a rabbit I would whisper excitedly, "There's one. Can you see it? Can you see the rabbit?"

My uncle would look close at the little animal and act as if he were going to shoot it, then he would say, "We'd better save him. We'll kill him on the way back."

We could hear the sound of leather as the sheriff adjusted his gun-belt. "Don't be too sure," he said. "He could be violent under certain circumstances."

"That's strange," my mother said. "I've never known anything, *anything*, that makes him violent, except being violent on himself. God only knows what voices he hears or what pain he gets, but he yanks at his ears like he's going to pull them off."

"Well, enough of this," the sheriff said, and we could hear him walk around our little house opening doors. "Where is he?"

"He's probably at the beer hall," my mother replied, "where he normally goes every day. Don't you think?"

"No, he's not there," the sheriff informed her. "I've looked everywhere except here."

"Well, I'll be," my surprised mother said. From under the house I could imagine her putting her fingers to her mouth like she always did when she felt surprised.

"You don't have any idea where he's at?" the sheriff asked.

"No," my mother replied. "But have you seen the cow? He may be close by."

"I didn't see the cow," the sheriff said. "But I wasn't looking for her either. Where was he supposed to take her?"

"I have no idea," my mother said, "but I think that lately he's been staying close to the mayor's house on that open pasture."

"And you're sure you haven't seen him?" he asked my mother again to make sure she wasn't lying.

"I'm sure," she answered and she was telling the truth.

We could see my grandmother coming across the yard. She lived next door. We could see her long black dress moving from side to side as she strode over to see what was going on.

"Are they here for Mercé?" she asked my mother as she stood outside.

My mother came to the window by where we were sitting and she talked to her. My grandmother was telling my mother where he was hiding. Of course I knew where he was hiding all along. He was under an old rug in a corner of the toolshed behind my grandmother's house.

In the morning he had come to the window by where I slept and he had scratched on the screen and awakened me. Today was the day they would take him, he said. He didn't want to go. "You've got to," I said to him. "Where are you going to hide?" "I'll hide," he said and he thought for a moment, as if he didn't know, "in the tool shed."

I felt sorry for him at that time. I wanted to cry. I didn't want them to take him away. And yet I knew that he needed help. Just think, I had told him, if you can come back normal how much better off you'll be. He still wanted to hide.

"And what if they find you?" I asked.

"They won't," he said. "What do you think?"

"If you think you can hide there forever, then give it a try," I said, although it scared me to think that I would have to lie about his whereabouts. What I didn't realize at the time, young as I was, was that they would find him very quickly and that there was no escaping the law.

Unknown to anyone, my uncle had panicked and fled the toolshed. The sheriff had already come outside and he was checking the yard. When he stood in front of the toolshed door my grandmother and my mother screamed, "Don't hurt him! Don't harm him! Please don't hurt him! He's a very gentle man."

The sheriff kicked the door open and had his hand on his pistol ready to draw it out if he needed to. He disappeared into the toolshed and we could all hear the commotion inside. My mother was screaming, as was my grandmother, imploring the sheriff not to hurt my uncle. From the noise inside it appeared that my uncle had been discovered. The sheriff seemed to be tearing the place apart. Finally, the old rug came flying through the door and my grandmother and my mother both screamed. They thought it was my uncle flying through the air. My grandmother fainted and fell to the ground, like a rag doll. The sheriff kept crashing things and I wondered how the place would look like after he got through. My mother ran inside the toolshed and my grandmother, who had gotten up and recovered, followed her, and my girlfriend and I could hear all three thrashing about and the greatest commotion I ever heard.

Then, suddenly, from behind me I picked up the faint smell of stale beer. It was my uncle's breath. He was under the house with us! He had escaped from the toolshed while the sheriff was inside our house.

I couldn't very well talk to him. My mouth was so dry and I was so scared, but the words finally came out and I asked him what he was doing. He didn't seem to know. He had the look that I had seen wounded rabbits have right before you step on their heads, as if they were pleading for help and knowing they can't have any. It was the sight of fear in his eyes, the feeling of being tracked down for the kill that haunts me still. What could I do? I was too little to do anything. He put his arms around me and we both fell to the ground and he started crying, sobbing. He didn't know what to do. He didn't want to go. My girlfriend started crying too.

The sheriff had come out of the toolshed and he looked like he had been in a terrible fight. My mother and my grandmother tried to fend him off with ropes and tools and whatever they could find. You see, they thought that he had killed my uncle. They were chasing him down the yard when, as luck would have it, my uncle began his trembling and started one of his crazy fits. He hit his head on a floor joist and he started bleeding. And thus he came out from under the house, crawling side-ways like a fast crab, bleeding from the head. He straightened out, grabbed his ears and began yanking and pulling them as he started his walk, shouting obscenities at the world. This time he included not only the mayor and the mayor's wife, but he also said some bad things about the priest and how the priest was fucking the nuns. And as if on order, the windows of the rectory closed as fast as possible.

Once he had shed the two women, the sheriff ran up from behind and tackled my crazed uncle. He caught my uncle completely by surprise, blind-sided him, and my poor uncle in the middle of his cursing gave out a loud grunt as the wind was knocked out of him. The sheriff quickly put my uncle's hands behind his back and hand-cuffed him. Still, my uncle persisted and yelled and screamed, and he rubbed first one ear and then the other into the ground until he caused them to bleed.

Once they realized that my uncle was alive, that the sheriff had not killed him, my mother and grandmother stopped beating on the man. And once they realized my uncle had been found and restrained, they ran over and tried to help the sheriff and my uncle to their feet.

My father arrived running. He had been at work. We could see that he was helping the sheriff get Mercé up and they had gone to the other side of the house to the water faucet. The sheriff cleaned himself up and my father, mother and grandmother cleaned up my uncle. He had quieted down now and was into the mumbling stage of his fit.

"Look at what you did to yourself," my mother said to my uncle.

"You could really hurt yourself doing all this."

"He can't help it," my father told her.

"Well, he wasn't so hard to catch," the sheriff said. And yet I feel sorry for you," he told my uncle.

"Come, we'll help you get him to the car," my grandmother told the sheriff.

"I'd appreciate it," the sheriff replied.

"Now, Mercé," my mother lectured him, "be good in Galveston. You're going to Galveston, did you know that? Maybe somebody there can help you. And it's very pretty in Galveston, did you know that? They have a beach."

My uncle shook his head.

"Well that's where you're going. Be good over there and behave. Try to control yourself and maybe you can come back soon."

When they helped the sheriff put my uncle in the back seat, he looked toward us under the house. I could see him plainly, but I could tell he was trying desperately to find me, so I came out a little ways to where the sun was shining under the house, and I could tell he saw me. He gave a terrible cry.

As the car drove away my father kept yelling for the sheriff to stop, but the sheriff never heard him.

"What did you want? my mother asked him, crying, as the car with my uncle disappeared from view. He replied that he wanted to find out what my uncle had done with the cow.

And my mother and grandmother cried some more. At first they cried every time they saw the cow. The poor cow could never figure out what there was about her that made them cry. She would look inquiringly from one side of herself to the other, as if looking for some clue.

My uncle came back a year later, uncured and ready to go. He did, though, carry a little card in a billfold my father bought him saying that he was not a menace to society.

Roberta Fernández

Andrea

something about you
  all of us
    with songs inside
      knifing the air of sorrow
        with our dance
          a carnival of spirits
            shredded blossoms
              on the water

Jessica Hagedorn

I

The most extraordinary images of Andrea had been neatly mounted inside the black triangular corners in the thick blue album. It had taken my mother almost fifteen years to piece all those pictures together; after that, she had carefully guarded her collection for almost as long as it had taken her to assemble it. She was so attached to her album that for as far back as I could remember she had been telling my sisters and me all about her cousin Andrea's dramatic life. My mother's retelling had made us very aware that the backdrop for Andrea's adventures had been set a long time ago, even before she had made her debut at the Teatro Zaragoza.

The photographs were our connection to that past. At first my mother had stored them in a large hat box but soon the constant arrival of Andrea's parcels caused it to overflow. The postmarks on those packages indicated that she had been in San Francisco and Santa Fe, Tucson and Albuquerque, cities my mother knew only from magazines and the movies. Mother was so good at describing those places, however, that I soon began to imagine myself journeying in Andrea's footsteps.

The album on Andrea's career had actually initiated me in this ritual already, for it had helped me and my sisters relive Andrea's experiences over and over. Andrea had assisted with this rerun by jotting on the back of each program or photo the information she thought my mother wanted to know: the name of the production, where it had been performed and the role she had played in it. Between the two of them, they had constructed a significant record of our family's history.

Over the years, the performer in the picture book had acquired a special quality for all of us; yet, in fact, my sisters and I knew Andrea only as the flamboyant character in the photographs. The last time she had visited my mother and my aunts, Patricia had been an infant and Adriana hadn't yet been born. I had been so little then that the only thing I remembered about her was a softly melodious voice which slowly became transformed into an enchanting personality who traipsed about in the limelight of make-believe and far-away.

But now she would be coming to see us once again. Tía Griselda and Tía Julieta had just told us that Andrea's visit would coincide with Violeta Aguilera's dance recital and knowing that Andrea would be in the audience during my first solo performance had really unsettled me. So, I barely listened to Tía Griselda's comments as she started to turn the pages of the album. By the tone of her voice in the background, though, I knew she had assumed the role of mother's elder sister as she described her early life in San Luis Potosí. As she talked, I preferred to concentrate on the sounds in my head—the steady clatter of castanets and Violeta Aguilera's strict counting of the *pasodoble.*

Still, I was unable to completely drown out the sound of Griselda's voice as she pointed to a portrait of Andrea's family. "Here's the entire family at Andrea's baptism. The picture captures the family relationships very well. There's Florencia holding the infant Andrea in her white baptismal gown. Notice how her gaze is letting the whole world know that this child was to be the center of her world. And here is Julián, the girl's father. See how he has his arms around Consuelo. They were very close to each other. For ten years Consuelo had grown up as an only child. Her father's favorite daughter you might say. The picture was taken in 1910. A few months later, they all headed northward. So while Andrea spent all her childhood in this country, Consuelo arrived fully formed. She was a very serious child and people tended to attribute her solemnity to an inability to adjust to a new culture. But you can tell from this picture that already in Mexico she had a very serious bent."

As soon as Griselda mentioned the expression on little Consuelo's face, the music in my head came to a stop. For some reason, every time I looked at this particular picture I became intrigued with the look on Consuelo's face. The sharp contrast it made with the dimpled, smiling seven-year old Andrea in the picture on the facing page could not be greater.

In the second picture, Andrea was standing in front of one of the large-framed houses at the local army compound. The house belonged to Mrs. Anderson, who taught piano classes in the local schools while her husband did his military duty. The third person in the photo was Mrs. Bristol, a poet of sorts from Connecticut. I knew that when Consuelo was thirteen she had done some housework for Mrs. Bristol and that the two women had taken it upon themselves to support Andrea's obvious talents by sending her to classes taught by the well-known dancer Pepita Montemayor.

I did not need to listen to Griselda's narrative to know she was not particularly fond of either Mrs. Anderson or Mrs. Bristol; so, I tuned her out altogether as the music once again filled my head. Instead, I pictured us—Pepita, Andrea, Violeta and me, four generations of dancers—moving to the sounds of the *jota aragonesa* as the steady, rhythmic chatter of eight castanets exploded in a crescendo over and over again.

The colorful ritual in my head ended when my sisters burst into laughter as they pointed to a picture of Andrea and Tía Julieta as young girls wearing long tunics tied at the waist with a cord.

"So you think we look funny?" Julieta asked them. "Well, let me tell you, we were marvelous in this *pastorela*, 'La Aurora del Nuevo Día.' We performed it at the St. Agustine Church plaza in 1921 when we were both eleven. Andrea convinced me to be her partner. I'm glad she did, since it's been my only performance in theater."

Griselda pointed to two more pictures. "Here, she's already at the Royal Opera House. In this picture, she's an Aragonese and in there, she's a *Tehuana*, a woman from Tehuantepec. She was thirteen then. Look at her *tehuana* headpiece. It's all made of lace and shaped like a huge balloon. Only her face showed through the opening. To me she looked like a smiling sunflower."

"Can we look at the picture of Doña Inés?" little Adriana piped in. "It's my favorite."

"You mean this one?" Mother turned to the back of the album, pointing to a photo of Andrea in a floor-length outfit and long curls gathered into a big cluster.

"That's my favorite," Adriana nodded.

"This one was taken at a theater in New York. Andrea appeared there in 'Don Juan Tenorio.' It was her last performance. November the 2nd, 1940."

"I'll show you the one I like the most," I said flipping through the pages. "I just love the way she's looking at us here. See how her hands are crossed at the back of her neck. Look at her funny little heart-shaped mouth. How I'd love to be wearing that long sequinned dress!"

"Hmmm," began Griselda. "She looks too artificial. The real Andrea was never like that. Today, she probably has no connection to that look. It's been fifteen years since she left the theater and that's really a long time to be away from all this."

"You're right. She is another person now," mother agreed. "The contrast was very obvious in the snapshot she sent us last Christmas."

"I remember. They looked like they were having lots of fun in the snow," Patricia interjected. She looked at mother with admiration, then asked, "How did you ever put so much work into this album? Me, I get bored with scrapbooks right away. But, Mama, you just kept making this one bigger and bigger. Didn't you ever get tired of it?" A wistful expression settled on mother's face. "You can't begin to imagine how much I loved touching all the material that kept coming in. Year after year. Sometimes when I was down in the dumps, the mailman would surprise me with a thick package. I never knew when it would arrive. But whenever it got here I'd show the materials to Mamá and Griselda and Julieta." She paused for a moment. "There was always such a sparkle in Andrea's face. For hours and hours we'd look at the pictures, imagining what her life must have been like. Then, many months later, when Andrea would come for a visit, we'd hear her version of things. I usually preferred what we had invented for ourselves. Our own stories were really much more elaborate than what she would describe to us."

She turned to Griselda, then to Julieta. "Do you remember when we got the first package? The mailman brought it in October of 1925. I was fifteen then and my life was so ordinary and boring in comparison to Andrea's."

Mother began to reminisce about Andrea's departure from home in early 1925. "That was the year she went to live in San Antonio. A year earlier Consuelo and Tomás had gotten married. He got a job in the advertising department at *La Prensa* and they moved to San Antonio. Then a little while later, Andrea and Tía Florencia went to live with them. Andrea had just turned fifteen then but she was already pretty well-known here. Pepita Montemayor had chosen her as the lead dancer in every one of her programs. She had even selected her as her assistant and took her to Mexico City for additional training. You can imagine how disappointed Pepita was when Andrea told her she was leaving. 'But you don't have any contacts there.' Pepita had warned her. Still, Andrea thought her career stood a better chance of taking off there. And she was right. It did.

"In San Antonio she found a job as an usherette after school at the Teatro Zaragoza, a grand theater at that time. This allowed her to continue her classes and also to get to know the dance companies that performed there."

Mother paused a bit and Julieta picked up the story. "At the Teatro Zaragoza she discovered a whole new world. Right after she saw 'Los Amores de Ramona,' she decided to dedicate herself totally to the theater. That's also where she had her first contact with *zarzuelas* and *sainetes*, the short pieces from Spanish popular theater. One day she read an announcement in *La Prensa* about a *zarzuela* called 'La Señora Capitana.' She auditioned and of course had no trouble getting accepted into the chorus as a dancer. With that bit part she was on her way."

"That's true, but remember that she went completely against Consuelo's wishes," Griselda interrupted. " '*No te metas más en ese mundo*,' Consuelo kept saying to her. In the end, though, Consuelo lost out and Andrea got her way."

As usual, mother quietly came to Andrea's defense. "With her earnings she signed up for voice lessons, and by 1927 she had started to work in operettas as well as in *zarzuelas*. I'm quite sure she had a small part in 'La Viuda Alegre' but I don't have a photograph of her in that role. *Más que nada*, she performed at the Teatro Hidalgo and at the Zendejas in plays written by Spanish playwrights and in a few works by some native Tejanos."

"How come she didn't stay in San Antonio?" Patricia asked.

"Well, in 1930 things got rough for the theater there. So Andrea and some of her friends decided to go West. They had heard that the Depression was not having a negative effect on the theater in Los Angeles in the same way that it was in Texas. On the way there, she performed in the Southwest—in Tucson and Santa Fe. Then she stayed in Los Angeles for quite a while. But by 1936 she was back in Texas touring through the small border towns: Brownsville, Rio Grande, Laredo, Eagle Pass, El Paso. She got as far south as Monterrey and Saltillo and, eventually, she made it to New York. There she found the Spanish exiles very excited about the works of a young playwright, García Lorca. But I don't think she ever appeared in any of his works."

As usual, Griselda suddenly changed the direction of the story. "By then she was already involved with Tony Carducci. After they got married in '41, they went to live in St. Louis, Missouri, where Tony's parents were living. There, Andrea said 'bye-bye' to the theater forever."

Mother then ended the familiar narrative. "In 1938 Consuelo lost Tomás in a horrible car accident. Four years later it was her turn to join Andrea and Tony in St. Louis. Ever since then, they have all been together. But Andrea has told me that Consuelo has never asked her about her fifteen years as a performer. She's just pretended all those years didn't happen."

"Consuelo has always been very stubborn," Julieta concluded.

"Here the three of us kept close watch over everything Andrea did. And her own sister pretended those things didn't happen just 'cause she didn't approve of them. *¡Qué extraña!* "

Surprising even myself by changing the cues, I said quite firmly, "Andrea should never have given up the theater."

"I think Andrea has been very satisfied with her decision," mother replied. "She's never looked back. Once she reasoned it out with me.

'*La rosa más bella dura poco.*' 'Every rose has its day,' she said. I have the impression that she was always happy while she performed. But after fifteen good adventurous years she wanted a stable life. Something she really hadn't ever experienced. '*No se puede repicar y andar en la procesión*' was how she summed up her decision. 'You can't serve two masters at the same time.' "

"I'm quite sure that if I had been in Andrea's shoes, I would never, never have given up the theater. Nor the dance," I insisted.

"Well, Nenita, you know what they say: *Cada quien cuenta de la feria según lo que ve en ella.* You see only what it is you want to see."

I knew I did not want to argue with Griselda; so, I looked for the photo of Andrea dressed as a *tehuana*. Turning the pages back to the year 1923, I heard the familiar mellifluous voice invite me to share the stage with her. The strains of "Zandunga" sounded faintly in the background and slowly we began to sway to its beat. As the music filled the room though, I could see that Andrea moved so much more lightly than I did, and slowly, slowly, I faded into the shadowy background so that the thirteen-year-old Andrea with the lacy white headdress could have center stage by herself, and she took it with full confidence. I closed the book and wondered what it would be like to finally meet this cameleon creature whose many days in the sun my mother had so carefully recorded. Shutting my eyes, I found that the lights on stage had dimmed but even then Andrea continued gliding, gliding so gently to the song that would sound in my head for a long, long time to come.

II

The 10th of July was marked in red on all our calendars. On that day Andrea would be arriving, not alone as we had first been told but accompanied by our cousin Consuelo. Tía Julieta had just informed us of the change of plans reminding us that this would be the first time since 1945 that both of them would be visiting us at the same time. On their previous visit the mood had been somber, for they had come to lay Tía Florencia to rest in the old cemetery next to the tomb of my grandmother, her only sister. To mark the change in tone for this visit, Memo—Julieta's husband—had purchased Mexican party-favors and at the train station he passed out handfuls of *serpentinas* and tin noisemakers to both adults and children.

In the distance we heard the train announce its arrival. A few minutes later, when it rumbled into the Missouri Pacific station, we waited for a sign to begin our welcome as passenger after passenger disembarked. Finally, a slender woman with short wavy hair, in a white shirtwaist stepped down and Griselda whispered, "Here they come." When a second figure appeared at the door of the pullman, Tío Memo gave a signal and we all sounded our noisemakers and sent the *serpentinas* spiraling through the air.

Tío Memo rushed to help Consuelo down the steps as billowing streamers wrapped themselves around her dark print rayon dress and her gray hair. The *serpentinas* looked even more dramatic against Andrea's dress and she quickly enhanced the effect by wrapping clusters of them around her neck. *¡Bienvenidas!*" we shouted in unison. "Welcome!"

There were so many of us at the station it took a long time before my mother's turn came to introduce us to her cousins. Then, I felt uneasy facing the stranger in the clean-cut white dress. Andrea's smile did not exude the least bit of the flamboyance I had learned to associate with the figure of the picture book, and as she embraced me I felt my back stiffen. Consuelo, on the other hand, seemed instantly familiar; in her aging face I immediately recognized the solemn look of the ten-year old girl facing the camera of that unknown photographer in San Luis Potosí. I was glad she'd be the one riding home in the same car with us.

When we got home, Andrea's presence continued to disconcert me; so instead of participating in the noisy gathering, I merely observed the scene before me. She clearly delighted in the attention and chatted freely about the trip. "It felt like the old days, traveling by train," she was saying, "I loved rolling along all those miles of tracks." Her spontaneity was contagious to everyone. Except me, I thought. Then I noticed that Consuelo did not say anything either until there was a lull in the conversation and Griselda asked her what she thought of the trip.

"It was pretty much like sis is describing it," she answered keeping to the role she must have played all of her life. I looked at her delicate figure, then decided to sit next to her on the floor, and as I inched myself towards her, she patted me on the back, then put her arm around my shoulders.

"Tell me about yourself," she whispered.

I whispered back, "I'll be a fifth-grader in September. But right now I'm preparing for my dance recital in Violeta Aguilera's class. It's next week. I'll be doing two solos and in three other numbers I'm one of the leading dancers."

I noticed she drew back a bit. "What kind of dancing do you do?"

"I'll be doing 'La Boda de Luis Alonso' by myself and with Cristina Ruiz and Becky Barrios, I'll be dancing two Mexican pieces, 'Tilingo Lindo' and 'Zandunga.' My other solo is my favorite. It's a Sevillana and I'll get to wear a white flamenco dress with bright red polka dots."

Consuelo looked away. Then she turned to me with her dark eyes. "Dancing may be okay for you now but you won't want to keep doing it later. It doesn't lead you anywhere. Take my word for it."

"That's what my teachers keep telling me. They say I spend too much time practicing. But I love it. I don't know what I'd do if I had to stop."

Just then Tía Julieta joined us. "We're breaking up the party," she said, "Memo and I are going to take Consuelo with us. After a few days we'll all trade visitors. For now Andrea will be staying here."

I felt a little disappointed, for I would rather have continued talking with Consuelo. But I decided to help my mother entertain Andrea as the three of us moved into the kitchen. Without saying a word, I brought out the blue album and placed it on the table. Andrea reached for it eagerly.

"Are these the photographs I sent your mother while I was on the road? *¡Qué gusto verlas!* You know, I don't have any of these pictures?"

She smiled as she turned the pages. "Tony's parents would have a fit if they saw them. Like sis, they never approved of what I did. I'm not even sure what it is they objected to. But I've concluded that they didn't quite like the idea of anyone feeling comfortable and free in front of an audience. For them that's exhibitionism. But I don't know if that was really their objection since they've never wanted to discuss any of it." Finally her light-hearted laughter sounded familiar.

"Tell me, Andrea, do you ever feel sorry you gave up the theater?"

"Would you believe I never think about it?" she responded.

"I felt the stage was my calling and I truly enjoyed performing but once I gave all that up to marry Tony I was determined never to go back on my decision."

She kept perusing through the photographs as she continued talking. "When I first met Tony in New York, he was very good-looking and very intent on becoming a success. I confess I liked both qualities about him. He was always as outgoing as I was and we had a good time together. At the beginning we didn't think we had too many things in common. He'd been born in Southern Italy and had come to New York when he was nine. Then, gradually, we realized we shared more than we had first thought. Even though we were born in different countries, we were both raised here. We grew up rather poor but in very supportive and traditional Catholic families. Our first languages were very similar. And so was the way we looked at the world.

"His parents and I get along fairly well now in spite of their early objections to me. Consuelo had always been very strict about how we should conduct ourselves as a family, and I think it was because of this I was able to adapt to their sense of propriety fairly easily. But, she gets along with the Carducci's much better than I do. Tony's younger brother and sister even think of her as a great-aunt."

"How come she always looks so sad?" I asked.

"Sis is probably the most solemn person I know," Andrea responded, "but I don't think she's a sad person. She's had a tough life and she's learned to be very self-contained. We have so little in common. I'm sure we've both done a lot of thinking about this. At least I have. You see I was brought here as a baby and all the time I was growing up I always lived in the present. Consuelo, by contrast, had been very close to our grandparents and to all the relatives she left behind in San Luis Potosí. Already as a child she tended to live in her memories. And I didn't share those memories. She still talks about being uprooted and keeps the Carducci children entertained for hours with stories about her life as a child. Me, I never had the home she missed. So, I've always managed to live pretty fully in the present."

Andrea paused for a moment, looking straight ahead. "All through my teens, Consuelo compared everything she was experiencing to life as she remembered it in her solid city of stone. Once she even went back to live in San Luis Potosí but by then our grandparents had passed away. What she found there no longer corresponded to what she remembered. That all happened right after Tomás died. Fortunately she had a good life with him. But when he was killed in that accident, she went into a deep depression. And it was then that she decided to go back to San Luis. She and Mama set out together to their old home. But after only a year there they came back. When Mama had her heart attack seven years later, Consuelo became quite desolate. Now she didn't have anyone with whom she could share her memories and since I certainly was no consolation for her she took to the Carducci's instead. They became her family. She's even learned Italian better than I have. Everyone loves her, especially my kids, Antonietta and Franco."

While we were talking, mother had been preparing dinner. Suddenly, she came to join us at the table. "Andrea, do you realize you have not even mentioned the death of your father? For Consuelo that was a major blow. You were only three when he died. Too little to suffer any major consequences. But Consuelo was thirteen at the time, and she was much closer to him than to your mother. For a long time after he died, she would wake up screaming in the middle of the night. To make things worse, we had become so poor following my father's death in the revolution. Then, your father passed away only three years after we got here, and Consuelo and Griselda were forced to seek work. They were still children really but luckily the people at the fort took them in as housekeepers. Those *americanas* thought they were treating the two teenagers like members of the family. But, you know, efforts like that never really work out. All kinds of underlying messages somehow come across. So, Consuelo always held herself aloof from the Bristols.

"That family had an entirely different relationship with you. From the first moment they met you, they took a strong liking to you. Consuelo got their hand-made-downs but they bought you lots of clothes. Later they even decided to pay for your dancing classes. You were too little to see what was going on there but Consuelo complained that they treated you like a doll. I think that's the real reason why she objected to your performing. Oh, you might say she was jealous but I always thought it was more complicated than that."

Mother paused, then looked straight at Andrea. "Mrs. Bristol and Mrs. Anderson not only doted on you but you obviously cared a lot for them. And one has to give them credit. They really did do a lot for you. Even after they got transferred, the Bristols and the Andersons continued to pay for your classes and your costumes. I think this was very hard on Consuelo. People were always doing things for you. But not for Consuelo."

Andrea became quiet for the first time since she arrived.

"Poor Sis," she finally said. "I do forget how different our lives have been. What's strange about it all is that except for the twelve years I was on the road we have actually lived together all of our lives. First here, then in San antonio, and now in St. Louis. The big difference between us lies in Consuelo's early years when I wasn't around yet. What it boils down to is we grew up in different countries and in different cultures. Odd, isn't it?"

"That's true," mother responded. *"Son las cosas de la vida."* They both became silent then. Finally, mother said, "Why don't you continue looking at your book? We spend a lot of time with it. It's one of our favorite pastimes."

"No, wait," I quickly interjected as I ran to my room. "I have something to show you first."

Moments later I burst into the kitchen in my *tehuana* outfit.

"Great!" Andrea laughed, clapping as I entered. "Your headdress is quite a modern version compared to the one I had when I was your age. Mine was more elaborate. But it was so difficult to keep clean. And even harder to iron."

"I still would prefer to have an outfit exactly like the one you wore."

"What difference does it make?" Andrea retorted. "It's not what you wear that's important. What counts is not the costume but the dance. It's in the movement of your arms, the control of your torso, the limberness of your legs. That's what really counts. Just like in life. It's also very important to adapt to your surroundings. *Por desgracia* your outfit comes undone. What do you do then? Your castanets are stolen right before you go on stage? You must adapt to the situation on the spot. That's what makes the difference, not your appearance. *Tú sabes, el hábito no hace al monje.* Clothes don't make the person."

She reached out for me. "Nenita, what you are wearing is perfect. Now, tell me, tell me everything about your program."

"The recital is on Wednesday. But in a few minutes I'm going to a dress rehearsal. Right now I'd like for you to tell me everything you remember about these photos."

"Or want to remember." She smiled the familiar smile I had learned to admire in the photos. "Gosh, I haven't seen these pictures in such a long time. I can tell you're very intrigued with them though. But you know something? I'm really quite unattached to them. I suppose that's why I sent them to your mother."

"Mother calls this her memory book. I remember everything she's told me about your work. But now you can tell me the things I still don't know."

"Don't count on it. It sounds as if you all know more about the Andrea I was once than even I can remember."

It became obvious right away that Andrea really did not want to talk about the experiences which had so stirred my imagination. Disappointed, I closed the album and said I needed to get ready for my rehearsal.

"I'm taking the album to my room," I said, picking up the book.

As I walked down the hallway, I suddenly realized that regardless of what Andrea might now feel about her past life as a dancer, the images in the album could not be denied. I paused for a second, then smiled as Andrea's past flashed by me, on the walls and on the ceiling. One after another I saw the pictures I knew so well—the child in the shepherds' play, the young dancer in the chorus, the full-fledged actress in Lope de Vega's plays. Mother was right, I thought. She's always said that for us this album has taken on a life of its own. Because of her incredible patience in putting this book together, it will always be more than just a set of inanimate images, more than a record of Andrea's career. Mother has said it will always be the repository of our own dreams and aspirations, of the past as it was and as we would have liked for it to have been.

I set the album down on its usual shelf and skipped off to my class.

III

On the day of my recital, Consuelo came to stay with us and as soon as she arrived I knew we would pick up where we had left off four days before. The minute we were alone she pulled out from her purse a gold chain with a tiny medal of the *Virgen de Guadalupe* and handed it to me. "A gift for you on a special day," she said. Thanking her I slipped it over my head, then said hopefully, "Andrea told me you speak Italian very well."

"*Sí. Mi piace molto parlare con tutta la famiglia di Tony.* It's very much like Spanish. The Carducci's have been very good to me and I felt that learning their language was such a small thing to do for them. Tony's parents remind me of my own relatives in San Luis Potosí. Grazia, his sister, is my dearest friend. *Mia cara amica. Uno di questi giorni andrò in Italia con lei. Capisce?* Did you understand what I said?"

"You said you were going to Italy. With someone, I think."

"*Con la sorella di Tony.* With Grazia, Tony's sister. I'd also like to have her visit San Luis Potosí with me."

"What's San Luis Potosí like? So far, we haven't gone there even though we're always talking about going."

"Oh, I guess you would find it a very tranquil place. I was very happy there once with my grandparents and my cousins. In spite of the revolution, they all decided to stay there when we came here. In those early years I missed them a lot. Then, much later, after Tomás died, I went back, hoping to retrace my steps and to recapture what I had left there. But by then Papá Enrique and Mamá Hortensia had died and my cousins and I had grown in different directions. At that point I felt I had no real family left. So back I went then to St. Louis to live with Andrea and Tony. Once there I became very involved with the Carducci's and their activities and now I'm quite comfortable with their ways. I'm even become a member of "Gli Figli d'Italia" and through the church I help out a lot in the San Giuseppe festivities. They're my family now. I hardly think about San Luis Potosí anymore although it's a beautiful city with many churches. I'll always remember it as the home I left behind."

"Is Andrea as involved with the Italian community as you are?" I asked.

"Not really. Andrea has many friends all over the city. She's always going someplace with someone or other."

"You two are so different. Whenever I look at the old photographs of the two of you I can't help noticing she was always laughing. But you, you seemed so sad." I kept looking at her face, then paused and quickly blurted out. "Everyone says you didn't like for Andrea to be in the theater. Is that true?"

Consuelo's eyes narrowed for an instant. Then she became very quiet. After a while she shook her head. "No one has asked me that question before even though I've always known they all thought I objected to Andrea performing on stage. But that was never the issue. I really love the theater. When I was little, Papa would take me with him on the train to Mexico City. We'd go to the *teatro popular*, the opera, the *teatro de variedad*. We quit doing that right before we came here because of all the social turmoil. But by then I had learned to associate the lights of the city with the theater.

When we first got here everything seemed so dark in comparison. And of course we were so poor we couldn't afford tickets for anything. Not that it mattered since nothing of the sort was happening here. Things changed a little after the war. In fact, Tomás and I went to hear Enrico Caruso at the Royal Opera House in 1921 when he stopped here on his way to Mexico City. That has always been a highlight for me. In St. Louis I used to go to the theater whenever I could afford it. No. No. It was never the theater in itself that I objected to."

Consuelo hesitated for a moment, then tapped my shoulder. "Before I go on, you should know that Andrea and I have gotten along very well ever since she and Tony invited me to live with them. We each know what we can talk about and what is best left unsaid. So what I'm going to tell you has no bearing on our present relationship."

She was about to measure her words. Then, inhaling deeply, she went on. "Andrea was spoiled by everyone when she was a child. I think that the woman I worked for—Mrs. Ernestine Bristol—added to the pattern that had already been set. Oh, they all meant well by their actions. Mama felt sorry for Andrea growing up as an orphan not knowing Papa like I had. Her teachers also treated her like something special. Then Mrs. Bristol messed her up even more. She never treated Andrea like a real person. I always thought she looked upon her as a cute little doll who could do unusual tricks. Take a bow, twirl to the left, give a good *zapateado*. Andrea loved to perform and she went along with all the requests."

"Wasn't she only five years old when she started her classes?"

"That's true. I knew then it was not her fault other people took advantage of her eagerness to please. I could also tell that the attention gave her the confidence she needed to continue getting better and better as a performer. But those experiences pushed her farther away from our reality. As I've already told you, we were extremely poor but Andrea never seemed connected to our circumstances. Someone was always taking care of her needs and she seemed to take that for granted. When she came to live with Tomás and me in San Antonio, she was obsessed with what she was doing and never contributed to the household. Her money went into voice lessons and clothes, into the social life that was more or less expected of young women like her. I soon learned not to expect anything from her, and I suppose I really resented that. But what bothered me most was the way she ignored Mama. Andrea simply took off to Los Angeles and all those other places, becoming more absorbed in her career. Months would go by without our hearing from her. I think she was much more in contact with your mother. Probably because Clarita doted on her accomplishments and made her feel important."

"There were so many other things I resented about her during those days. But it didn't do me any good to talk about them because she never seemed to be touched by anything that happened to Mama or me. When Tomás died she took off some days from work to come to the funeral but then she couldn't stay with me during the saddest period of my life. She had commitments in New York, she said. After all I had done for her. That really hurt me. And throughout all this time I was quite convinced she was telling everyone I disapproved of her for being an actress and a dancer. And as I've just told you, that in itself was never the real reason I was so disillusioned with her."

"What if you had been in her shoes? Would you have done things in a different way?" I wondered.

"Who knows? Never, by the longest stretch of the imagination would I have gotten myself into the theater. So, it's almost impossible for me to answer that question."

"Consuelo, you two really had a problem. Mother says that anytime we think someone is doing something that hurts us we should talk things over right away. Did you and Andrea ever talk about all this?"

"You tell me what I could possibly have told her. She said she had obligations and it was obvious that she did. One time we had an argument over her lack of interest in the family. She insisted she had kept us informed about her life. Then she went to the drawer where she knew I kept her few letters and pulled them out as evidence of her communication with us. I became so angry I tore those letters to shreds. That of course made her furious. She picked up the pieces, tore them into smaller bits, then flushed them down the toilet. Since then, we have never exchanged a word about all those years."

"There's still something I don't understand. Today, on the day of my recital you've just given me this beautiful medal. Isn't it some kind of blessing for tonight? I had the impression you didn't want me to be a dancer either."

She smiled for the first time. "You've got the right idea about the medal. But you've jumped to conclusions about the other thing. I'm really not entitled to an opinion on what you do. But do you really want to continue dancing for the rest of your life?"

"I don't know. I only know I love my dancing so much I can't imagine not doing it. Every day I spend hours practicing."

It means so much more to me than making good grades in school. part of me likes to study real hard but my great love is dancing."

"Well, you must do what is right for you. Tonight I'll be clapping for you as hard as I can. Who knows? You might even come to dance in St. Louis later if that's what you want. Do you ever think about visiting me?"

"Maybe I'll come just before you go to Italy. then you'll have to take me with you."

"*D'accordo*. We must keep in touch."

As though to seal a pact, she reached out to hug me, and as before, I felt in the presence of someone I had known forever and ever. While she held me, I imagined the two of us on tour in Rome, chaperoned by Tony Carducci's sister. Everywhere we went I performed my favorite pieces and the faceless Carducci sister-in-law took photographs as fast as she could click the camera. In the distance a tiny figure of Andrea was pasting the pictures in a beautiful silver-covered album.

The image disappeared as mother made her announcement, "Lunch is ready. After you eat you'll have to take your nap so you can be all rested up for tonight. Everyone wants you to do very well."

"Guess what, Mamá?" I said. "Consuelo has just decided to book me at all the opera houses in Italy and she's going to dance with me at the end of each concert while entire orchestras play 'Malagueña' for us."

"*Qué bueno*," mother laughed. "I better come along too, to make sure I get lots of material for my second memory book."

IV

That night, euphoric with all the congratulations and the flowers and chocolates I received after the curtain call, I was convinced that mother would indeed have lots of new material for her next book. Happy with this thought, I was running back to the dressing room holding the red roses that Consuelo had sent, when Andrea suddenly appeared in front of me with her camera. "I want this to be a really good picture," she said. "I've used up two rolls of film and now I have only one picture left. I want a close-up this time. Put your flowers on the floor. Now pretend you're dancing. Pose."

On cue I started playing the castanets while I danced some steps from "La Boda de Luis Alonso." At the exact moment when I held my arms above my head and crossed my wrists, I saw Consuelo among the well-wishers coming towards me. Tears were streaming down her face, and as I looked at her I felt a profound connection to her. Why is she crying I wondered. Aware that my smile had faded I suddenly experienced a tremendous tiredness and confusion. Before I had a chance to compose myself, I looked directly into Andrea's camera and at that instant she took the picture.

V

I never saw that picture although I could well imagine what I looked like in it. Other things were also left to my imagination as the years passed by quickly without my seeing Andrea and Consuelo again. Life did not turn out to be as predictable as it had promised it might be during those happy hours we had spent looking at the many dramatic transformations that Andrea had experienced against so many odds. As much as I had thought during the summer of our first and only encounter that I'd be following in her footsteps, I wound up not pursuing a career in dance. Consuelo didn't make it to Rome either as she had aspired. But Andrea and Tony did.

Over the years I tried to maintain correspondence with both Andrea and Consuelo but it was mostly Consuelo who answered me. During the five years following their visit I kept them informed of my latest accomplishments by sending them glossy pictures with notations of the dates and places of the performances and the numbers I had danced.

All of that came to an end in my junior year in high school.

For reasons I have not yet deciphered, I allowed myself to be convinced that I should put away my dancing shoes and concentrate on my studies. My teachers, the school counselor and my mother all thought I needed to be making plans for life after graduation. With various options facing me I did not know anymore if I wanted to be a dancer "for the rest of my life" as they put it, and I decided that their advice about more practical avenues made sense after all. When I graduated from high school I finished at the top of my class and made it to college just as I and others had expected of me. Every year, though, I made a point of visiting Violeta's best students to encourage them to stick with their dancing, no matter how strongly others might discourage them from doing so.

Off and on I would compare my decision with that of Cristina Ruiz and Becky Barrios. Cristina stayed with Violeta for many years, then opened up her own studio. Becky, on the other hand, went to college and majored in dance, much to her parents' consternation. She made it to New York and occasionally sent me press releases about her work. With those releases and clippings I gathered here and there, I tried to keep a scrapbook of sorts about her many successes. But compared to the one my mother had compiled about Andrea's life as an artist, mine looked rather ordinary and very much in keeping with my own generation's aspirations for fame in the big city, a fact which never entered into Andrea's fun-filled peregrinations. Becky's hard-won successes seemed meager when compared with what we all now were exposed to through the media, and there was nothing unique about what she was doing. So my album looked like hundreds of others that friends like me were pasting together for their more adventuresome acquaintances. My mother's album, by contrast, was simply one of a kind, in keeping with Andrea's career which had been bold and extraordinary in its day.

For a short while, the blue album was actually mine. When I graduated from high school my mother gave it to me, and although I was very moved by her gesture, I also had a slight suspicion she had passed it on to me as a token of my having given up, on her strong advice, what had been so precious to me for so long. At the dorm some of the other students occasionally leafed through the album and expressed surprise that I had a cousin who had been in theater so long ago. No one I knew then could say the same thing. In fact, no one I know now can say it either.

As the years passed, I became even more aware of just how special Andrea's early experiences had been, and for her fifty-fifth birthday I decided she should finally be reunited with the images of her youth. At that time I considered my gesture to be most magnanimous; hence, when she called to acknowledge receipt of the album, I was surprised to sense that she was not particularly happy that I had given it to her. "It really belongs to your mother," she said.

"You can send it back to her if you'd like," I told her but when the album did not come back I figured she had decided to keep it after all.

Already then I was aware of how much I missed looking through its pages and recalling my own youthful aspirations. But I also reminded myself that what had been captured in those black and white images were her accomplishments and not mine. I had done the right thing in sending it to her I kept telling myself. At times, though, I wondered why I had not kept at least one of the photographs but again I convinced myself that they belonged, as a unit, with Andrea.

I tried not to have any further remorse about the matter, and in fact, for a long time I managed to erase the album's existence altogether from my memory. It all came back in May of last year, however. At that time Becky Barrios called about an exhibit she was coordinating on women in dance. "Do you still have that marvelous album about your cousin which we found so inspiring when we were just starting out in Violeta Aguilera's class?" she inquired.

"I can come up with it," I reassured her.

Thus, I made my call to St. Louis.

Andrea was very happy to hear from me until I mentioned the reason for my call. Without the slightest hesitation she quickly said, "It's gone."

"What do you mean it's gone?"

"It's gone," she repeated. "It's been gone for a long time. About two years after you sent it, Antonietta was looking at it and left it on the kitchen table. Sis found it there and tore up all the pictures. Every one of them. Later she told me that she had shredded them into tiny pieces and put them in a bag. Then, she went down to the river's edge and sprinkled them into the water. As Sis described the scene I could see the little pieces of paper floating away like tiny white blossoms bobbing on the water."

"That's terrible," I barely whispered. "How did you feel at the time it happened?"

"I felt bad for your mother. You see, I always considered the album to be her own special way of expressing herself. I just sent her the photographs. But she was the one who arranged them in order in her picture book. Then she guarded the album like a relic. As far as I'm concerned, I simply don't think back on the things that are a part of my past. For over thirty years I have not been a performer. You, however, acted as though it were only yesterday that I was still dancing and acting in the theater. You refused to accept that I truly had set those years aside. They no longer exist as far as I'm concerned."

"What can I say?" I almost apologized.

"Look, I don't know if this will make you feel better or not but after Sis tore up the pictures, we had our first real conversation about the tensions of those early years. Her resenting my absences, and my frustrations with her focus on the past. Her resoluteness. With all the links gone to the part of me that so disturbed her, we both discovered we could now really be as close as we should have been all those years. I simply accept her as she is. Deep inside, I suppose I've admired the fact that she has never swerved from her very strictly defined value system."

I still could not say anything.

"Look at it this way. Even though Sis had not known I had the album, her finding it served one purpose for which it might have existed in the first place."

"May I speak with Consuelo for a moment?"

Andrea hesitated for a few seconds, then said simply, "She's totally deaf now. Promise me that you won't write to her about this either. She seems quite happy in her own memories. No need to disturb still waters. Just let things be."

I paced the floor for quite a while after I hung up. Finally, I picked up the phone and called Becky. I would offer to help her with the exhibit in any way that I could. After all, there must be more than one way to put the pieces back together again. Unlike the time I was fifteen, on this occasion I knew what I had to do and I would not allow anyone to dissuade me from it. A clear-toned voice inside my head kept saying over and over, "*De una espina salta una flor*. Something good comes out of every bad turn." Yes, I would reconstruct my own blue album even if those memorable pictures had disappeared long ago, gliding gently down waters I did not yet know. Right before Becky picked up the phone, the strains of "Zandunga" once again filled my head. And shadowy figures in lacy white head dresses beckoned me to join them.

Arturo Mantecón

The Cardinal Virtues of Demetrio Huerta

Alone at a bend in the silten Sacramento, surrounded by orchards of equidistant pear, sat the black-loamed farm of Demetrio Huerta, a small, meager bachelor with marvelous hands.

His hands had the narrow palms and long bony digits of a simian. His gibbon-like fingers were so absurdly thin and extended that, with his right index, he could extract a pebble from the bottom of a long-necked bottle of beer.

He planted every solitary seed in the soil of his farm with great care and elaboration. He would employ his thumb as a dibble and would rake the earth over the seed with the fanned fingers of his hands.

It was universally acknowledged amongst the bucolic residents of Free-port, Hood and Courtland that Demetrio Huerta possessed a near-miraculous gift for cultivating fruit, vegetables, nuts and grains, or any other land-rooted creature that feeds upon the light of the sun. He could grow watermelons the size of blue ribbon hogs, shining crimson apples as sweet or as tart as anyone could fancy, hillocks of huge, strangely shaped potatoes, asparagus as tall as the pickets of a white cottage fence, and lemons and limes that were bright yellow and green ovals of fresh, sweet fragrance and acrid delight. He could convince such southerners as avocados, mangos and chirimoyas to reconcile themselves to the cold winter nights and yield their abundance.

Demetrio Huerta considered his power over plants the result of an act of will. It certainly was not a matter of technique. He had no secret composts nor favored fertilizers; he never consulted an almanac. He had merely to desire a quality in his produce, and it was achieved. To him this seemed an easy enough thing to do, and it was difficult for him to understand why other farmers couldn't do the same. He felt that all they lacked was the proper forcefulness of thought.

He was fairly prosperous but not rich. He farmed only 8 1/4 acres and could harvest only enough for his own table and a few specialty markets in Sacramento. Most of the year he worked alone and would hire only one man during September and October. He never seriously considered buying more land or concentrating on one crop alone. Either action could have increased his income. He preferred variety in his crops and the solitude his small farm afforded him.

The solitude began to pall, however, as he approached his thirty-fifth year.

He had gone to countless kermesses, barbecues, jamaicas, tardeadas, weddings and nightclubs, and had always failed to meet a woman who would love him.

Pride prevented him from approaching ugly women who, as is sadly and humanly natural, would have accepted him readily. Behind his back, the beautiful, the pretty and the cute would laugh at his unpolished manners and lack of grace.

The sight of his grotesque hands sent shudders of revulsion through some, others, the pícaras, would laugh obscenely and surmise merrily as to what use he could put such long and probing fingers.

Demetrio would find fault with all who rejected him. This one was too boisterous, that one a glutton, another too vain and stupid. Thus he dealt with the injury and insult to his soul. He at last abandoned his futile socializing and set his mind to conjure up, to call forth from the great unknown of humanity, the woman of his life, the woman who would bear his impeccable children. He did not doubt that she would appear.

One cool evening of a very hot day in August, he was sitting on the porch of his clapboard house, leaning thoughtlessly against one of the spindly posts that upheld the overhanging roof; he was listening to a loud monotony of bullfrogs and watching the winking red lights of the towering television transmitters in the distance, when he saw a tiny figure afar atop the levee road. As the figure slowly came nearer, he could discern the fluttering hem of a yellow dress and the black long hair of a woman.

The woman stopped some 200 yards away and looked in his direction for five seconds or so, then continued on her way, but more briskly than before, until she clambered down the sloping gravel drive that led down from the levee to his home.

She at last was close enough for Demetrio to take in the features of her face, mobile and equine with a small, flat nose, pointed chin and porcelain white teeth—and her shape, big bosomed, small waisted and broad hipped. Her feet were dirty, calloused and bare. She carried a plastic mesh shopping bag with sturdy, riveted handles, loaded with clothing. She held two brown sandals in her left hand.

Demetrio's heart was racing, and he could not fathom why. She was quite plain. Her figure was sufficient to turn men's heads, but what excited Demetrio were her eyes, alien yet familiar, grey, smokey eyes that met his in a steady gaze that seemed to penetrate the mask of his concerted indifference with an invisible beam that could discover his thoughts.

"Muy buenas, señor. Tengo mucha sed. ¿Puedo tomar un poco de agua de la bomba?"

"Help yourself," replied Demetrio with downcast eyes. He was abashed by her brazen regard and embarrassed by his lack of fluency in Spanish.

"Thank you, mister."

She strode quickly to the long-handled pump that stood under a live oak twenty yards away from the porch. She withdrew a metal, enameled cup from her bag and rapidly swallowed nine cups of water. Her Bedouin-like thirst quenched, she walked slowly back to the porch, water dripping down the deep cleft at the point of her long chin, all the while grinning her expansive white smile and staring straight into Demetrio's eyes.

She assumed a bold, confident stance, hands upon hips and asked, in a manner without a trace of obsequy or flirtatiousness, if she could have a place to sleep for the night. She offered to prepare breakfast for him and to clean the house in exchange for something to eat in the morning. Demetrio told her she could sleep in a wooden shed, where he kept some shovels and hoes, if the prospect of a mouse did not worry her. He warned her that he had no work for her that would warrant an extended stay. She told him that the mice had more to fear from her than vice-versa and assured him that she had no intention of staying but was headed for Isleton where last year she had been promised work by Señor Hayashi.

She laughingly spurned his offer to escort her and walked toward the tool shed on her own. She turned and looked back:

"Buenas noches y duérmete bien, mi pequeño Demetrio."

He fell asleep, after staring for an hour, timid and lustful, out his bedroom window at the toolshed, dim and indistinct in the light of a crescent moon. It didn't occur to him that he hadn't told her his name.

Demetrio was awakened at dawn by the squeak of the pump handle and the gush and splash of the water. The woman was bathing at the pump. She was naked and wet, looking as glossy and slippery as a seal.

Demetrio crawled out of bed and knelt down by his bedroom window, peering over the sill, breathing rapidly through his parched open mouth. He hadn't felt such ferocious sexual desire since adolescence.

Hers was not an ideal figure—she was thick and squat, but voluptuous. Her thighs were smooth and solid. He had never seen anyone as callipygous. But, her breasts! Large, wide and broad-based, they followed the contour of her robust ribcage for a span and then curved away sharply, their big, blackish nipples pointed upward.

She lathered her body with soap, rinsed herself, toweled dry and retreated to the shed to dress.

Demetrio collapsed to the floor, exhausted by his own wild, libidinous thoughts.

Half an hour later, she came to the door of the house and reminded Demetrio that she was to cook breakfast. He let her in without saying a word, mortally ashamed of his secret voyeurism, and studied the faded pattern of the carpet. She smiled and went silently into the kitchen to work. In quick order, she set a pot of coffee, tortillas de harina, eggs with chorizo and sweet rolls before Demetrio, who waited sheepishly at the table. He begged her to sit down with him and avail herself of her own cooking. This she did readily, and with the appetite of a long-hunting wolf. He couldn't keep his eyes off her. He could manage only a few mouthfuls.

"¿Te gustó, Demetrio?"

"Yes, it did ... I mean, I did. Very much. Muchísimo."

"Good. I'm glad you liked it."

"When did you say you have to be in Isleton—at Hayashi's?"

"I don't *have* to be anywhere I don't want to be."

This was said with calm defiance. It was said with a smile.

"My house, uh ... The place really could stand some cleaning. You know, I'm a bachelor. It's kind of a mess. Do you do that sort of thing? Could you, I mean? Of course, I would pay you for your trouble."

"Yeah, tienes razón. Está bien sucia. Sure, I *did* offer to ... Didn't I? Pay me? ¿Cuánto quieres pagar?"

"I don't know. Whatever's fair. How long do you think it would take? A day maybe?"

"Pos, ¿quién sabe? Maybe a day. Could be longer."

Again a smile.

"Okay. I think we can work something out. And, of course I'll include your meals, and you can sleep in the living room if you want. The sofa folds out into a bed. Say, you know, I don't even know your name."

"I thought you knew my name. ¿No te lo dije? Es Fecunda. Fecunda Melga."

It took a week to clean Demetrio's house, but Fecunda stayed even longer. She just stayed on without a word passing between them as to whether or not she should. Both of them simply and tacitly concluded that it was the proper thing for her to do.

She continued to prepare his breakfast every morning, and each night she would sleep alone and undisturbed in the living room.

At last one night she entered Demetrio's room as he lay wide-eyed in bed. She knelt by his side and gently held his claw-like hand.

"Both of us know what is going to happen—what *must* happen between us. I love you, Demetrio. I know that you don't love *me*, though your passion may fool you into thinking that you do, but that doesn't matter. You want children, perfect, beautiful children, and I am that woman, that good soil in which your seed will take root. I am the woman you need."

She took him by the hand and led him outdoors to a newly furrowed field. They stripped themselves of the little they wore and lay together, he atop her, and first slowly, then faster and faster, they struggled together. They struggled to reach spasmodic oblivion, the expected mystery, the ecstatic denial of mortality itself.

With cries and groans they lost themselves in violent, shuddering pleasure. Then they were as still as corpses, and the deep furrows came alive and heaved up like a cold lava flow. They moved in slow black waves, and the two lovers disappeared beneath them asleep in their deadly embrace.

In the morning, they slowly emerged naked from the black soil and walked together back to the house through the slow rising, dewy vapors of the dawn.

One month later, a midwife in Thornton named Angustias confirmed that Fecunda was pregnant.

Fecunda was pregnant, in fact for three years, 36 months, during which she swelled to such elephantine proportions that she could not get out of bed. Demetrio's powers of plant cultivation had abandoned him shortly after coupling with Fecunda, but he was concerned only for the safety of his wife and the future of his child.

Fearing that Fecunda might explode before she gave birth, he summoned Angustias for diagnosis and advice. Angustias put her ear to Fecunda's huge belly and said that she heard four heartbeats.

"You have been pregnant nine months for each child. Your babies are bound to be rare and extraordinary!"

Fecunda was in fierce and fitful labor for two weeks. When her water finally broke, it streamed from her gaping vagina in a powerful torrent, knocking over a small table and lamp that stood at the foot of the bed. The four babies were blasted forth, one after the other, boy, girl, boy, girl in quick succession as blood spurted wildly in all directions, painting the walls and ceiling red. Four immense afterbirths followed, slipping off the pan held to catch them and falling wallowing, fetid and lugubrious to the floor.

The four babies were big, round, and buttery with soft, loose folds of fat about their arms and legs. They looked like the sort of cherubim that float heavily around the Virgin in cathedral oils. They had hair and teeth and eyes open and inquisitive. They were born with the facility of speech and loudly cried for their mother's milk in well pronounced and easily intelligible syllables.

Demetrio wept with joy at the sight of them.

"They're perfect in form and will certainly be perfect in all ways physical and moral, for I willed them to be so while they were in the womb. They will be the most naturally virtuous men and women to ever walk the earth and so must be appropriately named. My two sons will be called Prudencio and Fuerte, my daughters Justicia and Templanza."

Though they were fairly good when very small, Demetrio's children began to exhibit contrary qualities by age seven, the age of reason.

Justicia was a cheat at jacks, marbles, dominoes and other games. When any of her dolls were naughty, she would punish those that were innocent.

Templanza was an insatiable eater and would drink more Coca-Cola than was good for her. She would turn up her radio so loud that it would hurt one's ears.

Fuerte was a little weakling and a coward so fearful of the world that every morning he arose from his nightmarish sleep weeping at the thought of having to deal with life anew.

Prudencio was forever in trouble. He invariably chose the wrong time and the wrong place to blurt out the wrong words. He quickly lost any money entrusted to him. If he had not lived in the country, he would have been squashed by a passing car before the age of five.

As they grew into their teens, their ruling vices were amplified so that Justicia became a heartless, brow-beating bitch, forever choosing the expedient path of greedy, immoral gain.

Fuerte continued to be a hopeless coward, both physically and morally, without his former excuse of being a defenseless little boy.

Prudencio was constantly in predicaments of his own making, trouble much more serious now that he naturally found himself in a far more injurious world.

Templanza became a horrible, dissolute drunkard and cocaine fiend, who sold her poxy body to satisfy her addictions when she was not giving it away, for she was an inveterate, piggish slut. So much calamity, woe and disgrace did their children bring upon the family that Demetrio and Fecunda were in desperation for a remedy. They were considering handing their children over to the state, having tried everything in their power to rehabilitate their offspring. Fecunda predicted that the children would be their ruin.

One day it happened that Prudencio was on the levee aimlessly lobbing smooth stones into the muddy grey waters of the river when two men approached him, filthy and stinking of malice. One was fair and the other was dark. Both had beak-like noses, one short, the other long, so that they looked like a pair of baneful birds—a canary and a crow.

They confronted Prudencio and demanded money. Prudencio said he had none. They asked him where he lived. He pointed out his house down below.

"Who's home?" asked the dark one.

"My sisters and my brother."

"Where's your father?"

"Pruning the apricots with my mother."

"Any money in the house?" asked the fair one.

"I think so. My sisters say there is. They say my father has it hidden somewhere."

"Do *you* know where it is?" asked the fair one.

"No."

One look into his guileless eyes convinced them that he told the truth. The fair one drew a blue pistol with a curious, thin barrel from his evil-smelling trousers.

"What do you say we go to your house? Move it!!"

Prudencio stood stock-still and uncomprehending so the two men cruelly pushed and jerked him along down the levee and up to the door of the house.

They shoved Prudencio through the door and into the living room where his siblings were watching television. They screamed for money, threatening to maim and murder them all. Justicia, Templanza and Fuerte were astounded and could neither speak nor move. The fair one flew into a rage.

"Where the fuck is the money?!!!" he shouted, and he caved in the television screen with an explosive kick of his heavily shod foot.

Getting no response, the fair one knocked Prudencio down and kicked him in the groin. All eyes focused on Prudencio who gasped for air and squirmed in silent pain. While their attention was diverted, Fuerte edged slowly toward the kitchen and then made a sudden dash for the back door. He fled in pure panic through the fallow fields, rushing toward the apricot trees where his mother and father labored. He bleated for their help and ran for the margin of the orchard where he hid himself beneath a pile of fallen branches, for it occurred to him that his parents might try to enlist his aid.

Fecunda and Demetrio dropped their long handled pruning hooks and ran to the house. They entered the house to find Templanza and Justicia tied to chairs and Prudencio unconscious on the floor. The fair one stepped from behind the open door and put the barrel of the blue pistol to the back of Demetrio's head. The dark one sprang out of the kitchen, applying a half Nelson to poor Fecunda.

Demands and threats were repeated with enormous profanities. Fecunda told the thieves that there was money in her purse but nowhere else in the house. She pleaded that her children not be harmed.

The fair one proceeded to pistol whip Demetrio, who refused to answer any questions. Fecunda wept pitifully for her husband but would not give up the secret. The fair one forced Demetrio against the wall and pummelled his face until his mouth looked like some garish raspberry confection.

Seeing that Demetrio was unconscious, the two decided the children might be moved to talk if they saw their mother abused.

The dark one slammed Fecunda to the floor and knocked the wind out of her with a deft kick just below the ribs. He knelt down, reached under her dress and ripped off her panties. He pushed his pants down to his knees, opened Fecunda's legs and raped her in a curiously dispassionate yet violent way, calmly slapping her face and fiercely pinching her breasts as he heaved and thrust atop her. When he was spent, he gave her a terrific punch to her belly, and the fair one took his place with much more enthusiasm and sadism. Throughout this terrible violation, Fecunda begged her children not to reveal anything. This incited the thieves to greater cruelty, for now they knew there must be considerable money hidden.

The dark one took another turn at Fecunda, who at this point pretended to faint away, hoping the two men would relent in torturing someone who could not appreciate pain.

From the very beginning of her mother's ordeal, Templanza's face was flushed. She breathed in short inhalations through her half-open mouth, and her skin was slick with sweat.

"I know where the money is."

The dark one extricated himself from Fecunda's thighs. The two drew close to the manacled Templanza. The fair one spoke.

"So tell us where it is."

"Do to me what you did to my mother, only better, and I'll tell you."

They obliged her. They mounted her many times in many ways. When they were exhausted they used a candle, an empty R.C. Cola bottle and an English cucumber that Demetrio had grown to the length of a yard. Templaza kept moaning for more and more. They finally told her they could do no more, that she was to tell them where the money was or they would kill her.

"Well, the truth is I don't know where it is exactly, but my sister does."

Justicia rolled her eyes upward in exasperation.

"You stupid whore! I don't know where it is. Do you think if I knew I'd have stayed on this goddamn farm?"

She turned to the two thieves.

"Listen. I don't know where it is, but I do know what it's kept in. Let me loose, and I'll help you look for it. I don't have to tell you that I know this house and farm better than you do. You could give me a share. Whatever's reasonable, okay? We can burn this place down with these idiots in it. We could take my dad's car down south and split up there. I'd never rat on you because I'd be ratting on myself. Makes sense, doesn't it? So let me go. I'll help you find it. It's in a green metal box. Real late one night, I saw my dad open it, and there's a lot of money in it."

"A green metal box?" asked a revived Prudencio, lifting himself feebly from the floor.

"I know where it is. I though it was a fishing tackle box. I didn't know there was any money in it."

The fair one slapped Prudencio's face.

"Okay, kid! Just shut up and tell us where it is!"

"My father keeps it under his bed, underneath a floorboard. Just take it and leave us alone!"

The dark one scurried to the bedroom and quickly discovered the box. It was filled with one hundred and fifty $100 bills. The robbers clubbed Prudencio, Justicia and Templanza senseless. They spilled a small can of gasoline below the flimsy curtains in the dining room. They ignited the gas and waited for the curtains to catch. They fled in Demetrio's car, laughing and hooting uproariously.

As soon as they left, Fecunda arose from her feigned unconsciousness. She surveyed her house, a third of which was already involved in flames. There was no hope of saving it. She could have saved her children, but her heart had turned irreversibly against them. She burned with an absolute anger. She looked at their oblivious, prostrate bodies and spat black bile at them.

"I curse the day you were born. ¡Les odio! ¡Jamás nos causarán daño!"

She went to the kitchen for her long butcher knife. She stabbed each of them in the heart.

"¡Jamás!"

Murders accomplished, she dragged Demetrio by his heels outside to the safety of the humid lawn. She then brought out her dead children. She went to the toolshed and withdrew a pitchfork. She walked to the apricots where she found Fuerte cowering beneath the pruned branches.

"Please, mother! Please, no!" he whimpered, as she forced the points of the pitchfork into his chest. She put her foot on the bow of the fork and laid all her weight upon it, until the tines of it traversed his thorax and pierced the muddy ground.

She put his inert body in a wheelbarrow and rolled it back to the house. She found Demetrio awake and weeping for his dead children and flaming house.

"No llores, amor. They were no good. Eran todo lo que no es bueno. Con mis propias manos los maté, but I had to. They would have killed us in the end."

Demetrio continued to weep, but he was not disconsolate. He was relieved that Fecunda had accomplished what he had only dreamed of doing.

Fecunda fetched an axe and chopped off the heads, the hands and feet, the legs and arms of her four children. She wheeled the pieces of their bloody flesh out to a newly turned field and planted them in forty places. She returned to her husband, sat down and cradled his tearful head in her lap. She sang to him, soothed him, assured him that they would be happy.

They embraced until the night surprised them. Having nowhere else to sleep, they bedded down in the field where Fecunda had buried their children, the very field where they first made love. They made love there again. They coupled strenuously, alternately laughing and weeping with joy. When Demetrio finally ejaculated, his sperm flowed for an hour and a half. Forty gallons of semen flowed across the surface of the field in a sticky white sheet, before being absorbed by the thirsty soil.

When Demetrio and Fecunda awoke at daybreak, they found themselves in a shady grove. They looked up to see forty thick-trunked, magnificent trees. Dependent on the branches of each tree were forty glass-like globes. Within each globe was a ripening baby, each the smiling perfection of eternal goodness.

Judith Ortiz Cofer

The Black Virgin

In their wedding photograph my parents look like children dressed in adult costumes. And they are. My mother will not be fifteen years old for two weeks, and has borrowed a wedding dress from a relative, a tall young woman recently widowed by the Korean war. For sentimental reasons they have chosen not to alter the gown, and it hangs awkwardly on my mother's thin frame. The tiara is crooked on her thick black curls because she bumped her head coming out of the car. On her face is a slightly stunned, pouty expression, as if she were considering bursting into tears. At her side stands my father, formal in his high-school graduation suit. He is holding her elbow as the photographer has instructed him to do, and looking myopically straight ahead since he is not wearing his wire-frame glasses. His light brown curls frame his cherubic well-scrubbed face, his pale, scholarly appearance contrasting with his bride's sultry beauty, dark skin and sensuous features. Neither one seems particularly interested in the other. They are posing reluctantly. The photograph will be evidence that a real wedding took place. I arrived more than a year later, so it was not a forced wedding. In fact, both families had opposed the marriage for a number of reasons, only to discover how adamant children in love can be.

My parent's families represented two completely opposite cultural and philosophical lines of ancestry in my hometown. My maternal relatives, said to have originally immigrated from Italy, were all farmers. My earliest memories are imbued with the smell of dark, moist earth and the image of the red coffee beans growing row after row on my great-grandfather's hillside farm. On my father's side there is family myth and decadence. His people had come from Spain with tales of wealth and titles, but all I knew as a child was that my grandfather had died of alcoholism and meanness a few months before my birth and that he had forbidden his wife and children ever to mention his family background in the house, under threat of violence. My father was a quiet, serious man; my mother, earthy and ebullient. Their marriage, like my childhood, was a combining of two worlds, a mixing of two elements—fire and ice—that was sometimes exciting and life-giving, and sometimes painful and draining.

Because their early marriage precluded many options for supporting a wife, and with a child on its way, my father joined the U.S. Army only few months after the wedding. He was promptly shipped to Panama, where he was when I was born, and remained there for the next two years. I have seen many pictures of myself, a pampered infant and toddler, taken during those months for his benefit. My mother lived with his mother and learned to wait and smoke. My father's two older brothers were in Korea at the same time.

My mother still talks nostalgically of those years when she lived with her mother-in-law, Mamá Funda, as her grandchildren called her—since her name, Fundadora, was beyond our ability to pronounce during our early years—and Mamá Funda's divorced daughter, my aunt Clotilde, whom I am said to resemble. Three women living alone and receiving Army checks: the envy of every married woman in the pueblo. My mother had been the fourth child in a family of eight, and had spent most of her young life caring for babies that came one after the other until her mother, Mamá Pola, exiled her husband from her bed. Mamá Pola had been six months pregnant with her last child at my parents' wedding. My mother had been resentful and embarrassed about her mother's belly, and this may have had some effect on my grandmother's drastic birth control measure of relieving her husband of his marital duty soon after.

Anyway, my mother relished the grown-up atmosphere at her mother-in-law's house, where Mamá Funda was beginning to experiment with a new sense of personal freedom since her husband's death of alcoholism-related causes a couple of years before. Though bound by her own endless ritual of religion and superstition, she had allowed herself a few pleasures; chief among these was cigarette smoking. For years, the timid wife and overworked mother had sneaked a smoke behind the house as she worked in her garden (where she astutely grew mint to chew on before entering the house), occasionally stealing a Chesterfield from her husband's coat pocket while he slept in a drunken stupor. Now she would buy them by the carton, and one could always detect the familiar little square in her apron pocket. My mother took up the smoking habit enthusiastically. And she, my aunt Clotilde and Mamá Funda spent many lazy afternoons smoking and talking about life—especially the travails of having lived with the old man who had been disinherited by his father at an early age for drinking and gambling, and who had allowed bitterness for his bad fortune to further dissipate him—and telling family stories, stories that moralized or amused according to whether it was Mamá Funda or the cynical, New York sophisticated Clotilde who told them; stories my mother would later repeat to me to pass the time in colder climates, while she waited to return to her island. My mother never adopted the U.S., neither did she adapt to life anywhere but in Puerto Rico, though she followed my father back and forth from the island to the mainland for 25 years according to his tours of duty with the army; but always, she expected to return to *casa*—her birthplace. And she kept her fantasy alive by recounting her early years to my brother and me until we felt that we had shared her childhood.

At Mamá Funda's, Mother learned the meaning of scandal. She considered the gossip created by Clotilde's divorce in New York and subsequent return to the conservative Catholic pueblo, yet another exciting dimension in her new adventure of marriage. After her young husband had left for Panama, she had trouble sleeping, so Aunt Clotilde offered to sleep in the same bed with her. Clotilde had desperately wanted a child of her own, but her body had rejected three attempts at pregnancy—one of the many problems that had helped to destroy her marriage. And so my mother's condition became Clotilde's project; she liked to say that she felt like the baby was hers too. After all, it was she who had felt the first stirrings in my mother's belly as she soothed the nervous girl through difficult nights, and she who had risen at dawn to help her up while she heaved with morning-sickness. She shared the pregnancy, growing ever closer to the pretty girl carrying her brother's child.

She had also been the one to run out of the house in her nightgown one night in February of 1952 to summon the old midwife, Lupe, because it was time for me to make my entrance into the world. Lupe, who had attended at all of Mamá Funda's twelve deliveries, was by that time more a town institution than an alert midwife and on that night had managed to pull me out of my mother's writhing body without serious complications, but it had exhausted her. She left me wrapped up in layers of gauze without securing my umbilicus. It was Clotilde, ever vigilant of her babies, my mother and myself, who spotted the blood stain soaking through my swaddling clothes. I was rapidly emptying out, deflating like a little balloon even as my teenage mother curled into a fetal position to sleep after her long night's work.

They say that until my father's return, the social pariah, Clotilde, cared for me with a gentle devotion that belied all her outward bravura. Some years before my birth, she had eloped with a young man whom her father had threatened to kill. They had married and gone to New York City to live. During that time, all her letters home had been destroyed in their envelopes by the old man, who had pronounced her dead to the family. Mamá Funda had suffered in silence, but managed to keep in touch with her daughter through a relative in New York. The marriage soon disintegrated and Clotilde went wild for a year, leading a life of decadence that made her legendary in her hometown. By the time I could ask about such things, all that was left of that period was a trunk full of gorgeous party dresses Clotilde had brought back. They became my dress-up costumes during my childhood. She had been a striking girl with the pale skin and dark curly hair that my father's family could trace back to their ancestors from northern Spain. Piecing her story over the years, I have gathered that Clotilde, at the age of sixteen, had fallen madly in love with a black boy a little older than herself. The romance was passionate and the young man had pressed for a quick marriage. When he finally approached my grandfather, the old man pulled out his machete and threatened to cut Clotilde's suitor in half with it if he ever approached the house again. He then beat both his daughter and wife (for raising a slut), and put them under house-arrest. The result of his actions was an elopement in which half the town collaborated, raising money for the star-crossed lovers and helping them secure transportation and airline tickets to New York. Clotilde left one night and did not return for many years, until her father's death. But the tale is more complex than that. There was a talk at the time that the groom may have been fathered by the old man, who kept mistresses but did not acknowledge their children: for his pleasure, he nearly always chose black women. There was no way to prove this awful suspicion one way or another. Clotilde had been struck and blinded by a passion that she could not control. The marriage had been tempestuous, violent, and mercifully short. Clotilde was a wounded person by the time I was born; her fire was no longer raging, but smoldering—just enough to keep me warm until my mother came out of her adolescent dream to take charge of me.

The three women and a baby girl then spent the next two years waiting for their soldier to come home. Mamá Funda, a deeply religious woman, as well as superstitious, made a *promesa*, for the safe return of her three sons. She went to early mass every day at the famous Catholic church in our town, La Monserrate, the site of a miraculous appearance by the Black Virgin during the Spanish colonial period. Mamá Funda also climbed the two hundred steps to the shrine on her knees once a week, along with other women who had men in the war. These steps had been hewn out of a hillside by hundreds of laborers, and a church had been constructed at the top, on the exact spot where the woodcutter, Giraldo González, had been saved from a charging bull by the sudden vision of the Black Lady floating above a treetop. According to legend, the bull fell on its front knees in a dead halt right in front of the man paralyzed by fear and wonder. There is a fresco above the church altar depicting this scene. Pilgrims come from all over the island to visit the shrine of La Monserrate. A statue imported from Spain representing the Lady sits on a portable ark, and once a year, during her *Fiestas Patronales*, she is taken on her dais around the town, followed by her adorers. She is said to have effected many miraculous cures, and her little room, off to the side of the nave, is full of mementos of her deeds, such as crutches and baby garments (she can induce fertility in barren women). It was to her that Mamá Funda and other women prayed at times of danger for their men, and during domestic crises. Being a woman and black made Our Lady the perfect depository for the hopes and prayers of the sick, the weak and the powerless.

I have seen the women dressed in black climbing the rough steps of *La Escalinata* to the front portals of the church and I have understood how the act itself could bring comfort to a woman who did not even know exactly where on earth her son or husband was, or even the reasons why he was risking his life in someone else's war. Perhaps God knew, and surely La Monserrate, a woman, wife, and mother herself would intercede. It was a man's world, and a man's heaven. But mediation was possible—if one could only get His attention. And so there were *promesas*, ways to make your requests noticed. Some women chose to wear *hábitos* until their prayers were answered, that is, a plain dress of the color that represented your favorite saint, such a light blue for the Holy Mother or red for the Sacred Heart. The *hábito* was cinched at the waist with a cord representing Christ's passion. The more fervent would wear sackcloth underneath their clothes, a real torment in the tropical heat. The *promesa* was only limited by the imagination of the penitent and her threshold for pain and discomfort. In many households, women said rosaries nightly in groups, and this brought them together to share in their troubles. Mamá Funda did it all, quietly and without fanfare. She wore only black since the death of her husband, but mourning and penance had become an intrinsic part of her nature long before, since out of twelve pregnancies only six of her children had survived, having been taken from her as infants by childhood diseases that one generation later a single vaccine or simple antidote could prevent. But she had buried each little corpse in the family graveyard with a name and a date on the headstone, sometimes the same day for birth and death, and she had worn black, kept *luto* for each. The death of her babies had made her a melancholy woman, yet always ready to give God another chance. She lobbied for His favors indefatigably.

At Mamá Funda's house, my young mother and her baby were treated like royalty. Having served a demanding husband and numerous children, the older woman now found herself in a practically empty house with a new grandchild she could dote on and a daughter-in-law that was no more than an adolescent herself. My mother's only job was to play with the baby, to take me for strolls in fancy clothes bought with Army checks, and to accompany Mamá Funda to mass on Sundays. In the photographs taken of my mother and me during this period, I can see the changes wrought on the shy teenage bride in the short span she was taken care of by Funda and Clotilde: she is chubby and radiant with good health, she seems proud of the bundle of ruffles and bows in her arms—her babydoll—me.

By the time Father returned from Panama, I was out of diapers and ambulatory, Mother had regained her svelte figure, and Mamá Funda had thick callouses on her knees that deprived her of the pain she thought was necessary to get results from heaven. The safe homecoming of her son was proof that her pain had been worthwhile, and she applied her fruitful mind to even greater sacrifices toward credit for the other two who would both be wounded in an ambush while traveling in a jeep in Korea and would soon be back in Puerto Rico—slightly damaged, but alive. Funda's knees bore the scars like medals from many wars and conflicts. Aunt Clotilde found herself suddenly displaced as my "other parent," and returned to her own bed. All changed.

My first memory is of his homecoming party, and of the gift he brought me from San Juan, a pink iron crib like an ornate bird cage, and of the sense of abandonment I felt for the first time in my short life, as all eyes turned to the handsome stranger in uniform and away from me, in my frilly new dress and patent leather shoes trapped inside my pink iron crib, screaming my head off for Mamí, Tía, Mamá Funda, anybody . . . to come lift me out of my prison. When I ask about the events of that day, my mother still rolls her eyes back and throws her hands up in a gesture of dismay. The story varies with the telling and the teller, but it seems that I climbed out of my tall crib on my own and headed for the party in the back yard. The pig was on the spit and the beer was flowing. In the living room the Victrola was playing my father's Elvis Presley records loudly. I may have imagined this. My mother is sitting on his lap. She is gorgeous in the red silk dress he has given her. There is a circle of people around him. Everyone is having a good time. And everyone has forgotten about me. I see myself slipping through the crowd and into flames. Immediately, I am pulled out by a man's strong hands. No real damage: my abundant hair is a little singed, but that is all. Mother is crying. I am the center of everyone's attention once more. Even his. Did I sleep between them that night because my mother has finally realized that I am not a rubber dolly but a real flesh-and-blood little girl? When I ask, she says that she remembers only staying awake listening to me breathe the night of "the accident." She had also been kept up by the unaccustomed noise of my father's snoring. She would soon get used to both facts of life: that everyone of her waking hours would belong to me from then on, and that this solemn stranger—who only resembled the timid young man she had married two years before—would own her nights. My mother was finally coming of age.

_____

Miss Consuelo

"Just call me Miss Consuelo."

The petite woman sat in front of Professor Caldwell's desk with her diminutive legs crossed delicately, barely reaching the floor. Her rough hands clasped her knees with a charm and propriety the professor found rather touching. By then, Caldwell had adjusted his hearing to the woman's lively, rushed Mexican accent and could actually extract meaning from the foreign sounds that emanated from her voice as in "Jest cawl mee Mees Cawn-soo-ay-law."

Caldwell poured Consuelo some coffee into a foam cup and handed it to her politely. He was startled by her grave exaggerated gratefulness. "Oh, thaank jou so verry much!" She crooned festively as if such bouts of kindness were rare instances in her life. He installed himself on the swivel chair behind his desk and prepared himself to discuss Consuelo's novella, *Romance of the Guacamoles.* Caldwell had never read anything quite like it in his ten years of teaching Creative Writing and he couldn't come up with the rights words to fairly and objectively appraise it. Consuelo smiled heartily, directing her eager stare directly into his eyes, unaware of the discomfort it provoked in him. Caldwell stole a glance out the window. The day outside was calm and clear, the winter sun casting light on the well-kept campus of the Los Angeles City College. He took a sip of his own coffee and turned to this student whose presence often made him shudder for no apparent reason.

"The truth is, Consuelo ... "

"I sedd you can call me Meess Consuelo, Professor Cald-welk," she interjected, brightly brushing her loose curly hair back with her hands.

"Oh, but why 'Miss Consuelo'?" he groaned impatiently. "Consuelo Chavez is a perfectly fine name for a writer. Why would you want to be known as Miss Consuelo, of all things? Sounds like the name of a beauty pageant for god's sake!"

She smiled delightedly as if she'd been dying to answer such a question for a long time but no one had yet bothered to ask. "Because Meess Consuelo is my theeng, jou know, my own trademock, as they say. I whant the reader in *Maddmoiselle* or *Cosmopoleetan* to look at contents in the magg-zeene and say, 'Oh, jes, another story by Mees Consuelo.' Jou herd of Deer Abby, right? Same theeng! It's not her reel name, Deer Abby, see? Now let's tok about my storee, okay?"

"Ah, yes, that," he said shaking his head as if stepping out of a trance. "To tell you the truth, I don't think it's your ... forté ... "

"My fortt?" She looked unsurprised as if she'd heard it before and knew precisely how to respond. "Jou say roa-manz is not my fortt, Mr. Callwelk? Why roa-manz is my life! All those fancee dresses the heroine wear?" she asked gregariously. "Why, I've wore them!"

She didn't specify when and how she'd come across the ravishing and outlandish dresses with which she'd attired her fictional heroine. During the past twenty years, she had kept home for various well-known, self-described "bankable" actresses and had often been in charge of ironing, sometimes even patching the lustrous outfits that had so inspired her imagination. She believed the world couldn't possibly be such a grim place if she had access, albeit vicariously, to the wonders of modern fashion. On a week day, when the mistress of the home could be found somewhere doing tea at Trumps, Miss Consuelo would often be parading through hallways for the benefit of a spectacle of mirrors that endowed the average celebrity home with a circus-like atmosphere. There she'd stand in various silks and satin laces, buried beneath sizes too large for her with her head sticking out of thousand-dollar ruffles and pleats that were enough to transform Miss Consuelo into a fictionalist. But this source of inspiration didn't seem convincing enough to intellectuals like Professor Caldwell who believed—judging by his course lectures—that the storyteller's task was to endow his readership with horrid tales of middle-class perversion. He was an advocate of the minimalist school of writing in which flights of fancy and all forms of imagination were strictly forbidden. Miss Consuelo preferred her magic, her worlds of wonder, and she was quite confident that she'd find an audience for such a thing if only she ever managed to finish one story of the kind and even spell all its words correctly.

"So you've worn them," said Caldwell with a vexed look on his face. He noticed Consuelo herself wore a grey somber skirt giving her the look of one of Chairman Mao's idealized workers. A string of plastic-like beads of fake pearls wrapped around her neck looking like a cereal box gift.

"Fine," he said taking more sips of coffee. "Perhaps romance really is your life then," he added with a definite tone in his voice as if the woman were doomed to her fantasy. "But you haven't convinced me, Consuelo, that the story is close to you at all. You spend too much time describing the heroine's wardrobe, and don't go at all into her background. There's too much ado about rich lovers and their bloody struggles to win the woman's love, but not enough about their real feelings as men living in the post-nuclear world of Kafkaesque alienation. What I'm trying to say is, and I've said this a million times, stick to what you know."

Consuelo shrugged making a gesture with her face as if resenting the insinuation. "Oh, but what do I know really?" she asked.

The professor was suddenly encouraged by that touch of modesty, and continued, "Well surely you know about your family in Mexico, about crossing the border—illegally, I presume." She looked away, not bothering to confirm or deny. "About the people you've met in the U.S., about the exploitation you've experienced, the joys and woes of living in the Land of the Free."

She stared back with a hint of disdain in her eyes. "Whoo wants to know about all that?" she asked angrily. "My heroine Teresa Bella de Las Galbas is jest a, how do jou say, a hot potato, a sexee chick, and my readers want to know awl about her pashion, her foo-rious pashions, and so do I, Mr. Cammwack. Why can't jou help mee write her storee, nut mine? Forghet mine," she added defensively.

"Awl right," Caldwell retreated a bit, stopping himself as he feared he'd begun to sound like Consuelo. "Suppose you did end up writing about Teresa's furious passions, but then we would need to concentrate on basic spelling, diction, grammar, syntax, in whatever order you'd like, and believe me there's plenty of work to be done in these areas. How long have you been studying English, Consuelo?"

She looked outraged. "Why, I teach myself Eengleetch."

"In that case, I suggest a good solid course of Basic English Grammar. This open enrollment business does you a disservice, you're not really prepared to be in city college, not that many of our American students are, but anyway ... " He handed her back her manuscript. "I made some corrections—let me rephrase that, I made many corrections and I want you to go back home and retype the entire thing, for starters, then we'll worry about the aesthetics of it all."

Consuelo looked aghast at the comments on the script and the red-lining that stained that page. At first sight, one might have thought the professor's fingers had gotten cut on the fine edges of the paper and bled all over the manuscript. She saw nothing but bloody red, between the lines, on the margins, side, top and bottom, notes, comments, obnoxious exclamation points saying things like "Unconvincing introduction ... too many jewels around the heroine's neck ... not enough 'oomph' here ... " watch the run-on sentences ... this part's unreadable ... what's the point of these kisses in this scene, how do they contribute to their Kafkaesque alienation from the modern world? ... "

"I want it retyped by next week in neat orderly fashion and I also want you to buy a new ribbon for your typewriter."

Miss Consuelo looked up very much in a bind. She'd picked up the ancient typewriter at a garage sale were she'd also bought most of her furniture. She didn't even know if ribbons for the 1925 typewriter were still being sold in the market.

"Yes, Mr. Call-well," she said coyly trying to smile flirtatiously. She put a gum in her mouth and chewed noisily. "But I'm shoore the moment I feex the grammar, you'll fall for Teresa. She's hot and sexee, and eff you steel don't fall for her, what can I say?" She was on the verge of saying she was a misunderstood artist but decided that at that point in her career she should maintain a certain level of modesty more appropriate for someone who was virtually unemployed (though unemployed by choice, she hastened to add.) "Some people dawnt understand roa-manz," she finally said. "But I know I can make jou understand, Mr. Call-welld, I know I cann."

Caldwell watched her get up and agitate toward the door on the thin spiky heels, swaying her rumps in a hippo-like menacing motion. As soon as the door shut behind him, his fingers crawled instinctively toward a box of kleenex. His hands and face were awash in cold nervous sweat.

Miss Consuelo went merrily on her way, not too bruised by her encounter with the intellectual. In her two incomplete semesters at City College, she'd come across all types of people who read books and she wasn't intimidated by any of them at all. She found their bullying a lot less violent than those of the men she'd dated throughout her life. Their resentment at her talents took the form of red ink on paper rather than with fists on her face, which had happened occasionally with a few of her manlier lovers.

She stopped to brush her hair in a darkened window by the hallway that served as a mirror. She saw in her reflection a youngish woman in her early fifties with strong thick eyelashes that needed no make-up to rise up into the light of the world like stiff pieces of hay. She adored her eyelashes, thought they recompensed for a few deficiencies in other parts of her body, a mouth too big for its jaw muscles, a nose too small and too easily overshadowed by the mouth, a pair of buttocks too large for the tiny oblique legs, a pouch of fat that hung forth from her stomach—not enough to make her appear obese but that hinted nonetheless at a lack of balance or, worse yet by her standards, a lack of glamour. But the eyelashes! Oh, those eyelashes, so naturally wiry, stiff and sparkling like the tails of comets. She couldn't help but endow her heroine Teresa Bella with them as her special feature of allurement. That was realism in action, something she thought Caldwell might have appreciated if he hadn't been an old sourpuss. "I'm so inspired these days," she thought gleefully on her way to the bus stop.

Consuelo felt the stinging heat of the minestrone soup on her tongue and reached over for a glass of cold water to relieve the pain. She didn't mean to rush through the meal but resented the fact that biological functions of any nature exacted time on a life better spent fully on creative endeavors. That was a new realization for the day and she rushed to jot it down on a notebook she kept handy under the listing of "Real Isations."

Her tongue healing, her wisdom cautiously jotted down for the benefit of posterity, she took a long butcher knife and then dug through a piece of French bread that had grown obdurately hard after several days of being exposed out on the table. She was grinding her way through it like an inmate filing a prison bar. In a minute she held a full slice in her hands ready to soak in the remains of her canned soup. She was dunking, slurping, smooching, creating a rather lively atmosphere when her niece Perla Pesada arrived from work, rushing in with her own agenda in mind.

"I want everything spotlessly clean, Consuelo!" she demanded, slipping out of the concession stand uniform she wore at the local burger inn where she worked. "Marco's coming over any minute now," she announced, "and I don't have time to take a bath, I'm late!" She headed for the make-up table and started spraying herself with imitation perfumes.

"And if you don't mind, Consuelo, we really need to be left alone this time, please!"

Consuelo obliged with a smile, a nod, a quiet lament. Since she'd quit working full-time as a free-lance housekeeper for various Hollywood patronesses, keeping only one for occasional pocket money, Perla had been paying up to three-fourths of the rent and been making demands of time, space and privacy that a writer like Miss Consuelo could not help but comply with. She'd brought Perla from an impoverished section of Mexico City to rescue her, in melodramatic fashion, from extreme poverty and live in the United States only in relative poverty. She was rather glad the girl could provide for many of the expenses of the home and competently take over the role as teenage mistress of the house.

"And you may sleep in the bedroom tonight, Consuelo," Perla added, her arms loaded down by the heavy steel typewriter she hauled inside to the bedroom. Consuelo understood immediately that Marco would want to spend the evening in the living room close to the refrigerator. "If you must come out, please knock. Marco gets very upset when you suddenly sneak out and lurk around in that shocking nightgown of yours." She meant the panther-spotted pink gown inherited by Consuelo after one of her more famous Hollywood patronesses died of a drug overdose in the Holmby Hills.

"Well, it'll be nice to sleep on the bed again," murmured Consuelo. She'd never quite gotten used to the living room couch where she'd been sleeping during the past two months. But she realized that becoming a novelist, after all, did require sacrifices which gave her a clear sense of belonging among all the other struggling artists of the world.

"So," she muttered, "well, well . . . "

She was eager to find out precisely what sort of encounter was about to transgress under her very own eyes. This was Marco's third visit, clearly a "sign" of something. Perla's suitors usually rushed through the apartment like fads and fashions, rarely making it to a third round of visits. "How's Marco, dear?" she asked. "Anything exciting happening?"

Perla looked bothered by the insinuation in her aunt's voice. If she stood there spraying fragrance into her arm pits in front of the mirror, surely that demonstrated that Marco was good, real good. "He's just a friend," she answered in a discourteous tone of voice, irked even more by Consuelo's presence itself, her tininess, her daintiness, the manner in which she grinned unstoppably. "You will leave us alone, won't you, Consuelo?"

"But of course," said the aunt merrily, "I've got so much work to do now that I'm a professional."

Not long after, Perla, wearing a busy multi-colored dress with stripes of bright orange and dark striking blue, stood on the doorway welcoming her Marco inside. But Marco seemed color-blind or, perhaps, oblivious of all fashion and taste. He was a short, heavy-set Latin boy from East. L.A. who wore a hairnet on a bun-like hairdo. His lower lip seemed burdened by a thick bushy cluster of hairs that formed a triangle then trailed down to form a black goatee on the chin. Perla had met him at the burger store where he'd worked for a couple of weeks as a dishwasher. He'd been fired for allegedly stashing burgers into his pockets and feeding a gang of hoodlums, his family, he claimed. Perla insisted the boy was simply misunderstood, restless, rebellious and therefore masculine.

Consuelo was scrubbing away at the kitchen sink when Marco arrived, and she turned on the garbage disposal with perfect timing as Perla leaned over to welcome Marco in with a moist kiss. The sudden grinding, chewing and sucking of the device made them pull apart uncomfortably.

"She gonna be back there all this time?" Marco asked, looking again misunderstood.

"What are ya? Shy?" Perla threw him on the couch aggressively and, she thought, seductively. "Don't worry, you criminal, she'll be outa the way in no time, as soon as I snap my fingers, you'll see."

They turned and, to their surprise and befuddlement, they saw Miss Consuelo standing before them, smiling joyously, holding a tray full of soda, crackers and cookies.

"Enjoy!" she sang, placing the tray on the coffee table. "Now I am sorry I ken't keep jou cheeldren companee, but I'm afraid I huv a chupter of a novelle doo very soon. Excoose me ... "

As soon as she shut the bedroom door behind her, Consuelo leaned against it to hear the murmur of bewilderment arise out of the next room.

"What she say she gonna do?" Marco asked, perplexed.

Perla smacked her lips giving off a sarcastic sound. "Oh, just a novel," she answered looking ready to break out in laughter.

"A what?"

"Read my lips, pretty boy, a novel, a story, fiction, like the stuff you see at the supermarket in little racks, novels. She's gonna become famous, that's all."

A streak of wonder crossed the boy's face. "You mean we won't have to work any more?"

Perla clapped her hands letting out a harsh uneasy chuckle. "Yep, that's precisely what fame means, no work!" She wrapped her arms around the young man's shoulders, then did a rather balletic twist with her legs between his. "Now kiss me, you big cholo!"

But before lips met and entangled as they usually do under similar circumstances, they both suddenly jumped again, startled this time by the tapping sound of an ancient typewriter that penetrated the thin plaster walls much more fervently than any bit of lovemaking. Marco was beginning to grind his teeth as one would undergoing the drop-by-drop pace of Chinese water torture.

Perla pushed the volume notch on the television set and quickly drowned out the noise with the roaring spitting sound of a hard metal rock band on the music channel. Soon the couple was caught in another embrace too intimate, with rhythms all its own, to be affected by the sounds of mere typewriters keys hitting pieces of paper that the two lovers wouldn't have to worry about reading. As high school dropouts, they were free from such obligations. Free. Completely.

Betty Avisham took one step down the staircase, then another with indifference. Her auburn hair covered her eyes and she held on to the rail, not so much to prevent herself from slipping off, but to descend the staircase in grand dramatic fashion worthy of her. She held a glass of papaya juice and sipped from it, purified by its solemn glutinously healthy texture. She pushed her hair back, exposing her eyes which were reddened by a rather childish anger that made it genuine, instinctively painful. She was a middle-aged woman, an actress, who had learned by then that few roles were being written for stunningly beautiful women in approximately their early fifties. She could almost accept the fact as she—for the sake of consoling herself—

surveyed the grandeur palace-like ampleness of her Bel Air home, thanking the Lord for bringing into her life the fundamentalist minister who'd brought her in turn into the Lord's world of easy riches. This state of gratitude hadn't prevented her earlier in the day from taking a Chinese vase from the Ming period and throwing it wrathfully against the wall as a therapy of sorts.

As she reached the kitchen, she leaned to stare outside and observed as her maid, Consuelo Chavez, put the vase back together with Magic Glue, piece by piece. Betty sighed wistfully, yearningly. She didn't know what had gotten into her, perhaps the fact that Oscar nominations had been announced early in the morning, and she hadn't even been invited to read out the nominations. It was true that she hadn't been seen in films for nearly five years and that she even refused minor television material expecting a major aging-role to come along. But she'd been "big" once, as a supporting beauty, and tended to think that something was owed to her for her previous beauty, a little consideration perhaps now that her husband paid for extravagant parties to which even Hollywood pagans were invited. With all this in mind, she didn't think twice about picking up that ridiculous vase and allow the wrath of God to do the rest. But Lord, why that vase? Why hadn't she thought twice and picked up the imitation Manchu? Her husband had bought the Ming when the Chinese Communists had decided to dispose of their imperialist art (and to them anything made before 1949 was "imperialist.") He paid $100 for it and was now offering it for a million and a half on the secular market. What could he do now that the vase had been broken? Clearly a divorce from Betty Avishman would cost him twice as much, she figured.

She mixed herself a combination of protein, papaya and freshly squeezed kiwi juice and stood admiring Consuelo and her patient struggle with the broken pieces of art. But Betty also noticed Consuelo's expression was unusually sullen. She'd become accustomed to the all-consuming potency of the little woman's ninnyish grin, but more than an hour had transpired before she'd smiled at all. Even her eyelashes appeared limp and forlorn that day, abandoned to decrepitude. Clearly something other than Betty Avishman's troubles with ancient art was afoot. On the kitchen table she noticed a folder, which she quickly approached and opened with great curiosity. The first page read, "*The Romance of the Guacamoles, an Epick by Miss Consuelo.* Six Draft." The title page was immaculately clean, but the rest of the manuscript looked stained by blotches of red. It looked faded and was barely legible.

"Pleese poot that down, Miss Avitcham!"

Betty jumped as if a gun had been shot into the air, as if Mr. Avisham himself had walked in and inquired about his Ming. She turned around smiling nervously.

"I wasn't sure what it was," she said, "I'm sorry, dear."

She watched as Consuelo moved quickly to seize the manuscript like a censor and throw it into a cabinet which she immediately locked with her own combination padlock. "The Meeng will be done soon," she announced.

"Oh, I know, but Mr. Avisham won't be home till tomorrow anyway," said Betty turning on the blender, going through the motions of preparing herself another protein drink. "So I hear you're going to school, Consuelo?" she asked, still curious about the ominously entitled *Romance of the Guacamoles*. "Mrs. Presley called the other day and says she's having a terrible time replacing you; Mrs. Sellars said the very same thing, and Mrs. Newman has complained that the new girl can't do windows very well because she's pregnant. The point is we haven't really talked intimately for a while, have we?"

Consuelo was drinking a glass of cold water and was pointing at the Ming outside with an urgency to rush back to it.

"Never mind the damn Ming!" Betty cried impatiently. She sat Consuelo down on a wooden kitchen stool. "Let's do tea now, dammit!"

"But Meess Avitchump," complained Consuelo, "jou huv an appointee with doctor ... "

"Never mind the therapist, you're my friend and I'm paying you to talk."

Betty turned the water on, hoping Consuelo would get up and do the proper thing and volunteer to take it from there, but she didn't. Clearly this tendency to fraternize with the servants had become a risk in itself, thought Betty, who felt she'd initiated informality in Beverly Hills among the classes, though only one class officially existed in her city. She wanted to be called Betty, but Consuelo insisted these days on being called Miss Consuelo. They were both stubborn about it. Betty maintained on calling Consuelo by her first name while Consuelo herself called her "Meess Avitchump," a rather uneasy trade of names. Betty proceeded to mention *Romance of the Guacamoles* and hoped that some greater level of intimacy would blossom between the two women as long as they didn't break the social contract by assuming a truly sisterly disposition.

"*Roa-manz of the Guacamoles* ees awnly red eenk now," said Consuelo in reference to Caldwell's red-inked comments. "The Prawfessor inseests I layrn prawper Engleetch ferst." After her sixth revision of the first chapter, she hadn't been able to proceed toward the more passionate moments in the story. Caldwell would completely tear apart the very premise of the tale and ask for more comments of alienation, which she still could not understand as a concept, as a trick of the writing trade, or as anything real at all. By the sixth appointment that semester, Caldwell had simply gotten her off her seat, then walked her all the way to the registrar's office like a grammar school girl and had her enrolled in a Basic English course. The humiliation of it all still lurked in her mind, the very idea that at her age she'd need to start at the bottom with the recent high school graduates. When she tried to disobey and write down another "Creative Writing" course in her list, the registrar himself told her he had "orders" from above to deny her enrollment in such a course until after she'd taken the grammar course.

"The professor jest dawsnt understaand roa-manz," she lamented.

"But most men don't, dear," said Betty dropping lumps of sugar into Consuelo's tea cup, thinking that menial service had its air of nobility to it after all, as long as one didn't have to do it for a living. "Could I read your story some time? Could there be a role for me in it?" she added playfully.

"My heroine is joung," said Consuelo flatly not caring how it sounded. "She also ees Mexicana and beeootifool, and has all the man she want."

"Sounds like the type of thing my husband would want censored," kidded Betty knowing her jokes were falling flat on Consuelo's humorless face. "Now, now, Consuelo, it takes years, sometimes decades to get something right," she said, realizing Consuelo didn't particularly have *decades* per se to live, and neither did she for that matter. "Now I wonder why you chose this house to work part time, dear."

"Becawse jou ushually stay out of my way."

"Yes, we meddle only into our children's lives," said Betty laughing it up. An idea was brewing in her restless mind by then. "Consuelo, dear, have you heard of the Beverly Hills Minority Workshop?" Her friend Jane Simone Bracknell was the head of it, but the workshop was constantly in recess, she explained, because there were very few minorities in the city of Beverly Hills and they often had to be imported from the outlying communities. "Why, I must get in contact with Jane and tell her all about you." She started for the telephone when Consuelo stopped to ask what she meant by a "minority workshop." A workshop on how to become a minority? "I meant a minority writing workshop," she specified, "it's an attempt to attract fresh new voices into our sagging cultural landscape."

"Sagheeng?" wondered Consuelo who'd only heard the word in a more glandular context. By then, Betty was holding her august digital phone up to her mouth and talking enthusiastically into it.

"Jane? Jane?" she cried excitedly. "I think I got you some new blood for your workshop ... yeah, her name is Consuelo. She's Mexican, female and underprivileged. Precisely what you've been looking for. She's writing a novel, I believe ... what's the name again? ... Consuelo." Consuelo repeated the name indifferently. "Yes, *Romance of the Guacamole*. I don't know if it's a satire, Jane. Why don't you talk to Consuelo," she said and added proudly, "she's not just my maid, but one of my very best friends."

And this is how Consuelo became part of the Beverly Hills Minority Writing Workshop. Consuelo was scheduled for the following week for a thorough reading and a full critique of her work by members of the workshop. She was even asked to bring additional copies for possible submission to literary agents. "But smile, Consuelo," Betty urged her as she restlessly prepared herself to go out for mid-day coffee at L'Orangerie. "Smile, we haven't seen your teeth over an hour now. Next thing you'll be accepting the Oscar for best original screenplay."

Consuelo looked up suddenly as if struck by that word, "screenplay." "Screenplay?" she asked herself. She looked comforted by the idea of writing dialogue without having to complete full sentences. Screenplay, yes, the language of the sub-literate. She could already see herself completing a full first draft before next Tuesday and still be ready to be submitted to agents.

"And don't forget the Ming," cried Betty on her way out looking inspired by her one good deed for the day.

Consuelo spent the following week staying up late, ignoring her Creative Writing class and proceeding with the instruction of a screenplay. It was a *ceench*, she decided, the easiest thing on earth, nothing like it, as long as it moved, as long as it had action and essential moments of grand passion, which of course were never lacking in her oeuvre. But this frantic hectic pace of work didn't help Perla's sleep who was struggling, tossing and turning in her bed during those nights of cinematic genesis.

The niece had been banging on the wall for several minutes when Consuelo heard a sudden silence. In a matter of minutes, Perla had walked out of her room with a suitcase and an overcoat covering her skimpy lingerie. "That does it, Consuelo, I've had enough, I'm leaving. Did you hear me, I'm leaving."

Consuelo turned around, looking distraught, too mesmerized by Teresa Bella de las Galbas' lofty misadventures with men to take Perla seriously at all. She flared a smile at her instead, startling the girl with its oblique, appealing look that was completely uncalled for and out of place.

"That's it Consuelo! I'm going away, you'll have to fend for yourself. I'm going to live with Marco, my man Marco. If I have to spend my precious youth laboring away at a minimum wage to support some leech financially, it might as well be the man I love! I'm sorry, Aunt Consuelo, you brought me to the United States to lead a good life and the only way I'm going to lead it is without you. That much is clear." The front door slammed behind her, Perla was suddenly gone, and Consuelo was falling dead asleep, exhausted, beaten, over the ancient portable typewriter that served uneasily as a pillow.

There she stood, tight-lipped but well-roughed in fiery pink, her eyelashes sparklingly stiff, wearing a white polyester dress that wrapped itself delicately around her fleshy contours without pressing too tightly on them. It was the best she could do as she'd prepared herself in a hurry, in need to rush to the closest copy center and use the self-service machine which saved her a penny a page. The machine had often stopped, chewing up her originals, making a disposer-like grinding sound that threatened to swallow up her creative output until the saleslady walked over to save her work from such a fate. And finally, there she stood on the doorway to a dimly lit classroom at the Beverly Hills High School which served as the headquarters for the Minority Writer's Workshop.

"Is thees the war-shop?" she asked.

A blond young woman reached forward to greet her, introducing herself as Jane Simone Bracknell, originator of the workshop. A few other members walked forward to greet her with a zealous look in their eyes as if eager to touch her but stopping short. One young woman, a red-headed girl, arrayed in bright silken colors, introduced herself as one of the "remaining original Roosevelts," welcomed her enthusiastically and even called her "sister." The more people she met, the lighter, the fairer the skins became, and the more fascinated they seemed with her own dark "genuine" look of underprivilege. Yet, one of the young men hardly seemed to take notice of her, and eventually shook her hand only with a complete lack of deference. He was, as it turned out, a half-Mexican, half-Scandinavian boy, blonder and more blue-eyed than any other member of the club, but who called himself Jaime Ixtichpt de la Raza and introduced himself as a proud member of the "cosmic" race bearing Aztec extraction that Consuelo clearly could not see on his face. She noted an air of fierceness in his eyes, a clear indication that she was somehow in danger, that she had now reasons to be more frightened of the workshop than embarrassed.

Jane Simone Bracknell finally seized hold of Consuelo's script, was delighted by the solemnly shoddy look of it—"so proletarian," she mused. When she introduced the work by its name, the title netted serious laughter that immediately ceased when everyone noticed that Consuelo herself wasn't amused. The Roosevelt descendant was cast as Teresa and the rest of the workshop members were summoned to read various parts of Teresa's countless lovers. Jimmy Ixtichpt de la Raza himself decided to pass on the privilege. The script was read slowly, patiently as the readers strained to read from the depleted mileage left on the ancient ribbon. There was even an attempt on their part to give their lines feeling. Nobody complained as the work was read, nobody groaned, nobody laughed, no one offered a coffee break, and Consuelo finally noticed a pervasive silence in the air when the last mispelled word was read outloud as it was written, "The And."

Jane Simone Bracknell summoned all the participants, about ten alto-gether, to a courteous ladylike applause and offered donuts to Consuelo and everyone else before criticism was solicited.

"Well," Jane finally said, when the last donut was distributed. "That was so . . . romantic. They don't make them like that any more. Any comments from the peanut gallery?"

The Roosevelt girl claimed the story needed a "certain level of ontolog-ical phenomena. The romance doesn't come across as inspired by higher forces which minority communities are more akin to relate to . . . "

"My understanding," said another young man, "is that romance is only the language of a dying class structure and should be depicted only with the understanding that it serves an oppressive need . . . "

Another young woman, yawning, found herself awakening to some in-spired bit of wisdom and saying, "It needs more character motivation, a better exposition, and a more delightful denouement, if you know what I mean. Otherwise, it was okay."

A man in his thirties, balding, talking with a nasal accent bothered to get up and gestured nervously with his hands as he chose his words. "Let's face it, if the story's gonna be done at all in the real world, it needs a teenage heroine." He was being booed out already. "And I'm afraid that it also needs to de-emphasize its ethnicity, I'm sorry, I know this is the minority workshop and everything, and don't get me wrong, Miss Consuelo, I'm with ya all the way, I want you to win and make it big. But you can't listen to these amateurs who know nothing about the business. You're not gonna sell Trotskyism to the studios."

He was suddenly being attacked for opportunism, for philistinism, for appealing to the lowest common denominator, for sounding and acting pretty much like these people's parents.

Consuelo had barely understood anything that had been said up to this point except for the fact that one of the girls had found the story "OK." But finally, her heart raced as she noticed the strange-looking Jaime Ixtichpt de la Raza rise augustly out of his chair, nearly making it tumble on to the wooden floor of the classroom. Silence ensued as workshop members turned to look. "It's trash," he said with a deeply earnest look on his face. There was a feeling of shock and tension in the air. Everyone's eyes suddenly shifted and rolled downwards at the floor as they avoided Consuelo's gaze which searched immediately for support and refuge in the eyes of anyone willing to provide it. But she found none, as if these workshop members actually needed a Jaime Ixtichpt de la Raza to say what they really meant.

"A Mexican woman should express herself in relationship to her class, her gender and her ethnicity," he said. "And even if she refuses to do so, she needs to learn how to write a full sentence. Why can't she write in Spanish anyway?" An excellent question, thought Miss Consuelo, realizing that her sixth-grade Spanish grammar would do Teresa Bella de las Galbas no more justice than her English. "She's a phoney through and through," judged Jaime, "not a real minority at all, brown on the outside, white on the inside—like a coconut."

Jane Simone Bracknell leaned forward with her hands pressing through the donut box, nearly flattening it on the table. "Now please," she finally said. "We must hear the author explain her own work, it's only fair, I should think." Consuelo watched Jaime sit down, his arms folded and a neat smile of satisfaction drawing on his face. "We're listening, Miss Consuelo," said Jane politely. "We're all yours."

Consuelo hunched up her shoulders, smiling vaguely, faintly, inspecting her audience which—with the exception of the pseudo-Aztec—stared back in need of reassurance, in need to witness the author strike back decisively and heroically. She found herself instead sinking into her seat, her head beginning to lower slowly as her feet collapsed beneath her, and she passed out and fell neatly to the floor.

So this was the future. A week had passed since her fainting spell at the Beverly Hills Minority Writers' Workshop. She got off the bus that afternoon. Her nails were broken. She had caught up with her housekeeping. Mrs. Presley, Mrs. Newman, Mrs. Johnson, and the ex-Mrs. Johnson, as well as Betty Avisham. They were happy campers now. Consuelo's only pressing matter was to fill out the registration form for the next school semester. She desperately wanted to take yet another course in Creative Writing, but knew that the powers-that-be wouldn't let her until she finished the Basic English grammar course. She thought of the selfishness of men, of their need to exclude women from all fields of endeavor. She was feeling discriminated against, thought she might file a suit against the City College for preventing her, Miss Consuelo, from expressing herself creatively. She would appear on television, start a new life as a rights' advocate.

She was in a daze of anticipation for a new future, but forgot all about it when she reached the apartment building off Sunset. Her niece, Perla, was sitting by the steps of the entrance, her foot kicking a loose brick. When Perla saw her, her eyes shifted away in shame. Consuelo walked forward, her heart beating. She struggled against appearing too light-hearted, though she was smiling within.

"Fawrgat the key, Perla?"

"Yes, I did." The girl's eyes were focused elsewhere, into space. "Marco doesn't want me around. Doesn't like a girl who gets up in the morning and wakes him up."

"I knaw the type."

"He's got some crazy scheme now, like robbing an old ladies' home or something. I told him I didn't go for that. He said I was behind the times. I had to come back, Tia Consuelo. You can type all you'd like, I'll sleep in the living room. You should be glad you're in school. I'll contribute money for your books and supplies. I wouldn't want you to follow in my steps. Do I make sense?"

Consuelo shrugged, handing over a piece of kleenex. "I theenk so. Come on, I make you good deener, pasta and wine. We'll even use napkeens."

That evening, Miss Consuelo sat by the light of her desk, inspecting the registration form that was due the next day. Perla was stretched out on the living room couch, feet on the coffee table as she watched mind-numbing music videos and belched merrily on a full stomach. Consuelo sighed to see the girl so much at peace, so worry-free, so young, so unburdened by ambition like Miss Consuelo herself had once been. Her attention shifted back to the registration papers on hand. Only one class was written down for her by the city college counselor, eight full units of Basic English grammar for foreign students. She'd been in the United States over twenty-years and she still had to register as a foreigner.

On her desk, her copies of *Romance of the Guacamoles* laid inertly, unwanted. She'd been afraid to touch the script since that fated day in which it'd been read publicly to the Beverly Hills brats. She thought she'd never write again.

But that evening something magic occurred. A thought sparked in her mind, tantalizing her, luring her back to her world of wonder. If the critics wanted realism, she'd give it to them. She would add a maid to the story. A maid! How simple!, she marvelled. Why hadn't she thought of it before. A faithful maid would care for Teresa's extravagant wardrobe. Who else would know the inside story as well as the maid. The critics couldn't possibly complain that her story lacked veracity. But of course since she wasn't allowed to enroll in the writing class, she'd have to work on the script on her own like a true artist. Perhaps she'd return to the Beverly Hills workshop and dazzle the kids with a rewrite, making that Jaime Ix-Whatever-His-Name-Was sink in his own waste. She'd sell the script through her Beverly Hills contacts, and she started thinking that she might even play the role of the maid herself. Acting, she figured, had to be a lot easier than writing. People were always telling her she was a "real character" anyway and it was about time she acted out the role of herself on film. That's it, she thought, an acting class would highlight her following semester while she struggled through English grammar on the side. She looked up her schedule of classes and found precisely what she'd been looking for, a course in "Acting Fundamentals." There were no restrictions and pre-requisites for that class. Nothing prevented her from taking it.

So there she sat that evening as Perla snored in front of the TV set. Nothing could have been more inspiring to Miss Consuelo than finding herself with two professions to excel in. She swooned in pride to realize that her life had begun anew that night as she, without misgivings, with the clear insight that in her adopted country everything was possible, renewed her adopted professional name by adding yet another title to it, "Miss Consuelo, author and actress."

Rima de Vallbona

La tejedora de palabras

> A Joan, quien desde hace siglos
> se aventuró por los mares de la vida
> creyendo que iba en pos de su propia iden-
> tidad, cuando realmente buscaba, como
> Telémaco, al Ulises-padre-héroe que todo
> hombre anhela en sus mocedades.

> ... *hallaron en un valle, sitio en un*
> *descampado, los palacios de Circe, eleva-*
> *dos sobre piedras pulidas. Y en sus alrede-*
> *dores vagaban lobos monteses y leones,*
> *pues Circe habíalos domesticado admin-*
> *istrándoles pérfidas mixturas.*
>
> Homero

El violento fulgor veraniego de los ocasos de Houston estalló en mil resplandores rojizos en su hermosa cabellera, la cual lo dejó deslumbrado por unos momentos; era como si hubiese entrado en una zona mágica en la que ni el tiempo, ni los sentidos, ni la realidad tuvieran cabida alguna. Ella se dirigía hacia el edificio de lenguas clásicas y modernas cuando Rodrigo tuvo la fugaz visión suya de espaldas, aureolada por el brillo de una nunca antes vista frondosa mata de pelo. Iba cantando —o eso le pareció a él—, con una voz tan melodiosa, que por unos instantes se suspendieron sus sentidos y quedó petrificado.

—¿Qué te pasa que te has quedado ahí alelado como si hubieras visto un fantasma o un ánima de ultratumba?—, le preguntó Eva, mientras la de los hermosos cabellos subía con aire de majestad los tres escalones de piedra del edificio.

—¿Quién es?—, le preguntó Rodrigo señalándola con un gesto de la cabeza.

—¿Quién va a ser? ¡Si todo el mundo la conoce! Es la profesora Thompson, la de clásicas. Todo quisque en la U sabe de sus excentricidades.

Ella es precisamente la profe por la que me preguntabas ayer, cuanto te matriculaste en su curso.

Al abrir la puerta para entrar en el edificio, girándose repentinamente, ella fijó en Rodrigo una mirada de cenizas con ascuas. Fue cuando el resplandor de sus cabellos se apagó. Entonces él no pudo dar crédito a sus ojos, pues superpuesta a la imagen de criatura divina, se le manifestó de pronto como un ser grotesco: la juventud que antes había irradiado brillos mágicos en la luz del sol de los cabellos, se trocó en un marchito pelaje color rata muerta, grasienta, sucia. Lo que más le impresionó es que pese a la distancia que lo separaba de ella, le llegó a él un intenso y repugnante olor a soledad, a total abandono, como de rincón que nunca se ha barrido ni fregado. Sintió náuseas, lástima, miedo . . .

—Da pena verla—, siguió comentando Eva. —Viene a la U en esa facha de trapera, como las *baggy ladies* que con la situación escuchimizada de hoy y la derrota de sus vidas, llevan cuatro chuicas en una bolsa plástica, hacen cola en Catholic Charities y se pasan hurgando en los basureros. Sucia, despeinada, sin maquillaje alguno, el ruedo de la falda medio descosido, ¿no la viste?, así viene siempre a clase.

Rodrigo agregó:

—Camina con desgana, como si ya no pudiera dar un paso más en la vida y se quisiera perder en el laberinto de la muerte . . .

—Mejor dicho, en las regiones del Hades, donde habita el clarividente ciego Tiresias, explicaría la profesora Thompson, cargada como tiene la batería de añeja literatura y mitos griegos.

—¿No estás tomándome el pelo, Eva? Este espantapájaros con figura de mendiga no puede ser una profe . . . y menos de clásicas.

—¿Pintoresca tu profesorcita, eh? Verás las sorpresas que te guardan sus clases, Rodrigo. —Muerta de risa, Eva se alejó hacia el edificio de filosofía mientras le recomendaba andarse con cautela con la profesora Thompson porque . . . ¡a saber por qué!, pues las últimas palabras las borró en el aire el traqueteo del camión que pasaba en ese momento recogiendo basura.

Como si la profesora Thompson adivinara que hablaban de ella, en un instante fugaz la divisó Rodrigo mirándolo con fijeza detrás de los cristales tornasolados de la puerta. El no sabía si los reflejos del vidrio, al influjo del sol poniente, habían vuelto a jugarle una mala pasada; lo cierto es que cayó de nuevo presa del embrujo de la primera visión de ella: se le volvió a manifestar en todo el esplendor de su abundante y hermosa cabellera horlada de fulgores mágicos que le daban una aureola de diosa, como salida de un extraño mundo de fantasías.

A partir de entonces, siguió apareciéndosele a Rodrigo en su doble aspecto de joven embrujadora/vieja-hurga-basureros. El fenómeno ocurría aún durante las clases. Al principio, temiendo que los efectos de esa doble obsesión quimérica afectaran sus estudios, Rodrigo se vio tentado a dejar el curso sobre Homero. Sin embargo, una misteriosa fuerza venida de quién sabe donde, incontrolable, lo hacía permanecer en él. Para justificarse, se repetía, sin convicción alguna, que tenía razones muy sustanciosas: ante todo, curiosidad. Sí, curiosidad, porque en el diario contacto con sus compañeros esperaba que alguno de ellos le revelase a él que también padecía de tan extravagantes espejismos; pero por lo visto, nadie a su alrededor mencionaba nada tan absurdo como el mal que lo estaba aquejando a él. Sus compañeros se complacían en poner en relieve sólo la descharchada figura de mujer que ha llegado a los límites, al se-acabó-todo-y-ya-nada-importamás. No obstante, todos reconocían que, como pocos profesores, la Dra. Thompson daba unas clases fascinantes durante las cuales volvían a cobrar vida Ulises, Patroclo, Nausicaa, Penélope, Telémaco, Aquiles.

En efecto, mientras ella exponía la materia, era imposible escapar al hechizo de aquel remoto mundo, el cual se instalaba en el espíritu de Rodrigo como algo presente, actual, que nunca hubiese muerto, ni moriría jamás. En varias ocasiones Rodrigo experimentó muy en vivo que en vez de palabras, la profesora le iba tejiendo a él —sólo a el— la "divina tela" (tela-tejido-textura-texto); ligera, graciosa y espléndida labor de dioses que había venido urdiendo la "venerable Circe" en su palacio, también hecho por Homero de puras palabras. En clase, enredado en la hermosa trama que ella iba tejiendo con palabras, palabras y más palabras, Rodrigo se sentía feliz, más cómodo que moviéndose en su realidad de fugaces amoríos, de conversaciones fútiles, de películas violentas y eróticas, del dolor de haber sorprendido las infidelidades de su imperial padre, de la sumisión dolorosa de su madrecita tierna, benévola, resignada; también de las noticias alarmantemente feroces que lo atacaban por doquier desde el periódico, la radio, la tele, los mismos textos universitarios. La clase sobre Homero era para él un paraíso perfecto donde sorbía embebido el frescor de aquel río de palabras que arrastraba consigo todos sus pesares, angustias, preocupaciones, y lo dejaban limpio y prepotente como un héroe homérico.

Así fue como la profesora Thompson captó el efecto mágico que producía sobre Rodrigo la urdimbre de sus palabras. Sin perder ocasión, lo colmó de palabras para hacerle saber que ella lo comprendía; le escribió al pie de los ensayos que ella le corregía, en las traducciones que él le entregaba como tarea de cada semana y a veces en papelitos clandestinos. Las primeras notas pusieron énfasis en sus cualidades:

"Rodrigo, por lo que dices y escribes en clase, observo que eres muy inteligente; más que la mayoría de las personas. Lo raro es que también tu sensibilidad e intuición te permiten percibir datos sofisticados y multidimensionales que los demás no alcanzan ni a adivinar. Lo ignoras, pero en tu caso ocurre el fenómeno rarísimo de conjugar íntegramente el poder creativo e innovador de lo intuido y el analítico de la razón resuelve problemas. ¡Y yo, que siempre me he creído más inteligente y capaz que lo otros (perdona mi arrogancia)! Ante ti experimento la impresión de que has venido a mi vida como uno de esos héroes míticos que estudiamos y que aparecen para romper con todas las reglas de lo normal y corriente e instalarse vencedores en el centro del mundo. Lo que te digo es una verdad que debes imponerte y de la que debes sentirte orgulloso, como yo lo estoy, porque juntos, las dos formamos una pareja separada del resto de la raza humana. Y por favor, no hagas esfuerzos — los cuales serán vanos— por escapar a ese destino, como estás intentándolo desde que te conocí".

Rodrigo no salía de su asombro ante tal análisis, el cual denotaba un gran interés en su persona. Además, le pareció que la profesora entendía aquel "destino" plantado en medio del papel, en el rígido e inapelable significado griego y que ella, quién sabe por qué hechicera capacidad, le advertía el contenido de su oráculo. Para complicar más las cosas, en carta adjunta al ensayo sobre el descenso de Ulises al Hades, ella le puso:

"Por lo mismo que eres tal como te analicé en otra ocasión, es muy difícil que encuentres una respuesta *simple* a tu obsesiva pregunta de quién eres. No olvides que cualquier respuesta satisfactoria será siempre *muy compleja*. Recuerda lo que el existencialismo afirma, que *cada uno es lo que escoge ser*. Ulises escogió ser héroe. Tú te debates entre la ventura ilimitada de Ulises y las reducidas demandas inmediatas del joven Rodrigo, atrapado en los avatares supérfluos de la vida burguesa de su familia, la cual no le calza en nada. Yo, en tu lugar, estaría furiosa por la injusticia cometida por la familia que se roba hasta la libertad de cualquier ser humano, todos tenemos el deber ineludible de defenderla si no queremos quedar alienados".

Sin ton ni son, siguió pasándole notitas. En una de ellas hacía énfasis en la *desesperada necesidad* (así, subrayado) que él tenía de establecer una sana y completa relación íntima con alguien. Lo curioso es que Rodrigo nunca aludió a eso ni a nada de lo que ella decía, aunque se vio forzado a reconocer que había un gran fondo de verdad en lo que la Dra. Thompson conjeturaba. Sin duda alguna la mujer tenía algo de hechicera o se las sabía todas en el campo de la sicología. Entre otras cosas, ella le dijo que le daba lástima verlo tan impotente para proteger de las imposiciones de su familia lo que era para él inapreciable, como la íntima e íntegra relación con alguien. Agregó que le destrozaba el corazón, porque de alguna manera el cumplimiento de su destino (¡y dale con el destino!) rompería las amarras con los principios pequeñoburgueses de su familia. Acompañando la notita, en sobre aparte, y para mayor sorpresa de Rodrigo, venía la llave de su casa y un mapa: "Este es el mapa que te llevará, muchacho querido, a través del laberinto de autopistas de Houston hasta mi morada salvadora de la muerte existencial que te imponen ellos, los que diciéndote que te quieren, te están destruyendo", puso al pie del mapa.

A partir de entonces la profesora Thompson no perdió oportunidad para escribirle papelitos de toda clase, en los que analizaba con agudeza la idiosincrasia de Rodrigo: la intensidad de sus problemas y emociones, su sensibilidad exacerbada, no comprendida por muchos que hasta lo llamaban neurótico, sicópata, en fin, todos esos membretes que se le ponen a la conducta que no se comprende porque está fuera de los alcances de las inteligencias comunes. En otra carta le decía:

> "No temo de manera alguna la intensidad de tus emociones y arrechuchos y por lo mismo prometo no abandonarte jamás. Has de saber, Rodrigo del alma, que conmigo puedes desplegar la amenazadora gama de tus pensamientos, iras y emociones. Yo te comprendo y comprendo tu frustración. Conmigo podrás ventilar todo lo que has vivido reprimiendo por temor a malentendidos.
>
> Te sobran razones para creer que lo que ves, percibes, piensas, sientes, es equivocado. Sin embargo, *nada de eso es equivocado*, sólo diferente a lo que los demás ven, perciben, piensan y sienten. Debes tener más fe en ti mismo, Rodrigo, muchachote tan de mi alma. Has de saber que mi tarea a tu lado es la de trasmitirte, infusionarte, saturarte de fe en tu talento y en la extensión de tu potencial. La otra tarea mía consiste sobre todo en librarte de tu familia y de las absorbentes obligaciones sociales que ellos te imponen; te prometo cortar del todo las amarras que te tienen maniatado y no te permiten entregarte a mí. La última de mis tareas reclama que tú y yo gocemos de momentos privados y que vengas a verme cuando las presiones del mundo exterior te hagan daño, para que ventiles tus frustraciones y pesares conmigo. Tú no lo quieres reconocer, pero

desde el día que te vi a través del cristal de la puerta del edificio de lenguas, capté en tu mirada un anhelo intenso de morir, de acabar con tu preciosa vida para siempre. Desde entonces, mi amor por ti ha ido creciendo y creciendo. Y porque te amo, Rodrigo, mi Rodrigo, porque has llegado a ser todo para mí, lucharé a brazo partido y hasta daré mi vida entera por salvarte de ti mismo".

Al leer aquello, Rodrigo siente que un raro vacío se ubica en su ser y que la vergüenza, el rechazo, la rabia, el desprecio hacia la vieja-hurga-basureros se apoderan de él. Sin embargo, el penetrante olor a soledad que despide ella le recuerda (¡extraña asociación sin fundamento!), la soledad de su frágil madrecita siempre empequeñecida por el fulgor juvenil de las amantes de su padre. Entonces se le viene al suelo el ánimo que lleva para dejar la clase de Homero, para enfrentarse a la profesora Thompson y gritarle las cuatro verdades de que se mire en un espejo y compruebe que con su imagen cincuentona, surcada ya de arrugas, sin belleza alguna, es ridículo pretender seducir a un mozalbete de su edad. Una vez ante ella, Rodrigo baja la vista y el aprendido código social de gentileza-hipocresía-disimulo, se le impone de nuevo y sí, señora, ¿en qué puedo servirla?, déme la cartera que está muy cargada de libros, para llevársela, le abro la puerta, no tenga cuidado, sabe que estoy a sus órdenes, usted sólo tiene que mandarme. Así fue como después de una de las clases, y so pretexto de que con los atracos y violaciones que abundan por los alrededores de Montrose, Rodrigo la acompañó hasta su coche.

—¿Dónde estás estacionado, Rodrigo?—, le preguntó la profesora Thompson cuando ya estaba instalada, con el pie en el acelerador.

—A unas cuantas cuadras de aquí, pues hoy me costó encontrar espacio cerca. Debe tener lugar algún concierto o conferencia para que haya tanta gente por aquí.

—Te llevo. Entra.

Fue con miedo, mucho miedo, que Rodrigo entró al destartalado Chevrolet de los años de upa. Las piernas le flaqueaban porque en ese preciso momento recordó otra de las cartas en la que ella le decía que para defenderlo de la muerte (¡del Hades!), la cual pululaba en todo su ser, él debería abandonarlo todo, absolutamente todo y retirarse a vivir con ella en su mansión (sí, había escrito "mansión", y a él le pareció raro que con esa facha tan desgarbada tuviera una mansión) de Sugarland, donde sólo sus gatos le quitarían a ella poco tiempo para dedicárselo sin medida a él. Ahí, en su mansión, ella le daría cuanto él necesitara y pidiera:

"Para darte la paz que necesitas, Rodrigo, sólo para eso te

llevaré a mi paraíso al que nadie más que mi legión de gatos entra ni entrará. Podrás darles mi teléfono a tus parientes y amigos para no cortar del todo amarras con el mundo de afuera. Allá, conmigo, verás cuánta paz y dicha alcanzaremos juntos, *porque sabes que te amo con un amor rotundo y total, como nadie te ha querido antes, ni siquiera tu madre*".

A Rodrigo no le cabía duda de que ella era una hábil manipuladora de palabras, palabras que iba tejiendo a manera de una tupida red en la que él se iba sintiendo irremisiblemente atrapado, como ahora dentro del coche. En cuanto entró, le vino de golpe un violento tufo a orines y excrementos de gato que lo llenó de incontenibles náuseas. En seguida comprobó que mientras impartía clase por cuatro horas, la profesora Thompson había dejado encerrados a dos de sus numerosos gatos que se quedaron mirándolo con odio y rabia (al menos así le pareció a él cuando atrapaba en la oscuridad el oro luminoso de sus pupilas felinas ... ¿Y si hubiese sido más bien lástima lo que le trasmitió el oro encendido de sus ojos? ¡Había un fondo tan humano en su mirada!).

En ese instante, en la penumbra del desmantelado y ridículo Chevrolet ella volvió a aparecer ante Rodrigo en todo el juvenil resplandor pelirrojo del primer día. Entonces él experimentó con más fuerza que antes que ya nada podía hacer para defenderse de ella, que de veras estaba atrapado en la red tejida por ella con palabras, palabras, palabras y palabras, escritas, susurradas, habladas, leídas, recitadas, palabras, y no, yo quiero irme a casa, déjeme usted, señora, se me hace tarde, mis padres me esperan a cenar, no seas tontuelo, mi muchachote querido, que ellos sólo te imponen obligaciones y yo en cambio te daré el olvido y abolición completos de todo: dolor, deberes, demandas, reprimendas, ¿ves cómo los vapores de este pulverizador exterminan el penetrate olor gatuno del coche?, así se disipará tu pasado en este mismo momento, vendrás conmigo a mi mansión cerrada para los demás y a partir de ahora, sólo tú y yo, yo y tú juntos en mi paraíso ... nada más que tú y yo y el mundo de afuera eliminado para siempre.

* * *

—¿Se enteró usted que desde el jueves pasado, después de la clase suya, Rodrigo Carrillo no ha regresado a su casa, ni ha telefoneado a su familia?—, le preguntó a la profesora Thompson Claudia, una de las alumnas del curso.

—¿Ah? ¡No lo sabía!

—Como acaba de pasar lo de Mark Kilroy y la macabra carnicería ... digo, el sacrificio satánico en Matamoros, la familia Carrillo y la policía lo está buscando temerosos de que haya sido otra víctima de los narcotraficantes.

—Se teme lo peor, dicen los periódicos, y lo malo es que no han dado con la menor pista—, con voz llena de ansiedad, comentó Héctor, el amigo íntimo de Rodrigo. —Sólo saben por nosotros que estuvo el jueves en esta clase y que después ni siguiera entró en su convertible que encontraron estacionado en el mismo sitio donde lo había dejado al mediodía, cuando regresamos juntos de tomar una piscolabis. Como anteayer se descrubrió por estos barrios otra banda de traficantes de drogas que también practicaban cultos satánicos, se imaginará usted cómo está de angustiada la familia.

—¿No la interrogó a usted la poli como a nosotros?

—Oh, sí, sí, pero qué podía decirles yo? Rodrigo debe estar con alguno de sus parientes en Miami, de quienes se pasa hablando. Tengo la corazonada de que esté donde esté, no corre peligro ... ningún peligro. Sigamos con Homero. Comentábamos el pasaje en el que Ulises y sus camaradas llegaron a la isla Eea.

Héctor fijó la vista en el libro donde se relata cómo los que se alejaron de la nave oyeron a Circe que cantaba con una hermosa voz, mientras tejía en su palacio "una divina tela, tal como son las labores ligeras, graciosas y espléndidas de los dioses" ... Al posar de nuevo la mirada en la profesora Thompson, no podía dar crédito a sus ojos: en lugar de la mujerota alta, fornida, jamona, desaliñada, en la penumbra de la vejez, de rasgos duros y amargos, apareció ante él ¡increíble!, ¿estaría soñándola?, como una bella y atractiva joven de abundante cabellera rojiza —aureola rubicunda que le daba un aire de diosa prepotente. Además, en vez del vozarrón al que él se había habituado, con voz melodiosa que a sus oídos parecía un cántico divino, ella seguía relatando cómo los compañeros de Ulises fueron convertidos en puercos por Circe ...

Pablo La Rosa

Chronicle of the Argonaut Polypus

Of all the land and sea animals known to man, the polypus is perhaps one of the least understood and most needlessly feared by humans. A spineless, disproportionately large-headed creature with shifty eyes, the polypus prefers to scrape along murky bottoms and to hole up where light barely disturbs the darkness. But in spite of its menacing appearance, this cephalopod is a harmless being that feeds on weaker life forms entrapped by rows of suckers hidden in the lower half of its tentacles, which deliver the captured prey to a mouth equipped with a sharp, file-like tongue used to crush crustaceans, its favorite food. The polypus is not therefore the man-eating monster described in old mariners' and fishermen's tales. In truth, the polypus will avoid confrontation with superior adversaries, and when threatened or frightened its skin changes color and its jets spray ink to blind the enemy and cover its retreat. It is, however, in the peculiar way we copulate that our true nature is revealed with greatest clarity. This has been amply documented by a famous underwater explorer, the one who has filmed those incredible aquatic ejaculations, ranging from the foamy cascades of the sperm whale to the insoluble, oily droplets of the unfortunate crab.

I began to feel like a polypus a few days after I left my wife and children. At first I felt like an alienated octopus, if that makes any sense. I haven't counted how many suction cups we have, but after abandoning my family I had the sensation my tentacles had come unglued and that they were spinning wildly, like blades adrift in a sea of wind. My only support was my own body, flaccid and slippery. I am afraid a polypus can't survive long in such a helpless state.

This wasn't the first time I ran away. I had done it twice previously and on both occasions went back before a month elapsed begging forgiveness. But those brief excursions left a longing for freedom deep inside that neither wife nor children could quench. She blamed herself, but now I'm convinced it'd have been the same with any other mate. After fertilization of the eggs, unlike its female counterpart who won't abandon the nest until the very last offspring has emerged from the embryonic stage, the male polypus continues his nomadic existence in the marine desserts, impregnating all willing females he finds along the way. But I can no longer fertilize egg clusters, for my semen is as sterile as the sands of the Dead Sea.

To help me remember who I am, or at least who I was a few months ago, I opened my passport to review the vital information. I still look entirely human in the photograph. My wife always claimed I have sneaky eyes and she's right; I've never been able to look at a camera in the eye. Undeniably, those are polypus eyes, or at the very least the eyes of a squid.

I must have mutated greatly since the photo was taken. The first time I cashed traveler's checks the clerk didn't pay any attention to my face; she merely compared signatures on the checks to the one in the passport. But the last time the cashier made me endorse the checks front and back; he obviously was having difficulty reconciling the face on the document to the one facing him. Finally, he wrote down my passport number on a notebook and asked where I was staying. I gave him a fictitious hotel named after some obscure pre-Colombian ruins.

According to the visa stamp I crossed the border a little over two months ago. I got paid on the first and from the bank I went straight to the bus station. I prefer this mode of transportation not so much because it's cheap as for the type of people that use it. It was actually in a bus where I met the female who taught me to use my hectocotylus in a primitive manner. But that was years ago and I had no inkling whatsoever of my destiny.

After a forty hour trip I arrived at the capital of this underdeveloped nation. I decided to come here because I can make my dollars stretch, and because in a few hours I could reach the sea if I so desired. (I've always felt a tremendous need to be near water and couldn't explain it until now.) However, the real reason I came here was so that I could immerse myself in a cultural dejá-vu. Underdeveloped societies tend to imitate trends and fashions that were in vogue years before in the industrialized world, and I thought I might be able to take advantage of another sexual revolution. Until recently, though, I had the luck of a celibate monk.

It would appear from my experience here that homosexual liberation precedes the heterosexual revolution. I've been courted by gays since day one. They see me alone and conclude I must be gay too. I've been asked to the movies, to dances, have even been offered monetary rewards. I truly appreciate their brotherly love, but they must understand that we polypi are restricted to heterosexual copulation. In years past I may have resented all their attention, considering it a threat to my masculinity, but now I welcome it since gays are among the few who are not disgusted by my appearance.

Until the other day, the only women who didn't avoid me were the beggars. Not even prostitutes got near. I was desperate; my suction cups sucked on one another for lack of a strange body on which to find support. I visited anthropological museums, modern art museums, the avant-garde bookstores where one should find those trail-blazing females of the erotic revolution, but I didn't make contact. Either there are none in this country, or they are still in the underground phase.

Finally I met her one afternoon. I am a romantic polypus so I believe in fate. I was at an outdoor cafe pretending to read a poetry journal when I had a feeling. I looked up exactly at the moment she looked at me. She stopped as if to read the menu posted at the entrance and then sat at the table next to mine very naturally. She ordered a capuccino and I kept pretending to read my magazine. At last I got tired of the game and simply asked her if she was travelling alone, for obviously she too was foreign. We talked for a good hour. My vocal cords hurt, I thought because I hadn't had a sustained conversation in weeks. Now I know it's because I'm losing my ability to speak.

Not only my voice. My mental faculties are faltering and along with them language itself: I close my eyes and I see submerged landscapes, the skeletons of sunken galleons in the Sea of Antilles, or Ionic amphoras that once upon a time gave me shelter in the Mediterranean or Red Seas. I fear that soon I will cease to be human altogether and won't be able to use the ink from my glands to finish these chronicles.

That night I couldn't sleep. I was brutally frank and asked her to spend the night with me. She thought about it briefly but denied my request, claiming she was very tired. However, she said she'd like to see me the next day. I went to her hotel at first light. The night clerk didn't allow me to go up to her room; he phoned her instead and while I waited he didn't take his eyes off me. When she at long last came down to the lobby I grabbed her hand and led her to a nearby park. I told her everything; that I was married with children, that I was desperate, that I believed I was turning into a polypus. When I finished my confession she stroked my hair and sank into deep thought. Then her blue eyes came to life and she said:

"I have an idea. Let's leave for the coast this afternoon. We can get better acquainted by the sea."

My thoughts are becoming more and more incoherent as my mind gets into an extremely desultory mode. It must be apparent, because people eye me with fear and even street vendors go out of their way to avoid me. Since she disappeared I hardly leave the hotel room. I step out only to quench this thirst for sea water that burns my insides and to take my mid-day seafood meal at a bay side restaurant. At night I lie awake thinking until very late, so late the only noise heard is that of the rats and the waves eating away the foundations of the port. I go into the bathroom to be surprised by the mirror; I catch a glimpse of a shocked, unrecognizable face that doesn't match the memory I have of myself, because I've been evolving backwards and what

I was years or months ago has no resemblance to what I am now. I turn out the lights and spend an eternity sucking on the sheet's edge. Then I am overwhelmed by desire and would masturbate into oblivion if not for the fact that we polypi can't masturbate, all the tentacles notwithstanding. Besides, I lost my hectocotylus and I must wait for another to grow.

I wonder how long that might take. I fear this cavity may be permanent, leaving me a polyped eunuch for the rest of my new life; that this coagulated mass of blood vessels might not be able to decipher the genetic code for hectocotilar regeneration and that my pentatentacle has been irreplaceably lost to the treacherous female. She lured me to the sea so I could impregnate her, but she didn't know a surgeon removed my seminal vessels the day after my last offspring was born. She's probably holed up in a ledge of the continental shelf, awaiting futilely the birth of thousands of our offspring.

We made the bus trip in silence. She fell asleep on my shoulder and I had to keep touching her to make sure it all wasn't a dream. Throughout the ride I had the impression I was a silent movie spectator, that the landscape of volcanic rocks and malnourished fields was only an illusion projected on the window. As we approached the coastal plain my skeleton softened; each time a whiff of saltpeter-laden breeze seared my nostrils my body tissue thinned. When I saw the ocean in the distance I understood this was a journey with no return. I must have trembled, for she awoke and caressed me.

We caught a taxi and I asked the driver to take us to a second-class hotel with a beach front. On the register form I marked we were married, but I could tell the clerk didn't believe it from her sardonic smile. I asked for a room with natural ventilation, with a balcony overlooking the ocean. The clerk insisted I pay in advance after remarking sarcastically that air conditioned rooms weren't that expensive.

We spent three days in an agonizing apprenticeship. I believed I made love rather competently, but my method was human and she had to teach me the way polipi mate. As soon as the bellhop left us alone in our room, I embraced her violently and tried to kiss her in the neck. She rejected my overtures, and this really confused me. I looked at her right in the eyes, begging for an explanation. I had thought we wouldn't be wasting time on childish psychological foreplay.

"I get more pleasure from a warm bath than from making love with a man," she said.

I answered I didn't understand.

"I mean that most men make love as if they were racing. They struggle so hard to cross the finish line first."

I felt ashamed. Her words made certain lightning-quick copulations from my youth come to mind.

"Forget it, it's not your fault. Undress."

We undressed without touching. I was accustomed to having to undress the female as a prerequisite to love making and it took great effort to hold back. She instructed me to sit at one end of the bed, and she took a yoga position at the opposite end. We looked at each other for over an hour. The sun was setting and the constant crash of waves was hypnotizing. I watched as her skin changed hues. Two red circles grew around her eyes. My body started moving towards her. Our tentacles met cautiously at first; then mine explored her supple cephalopod body and we became one. I felt her abdomen open under mine, allowing the hectocotylus to penetrate fully. We remained motionless for a very long time. When we separated, the sun had set hours before.

I turned on the lights. She had returned to her human form. I looked in the mirror with horror, but I too had regained the body of a man. We dressed and went out on the streets, sharing an unspeakable secret. We hadn't eaten since morning and were famished. We found an outdoor restaurant and chose a table sheltered from the bustle. The waiter approached with a menu.

"We know what we want," my lover spoke, "oyster cocktails and Valencia-style paella for both."

She looked at me with her woman's eyes, fathomless and blue like the sea.

I don't have much time left. This morning, the sight of an Indian woman breast feeding her child filled me with a nostalgia for things mammalian. I wrote a long letter to my children but after reading it I realized it was full of sentimental nonsense. I tore it up.

On the third night, we waited till all was quiet before slipping down to the beach. Out at sea, the lanterns of the fishing boats flickered, the same travelers that catch my kind with their treacherous nets. We undressed by the water. She took me by the arm and led me away from the shore. The cold didn't affect us and we floated easily, swept by the tide. Soon our bodies began to irradiate a reddish-green phosphorescence. Her abdomen opened to mine and my tentacle sought its primeval sea warmth. We went under the surface. I was able to breathe submerged; I was able to breathe through water as in the beginning of life. I was enveloped by the mother sea and part of me was surrounded by another sea. Suddenly her abdomen shuddered and tightened. Her inside walls began contracting as if giving birth in reverse. Then her abdomen closed and severed my hectocotylus. She fled in a cloud of ink, abandoning me in the ocean's immensity.

I've just come out of the shower. My skin dries off quickly if I'm not careful; I must constantly drag myself to the bathroom, attach my suckers to

ool brackish water run down my body and saturate my
:k to bed dripping and cover myself with a wet sheet. I
with the tip of my right upper tentacle. I know the end
existence is near. Tonight my transfigured body will slither
through the window and on to the beach. When the cleaning woman opens
the door tomorrow she'll find my bodily remains. Scattered on the floor
nearby she'll see sheets of a manuscript written in an opaque ink of unknown
origin. The police will look for a pen but will never find one. They might
discover the trail of spittle I'll leave on the sand as I make my way toward
new seas, toward new archipelagoes inhabited by voracious females ready
to swallow my sterile yet virile hectocotyli. It is possible that if I continue
this evolution in reverse, some day I will become an argonaut polypus. In
that ideal state my isolation will be absolute, because the hectocotylus of
said species has the unique capacity to become detached from the body and
gain a life of its own as soon as it reaches maturity. To be nothing but a
phallic being, to know not why nor how, to have but one mission in life
with no questions or answers, to enter the womb of an unsuspecting female
without the need for excuses, and nothing else.

Elías Miguel Muñoz

Carta de Julio

A *Thalia Dorwick*,
naturalmente

"En la mentira infinita de ese sueño . . . "
(Julio Cortázar, "La noche boca arriba")

La editorial se encargó de proveer los ingredientes: vocabulario, tiempos verbales, modismos, tono y glosario para las expresiones coloquiales. Que divierta, que excite, que despierte interés, me pidió la editora. Que el texto agarre a los alumnos y que no los suelte hasta que lleguen al último silencio. Que se olviden, al leer, que están leyendo en otra lengua.

¿Qué te parece un relato fantástico?, preguntó la editora, amorosamente autoritaria, como siempre. Un librito de lectura para complementar los grandes métodos comunicativos del momento. Amplio mercado. Grandes ventas. Luego me sugirió el título y la anécdota, por supuesto:

Quinto sol se llamaría el relato y su protagonista sería un joven mexicano, Daniel Flores, estudiante de historia en la UNAM. Buena descripción del Distrito Federal, Chapultepec, museo, etcétera, sin mencionar la polución ni el desempleo. Vida de estudiante pobre pero no tan pobre para que los chicos puedan identificarse, etcétera.

La peripecia: Daniel se cansa de la ciudad (no porque esté pasando hambre y comiéndose el cable, nada de eso; ni tampoco porque sea un nene de la Zona Rosa, engreído y ávido consumidor de chichifos). Agobiado por la gran metrópolis —pobrecito— Daniel decide regresar a su pueblo natal, Ayapango, ubicado entre los dos volcanes, justo a lado del Paso de Cortés. El estudiante añora —¡dígame usted!— el calor del hogar y la comida de su madre.

Al caer extenuado en el lecho hogareño, volcado sobre la nada oscura del cansancio, Daniel viaja al siglo dieciséis, a Tenochtitlán, para enfrentarse a los blancos. Una vez pasado el susto de estar en otro tiempo y habitar otro cuerpo, Daniel asume feliz la vida de Tozani, joven guerrero azteca. Luego vislumbra un plan descabellado, ambicioso y tentador: destruir a Cortés y evitar la masacre.

*   *   *

¿Cómo podía yo contar la historia de un estudiante mexicano? ¿Qué diablos podía decir de un país donde ni siquiera había estado? ¿Qué sabía yo de tortillas calentitas y volcanes? Una cosa era sacar un relato de los libros, (Soustelle, Gary Jennings), reescribir lo que ya había sido machacado, y otra muy distinta era ponerle algo de mí a la narración, darle un poco de vida. Porque yo no concebía la escritura de un texto —así fuera un proyecto menor, esencialmente lucrativo, para una gran casa editorial— sin que llevara algo real, algo *auténtico*. Podía partir de mi experiencia del destierro. Cubanito refugiado. El dolor de la ruptura, supuse, siempre es el mismo. Sólo tendría que disfrazar levemente los hechos, darles color local, mexicanizar mi exilio cubiche. En realidad, pensé, no era un proyecto irrealizable. Me documentaría conversando con un par de *cuates*, un profe de español y un artista. Después me dejaría arrastrar, llenando de palabras (preasignadas) la fascinante anécdota.

Fue así que me vi describiendo a un personaje que sueña y se desplaza, que *se pierde*. Fue así que me adentré en su pesadilla. Daniel regresaría a su pueblo (¿cómo deseaba yo regresar al mío?) para vivir la más desafiante de todas las aventuras.

*   *   *

Algunos detalles de intrahistoria y *backstory*: resulta que Tozani está casado con una hembra buenísima, azteca de pura cepa, ojos verdes y curvas tremendas. Y Daniel mosquita-muerta se coge a la esposa del guerrero, haciéndose pasar por él y sacándole un *fringe benefit* a su aventurita.

Luego resulta que el Emperador nombra a Tozani "Águila de Luz", un gran honor, y le pide que vaya al encuentro de los dioses blancos, llevándoles ofrendas. Pero Tozani (que en realidad no es Tozani sino Daniel Flores) sabe muy bien que no se trata de seres divinos, sino de seres muy "humanos": los españoles. Y claro, Daniel, siendo estudiante de historia, está muy enterado de todos los sucesos. De hecho, una de sus fantasías ha sido siempre desplazarse en el tiempo y salvar su civilización, la otra, la *verdadera*.

En fin, que Daniel-Tozani le confiesa enternecido a su esposa, en víspera del encuentro, que no piensa agasajar a los blancos, sino destruirlos. ¡No lo hagas, esposo!, ella le implora. Pero Daniel-Tozani no la escucha. Sólo le pide un lindo recuerdo, por si acaso no vuelve. Y ella le agarra la onda, entregada y obsequiosa. La mañana siguiente Daniel —encarnando a Tozani— parte en pos de su historia, dispuesto a pelear por el triunfo de sus antepasados.

Como todos sabemos, *c'est domage*, Daniel no logra su objetivo. Le pega un buen susto a Cortés, eso es todo; casi mata a Alvarado, y le da un sendo trastazo en la cabeza a la Malinche. Lucha como todo un hombre, comandando a sus soldados. Pero pierde y tienen que hacer retirada, él y unos cuantos sobrevivientes, rumbo a Tenochtitlán. Y allí, pues nada, que lo regaña duramente el Emperador. Porque Daniel-Tozani es muy "echao p'alante" y lo primero que hace cuando regresa a la ciudad es decirle a Moctecuhzoma que está equivocado (¡habráse visto mayor atrevimiento!), que Cortés no es Quetzacoatl, dios creador de los aztecas, que regresa buscando su reino, sino un vil hombre apestoso e ignorante. Y el Emperador que se encojona (y no era para menos), temeroso de la ira del creador. Y condena a Tozani a la pena de muerte, bajo el filo de un cuchillo de obsidiana. Su corazón en sacrificio a Huitzilopotchli, dios de todas las guerras.

* * *

Quinto sol no vio nunca la luz. Sé que todavía lo usan por ahí, en algún college de Orange County. Sé que el manuscrito va de mano en manito, como los chismes y las malas noticias.

Al cabo de los años —siendo ya todo un "señor escritor"— me doy cuenta que el relato no fue escrito para ser publicado, y mucho menos para que los amigos de la gran editorial incrementen sus ventas; mucho, muchísimo menos, para que miles y miles de gringuitos tengan una grata experiencia de lectura en su *second language*. La razón de su escritura fue otra.

* * *

¿Rescatar algo del texto? Tarea difícil, porque no guardé copia del manuscrito (en aquellos días todavía no "salvaba" las palabras en los *files* de un ordenador).

Creo que empezaba más o menos así, en primera persona:

Mi vida en la capital (donde yo no había estado, lo repito) se hizo difícil. Extrañaba a mis padres (mis verdaderos padres habían quedado atrás, en Cuba); extrañaba la vida tranquila de Ayapango (Ciego de Ávila), la comida casera, las tortillas calentitas amasadas por mi madre (chicharrones y yuca), el enorme nogal del patio y sus nueces que caían como lluvia (un cocotero); el olor a humo de la cocina, la lucha diaria con las ardillas (en la realidad de mi recuerdo, cucarachas) y los animales que querían devorar el maíz almacenado (comida que mi padre compraba en contrabando); el techo de dos aguas (un chalet que mi familia hizo construir a raíz de la Revolución). Pero lo que más extrañaba de mi pueblo era la vista imponente de los dos volcanes, Ixtaccíhuatl y Popocatépetl (en la experiencia de mi patria, el Pico Turquino).

En algún momento del relato llegaba el cruce del umbral, en tercera persona:

Se quedó dormido hacia las tres de la mañana. Y soñó con la Piedra de Sol. Podía penetrarla, recorrer dentro de ella el tiempo. Vio su propio rostro retratado en la superficie de la roca, junto a Tonatiu, dios del sol. Al penetrar la piedra sintió un calor intenso. Y escuchaba, mientras viajaba al mismísimo centro, un susurro lejano que decía Tozani. Voz de mujer que le dice y le grita ¡Tozani!

Abre por fin los ojos y ve su cuerpo, está casi desnudo; lo cubre un taparrabos de tela muy áspera. No siente el olor dulce del café de su madre, pero escucha una voz de mujer ... Tozani ...

Una calle amplia, casas de paredes muy blancas, jardines, y a lo largo de toda la avenida el agua, el lago, hombres en canoas, hombres vestidos como él, taparrabo y manto, hombres cubiertos de plumas, vestidos con pieles de tigre, con lanzas; hombres, mujeres y niños que lo miran y sonríen ...

Una escultura esplendorosa, el rostro de Tonatiu, su mirada fija en el vacío, la boca abierta, con hambre de tiernos y jóvenes corazones.

Las colas de dos serpientes se juntan en la fecha sagrada de la creación ...

* * *

Quiero pensar que Julio tenía razón, que estaba en lo justo, que mi librito era demasiado plagio de uno de sus cuentos. *Usted me pidió mi opinión y se la doy con toda sinceridad* ...

A veces digo no, te equivocaste, che. Lo tuyo es lo tuyo y el *Quinto sol* es mi parto. No pensarás que sólo vos podés hablar de los aztecas y los viajecitos en el tiempo. ¿Dónde se ha visto autoridad igual, chico? *La trama de ambas cosas parecería revelar una influencia excesiva de mi relato* ...

La sabia editora de la gran editorial husmeó desde el primer momento el parecido. Aquí me huelo yo Julio encerrado, dijo poco después de leer el manuscrito. Un *tour de force*, sin duda, te felicito. Es exactamente lo que te pedimos, pero por si las moscas pide permiso, mándaselo a Cortázar a ver que opina.

Y yo, obediente escribidor agarrado con las manos en la masa, así lo hice.

Un día, sin poder sobreponerme a la sorpresa, recibí contestación. Una carta frágil de puño y letra, papel de cebolla, tinta negra, caligrafía nerviosa, palabras gentiles, dignas de Julio. Una carta escrita el 18 de septiembre de 1983, poco antes de su muerte.

Sumido en la vergüenza de mi plagio, guardé la misiva. Usted tenía razón, le dije a la editora, mordiéndome la lengua. Hay Julio encerrado en mi relato.

* * *

Uno de los guardias mira a sus alrededores, pero no me ve. Ya casi llego al escondite del "dios" blanco. Un soldado a la entrada. Un golpe de cuchillo y cae al suelo. Agarro su bayoneta.

"¡Buenas noches, señores!", les apunto. "¡Quietos todos!" Alvarado se me tira encima; le disparo. Cortés y Malinche se miran y me miran, incrédulos. "No esperaba esta visita, ¿verdad, capitán?", le pregunto en su idioma. Malinche tiembla. Cortés mira a Alvarado, muerto o mal herido en el suelo. "El menor movimiento y los mato a los dos", les grito.

"El indio aprendió nuestra lengua, Malinche", dice el Conquistador. "Es increíble, ¿no crees? Esta gente es mucho más inteligente de lo que yo pensaba . . . ¿Cómo te llamas, indio?"

"Tozani, Águila de Luz".

"Entonces, Tozani, supongo que ya conoces nuestros planes".

"Sí, sé lo que vas a hacerle a mi pueblo".

"¡Imbécil! Nada pueden tus armas primitivas contra mis cañones".

"Un paso más y disparo", le digo, y jalo a Malinche, envolviendo su cuello con un brazo. "Si te mueves la mato, y no tendrás cómplice para tu invasión".

"¡Corre, Hernán!", grita la amante. "¡Corre a luchar con tus hombres!"

"¡Traidora!", con el filo de mi mano le golpeo la nuca y cae desmayada. "Ahora no tenemos testigos, hombre blanco".

"¿Testigos de tu muerte?"

"No, de la tuya, porque voy a matarte, Hernán Cortés".

* * *

Releí la carta cuando ya empezaba a dolerme un poco menos su muerte. La encontré donde acabo de encontrarla hace un momento, acariciada tiernamente por dos páginas de *Salvo el crepúsculo*.

Porque de pronto quiero reclamar un pedazo de Julio, dejarlo vivir otra vez, a mi manera. Decir, por ejemplo, que por mucho tiempo me sentí personaje de Julio, títere suyo, admirador febril y subyudado, sombra de un texto de Julio.

¿Cómo evitar su influencia, deshacerme de él? ¿Quién, en su insano juicio, podía darse el lujo de despedir a un *tal* Julio, de cantarle por fin una buena milonga?

* * *

Cinco soldados me sujetan y me empujan a lo largo de la Gran Plaza, hasta la Pirámide. Escucho los gritos de la gente. *¡Ayyo Ouiyya!* Se despiden de Tozani, único guerrero capaz de desafiar al poderoso Uey-Tlatoani Moctecuhzoma. El que encaró a los invasores, en vez de ofrecerle ofrendas y regalos.

Entramos al templo de Huitzilopotchli. Está oscuro y apesta a sangre seca. Encienden las antorchas y me atan a una cama de piedra. Cierro los ojos, exhausto, vencido. Me arrancan la poca ropa que llevo y quedo desnudo. Sobre el suelo, a mi lado, colocan mis armas, llenas de polvo . . .

Y aparece un hombre vestido de plumas, rostro blanco; en su mano derecha la obsidiana. Detrás de él, Moctecuhzoma. El Emperador hace un gesto y el sacerdote me dice "¡Ayyo! Estamos preparados para concederte una última palabra, Tozani. Habla".

"¡Sí! Hablaré", le grito. "¡Los blancos no son dioses! ¡Y Moctecuhzoma es un cobarde!"

El Emperador le arrebata al sacerdote su cuchillo. Sus ojos encendidos, sus manos temblorosas. Esta vez será suyo el honor de abrirle el pecho a un prisionero.

"¡Moctecuhzoma es un cobarde!", le grito.

Una serpiente me recorre la sangre y me desgarra las entrañas. Un sueño intenso. *Cobarde.* Me hundo hasta el centro, *cobarde*, hasta el profundo centro de una piedra . . .

Ahora sé que Daniel Flores nunca despertará.

* * *

Estimado amigo:

La lectura de su novela muestra una semejanza considerable con mi relato "La noche boca arriba". No solamente en el plano de lo fantástico, sino en el hecho de que éste se cumple dentro de un contexto histórico equivalente al de mi cuento, o sea el mundo mexicano de las culturas precolombinas.

La trama de ambas cosas parecería revelar una influencia excesiva de mi relato, que cualquier lector de su novela no tardaría en sentir.

Usted me pidió mi opinión y se la doy con toda sinceridad, a la vez que alabo la vivacidad con que se desarrolla su relato y los muchos aciertos que tiene.

Le envía un saludo cordial,

Julio

* * *

Sé que él era gigantesco de estatura, que tenía ojos enormes de niño solitario, que era tierno. Nunca llegué a conocerlo (en persona, quiero decir). Y sin embargo, cuando murió fue como si la vida no valiera, como si de pronto se esfumaran todos los cuentos del universo.

Se me murió un amigo, coño.

El pedido de la editorial, las largas horas de plagio recreativo, de sudor en las sienes, los sueños de ver mi relato convertido en texto de lectura para los chicos (sueños que ahora tan poco me importan), todo se combinó para que yo, al estilo de Julio, recibiera el anuncio de su fin.

Rosaura Sánchez

Tres generaciones

Esta tarde cuando llegué estaba de rodillas ante unos geranios y unas gardenias y refunfuñaba por lo que yo llamo "el tomate imperialista" que siempre se anda queriendo apoderar de todo el terreno. Se han puesto demasiado grandes las plantas y como que quieren tomarse el jardín.

—¿Y por qué no las cortas?

—Voy a dejar que maduren los tomates y después adiós plantas. No volveré a sembrarlas. ¿No ves como lo invaden todo? Mejor pongo unos chiles allí, aunque no hay mucho campo. Ay, no es como el solar que teníamos allá en Texas.

Las plantas han adquirido personalidad para ella. Al limonero le pide disculpas por haber dejado que la madreselva largara sus raíces por donde no debía. El pobre limonero enano que yo planté antes de que ella se viniera a vivir con nosotras no ha muerto pero tampoco crece, ya que las raíces de la madreselva que ella plantó han acaparado el poco terreno que había para ese lado del patiecito. Otra planta imperialista, pero ésta por la superficie subyacente, por donde no se ve ni se sospecha. La planta de tomate en cambio lo hace a los cuatro vientos y es obvio que sus ramas se extienden por todos lados, pero la madreselva se mantiene acurrucada contra la cerca, como si nada. Es como la diferencia entre la dependencia y el colonialismo, le digo, pero no acaba de entenderme. Mi madre sigue sacando las hierbas malas y regando, mientras piensa en podar la bugambilia, para que no le quite el sol al malvavisco que está a sus pies. Y yo no sé por qué le salgo con esas frases absurdas, como si me quisiera hacer la interesante, porque después de todo, la terminología, fue lo único que me quedó de aquellas clases universitarias de estudios del tercer mundo. Y pensar que en un tiempo creí que podría ser mi especialidad, pero al final, me fui por lo más seguro, y estudié comercio. Pero ella, ahora que está sola, parecería haber estudiado jardinería. Se la pasa trasplantando, podando, regando y conversando con las plantas porque yo y mi hija casi nunca estamos en casa más que para dormir. Y no es que no quiera yo también ponerme a trabajar en el jardín, sino que el trabajo, las reuniones, los viajes fuera de la ciudad me tienen siempre ocupada, siempre corriendo. Como ahora mismo.

Quería mostrarle lo bien que va la hortensia pero ya se metió. Seguro que estará allí con la computadora hasta las altas horas de la noche; a veces ni quiere bajar a cenar. Y la Mari, perdida anda esa muchacha. Ya traté de decirle a Hilda que algo anda mal, pero ni caso me hace. Cosa de adolescentes, me dice, ya se le va a pasar. La Mari se encierra en su cuarto y cuando sale tiene los ojillos todos rojos como que ha estado fumando o tomando alguna cosa de ésas, de esas mugres que hoy consiguen fácilmente los chavalillos. Ay, cómo me hace falta aquel hombre. El sabría cómo hablarle a su nieta, creo, pero a mí ni caso me hace. Por eso me la paso aquí afuera con mis flores y mis arbolitos. Y a veces doña Chonita se viene a platicarme alguna cosa y nos tomamos un poco de limonada mientras le muestro las matas y así se me pasa el tiempo. Voy a tener que comprar un poco de alimento para las plantas porque esta mano de león, por ejemplo, no quiere prender. Recuerdo las que sembraba mi mamá en el solar hace ya tantos años. No eran estas miniaturas raquíticas. Esas sí que eran flores. Jardín más chulo no había en todo el barrio.

Tan pronto como me cambie, me pongo a la computadora. Pobre de mi mamá, me da no sé qué dejarla sola allá abajo, pero por lo menos se distrae con el jardín; a veces se va con alguna de sus amigas de la iglesia al cine o de compras. Pero más sola que yo no puede estar porque desde que me dejó Ricardo . . . aunque de eso ya hace tanto tiempo que hasta ridículo me parece recordarlo. Tampoco puedo quejarme, porque mejor nunca estuve. Me mantengo ocupada y tengo mis amigos y mis amigas en el trabajo. Y a veces salgo con Alfredo y cuando podemos, nos vamos de paseo. Pero ninguno de los dos quiere volverse a meter en problemas. El divorcio como que le deja a uno un mal sabor en la boca. Así estamos mejor, nos divertimos, nos vamos de viaje los fines de semana cuando hay tiempo y cuando no, cada uno a su trabajo y a sus obligaciones, y hasta la próxima, sin compromiso, sin recriminaciones, cada uno libre de hacer lo que se le antoje. Por lo menos es lo que me digo y lo que contesto cuando me preguntan que por qué no me he vuelto a casar. Porque con Ricardo fui muy celosa, aunque tal vez todo eso fue un error desde el principio. Si no hubiera salido encinta, no nos habríamos casado, seguro. Pero ¿qué otra opción tenía yo? Porque el sólo pensar en lo de Antonia y en el trauma que fue todo aquello me daba escalofrío. Los tiempos cómo cambian y no cambian, porque el tema sigue candente, y hasta quieren recortar los fondos para esas clínicas, pero en aquel entonces todo era prohibido, no había clínicas para el aborto, y a menos que una tuviera plata para irse al otro lado, para hacérselo allá, tenía que acudir a alguna curandera para que le diera un remedio o a lo que acudió Antonia cuando supo que el marido andaba con la vecina. Desde entonces no tolero ver los ganchos de alambre para la ropa. Todos son de plástico. No, no pude hacerlo. Pero si hubiera sido más fuerte, más inteligente, me las habría arreglado sola, aunque en casa me hubieran desconocido por el escándalo. Y por eso, nos casamos porque tuvimos que. Pero nunca estuvimos bien. Al año ya estábamos divorciados y así se ha criado Mari, sin padre, sin la ayuda económica que nos vendría bien si Ricardo se portara como debería. Pero pronto se volvió a casar con la gringa ésa y ya después no me aventó ni con un centavo. Por eso tuve que trabajar y dejar a la niña aquí y allá, buscando siempre quien me la cuidara hasta que ya pude ponerla en una guardería infantil. Ahora también está mi mamá. Cuando quedó viuda, me la traje acá, porque después de tanto año de trabajar en la costura de blue jeans, ¿qué le mandan? ¡Unos trescientos dólares por mes del seguro social! Ni para comer le alcanza; por eso me la traje a Santa Ana donde no le ha de faltar techo ni comida. Esta impresora es bastante lenta, no como la de la oficina, pero imprime más o menos bien. Voy a tener que comprarme una nueva, de laser; así no tengo que llegar como loca por la mañana haciendo copia de todo antes de la primera reunión a las 8:30; no sé por qué me las ponen tan temprano. Uuy, cómo se pasa el tiempo. Creí que eran las 7:30 y ya van a ser las nueve. Al rato bajo a comer algo. Ay, esa Mari, aún no ha llegado de la escuela. ¡Estas no son horas! ¿Dónde se habrá metido? Voy a tener que hablar con ella cuando llegue. Una chica de 13 años no tiene por qué andar fuera tan tarde. Se le hace fácil todo.

¡Ay, la que me espera! Tengo que apurarme porque si no, mi mamá se va a poner sospechosa. Pero si está ocupada ni se ha de enterar. Pero cómo iba a venirme cuando todos estaban mirándome, viendo si le entraba duro o no. O soy de la clica o no soy; por eso por fin probé la nueva combinación. Es como volar. What a blast! Pero después, qué bajón. Por eso no podía venirme, hasta que se me pasara un poco. Cuando sepa mi mamá que hoy no fui a la escuela, se va a poner furiosa, pero y qué. Que se enoje nomás. Ya realmente no me importa nada, nada más que volver a fumar la combinación. No sé cómo pudo conseguirla Daniel. Generalmente sólo trae marihuana o "crack" pero hoy de veras se aventó. Su papi debe ser muy bueno porque cada semana le afloja la lana para que se divierta. Para que no lo moleste dice Danny, pero no sé por qué se queja porque con lo que le da su papá pues siempre tiene con qué hacer sus compras. Sabe exactamente dónde venden lo que quiere; yo he ido varias veces con él y es casi como "drive-in service" porque nomás para el carro en medio de la calle y siempre corre algún chico con el paquetito, pagamos y vámonos. Después nos vamos a su casa o a la de Jenny. Uy, ya van a ser las nueve; creí que eran las siete, como ya se hace noche bien temprano. Ojalá que la abuela no me haga preguntas como siempre; le gusta fastidiarme nomás. Allí está siempre esperándome y mirándome con esos ojos. No sé por qué no se va a ver televisión o lo que sea y se deja de meterse en lo mío.

Ay, esta niña que no llega. Allá en mis tiempos todo era muy difícil. Mi papá ni nos dejaba salir a ninguna parte. Por eso ni primaria terminamos las mujeres. Eran los tiempos de los trabajos en la labor, en la pizca de algodón o la cosecha de betabel. Nuestros viajes eran de un rancho al otro hasta que volvíamos a San Angel para la Navidad. A veces teníamos que pararnos en los caminos para dormir y calentar algo para comer. Ya después en el rancho, a mí como era la mayor, me tocaba todo. Tenía que levantarme a las cinco y media para hacer el desayuno y el lonche para mediodía. A veces le digo a la Mari que no sabe lo que es fregarse, que antes no teníamos baño dentro de la casa, que teníamos que pasar al excusado que estaba cerca del callejón y se ríe, diciendo que eso es horrible y que ella nunca aguantaría tal cosa. Ni lo cree ni le importa. No conoce la pobreza ni quiere saber que todavía hay pobreza por el mundo. Los jóvenes de hoy no saben nada, ni se enteran de nada, ni piensan en nada más que andar de parranda y tal vez cosas peores. Piensan que son cuentos de hadas. A ver qué le caliento a Hilda, si no le hago algo se la pasa con puro sánwiche de pavo.

¡Cómo cambian los tiempos! En los míos, a mí me tocaba hacer las tortillas, la lavada, la planchada, porque generalmente mi mamá estaba encinta y no podía con todo el trabajo. Para mí no hubo escuela ni nada, puro trabajo bruto, como el burro; por eso cuando yo tuve a la Hilda me dije, ésta no va a sufrir como yo; por eso la mandé a la escuela aunque todos me decían que hacía mal en mandarla, que para qué, que me iba a salir mal, que seguro la iba a tener que casar a los 15 años por andar de pajuela. Pero no fue así, estudió su carrera, se graduó y se puso a trabajar. Fue mucho después, cuando ya era una mujer de 25 años, que salió encinta y decidió casarse, porque no quería abortar, no quería que le pasara lo que a Antonia, aunque mi hija podría haber ido a alguna clínica en la frontera, si hubiera querido. Pero luego le tocó la mala suerte y el marido la dejó. Es lo que ella dice, pero a veces hasta creo que sólo se casó para tener la criatura porque siempre ha sido muy independiente la muchacha. Gracias al estudio pudo mantenerse sola, porque nosotros no estábamos en condiciones de ayudarle. ¿Qué habría sido de ella si no hubiera tenido el trabajo? Habriá tenido que vivir del Welfare como más de cuatro en el barrio.

A la impresora le tengo que cambiar la cinta. Y la Mari, ¿dónde andará que no llega? Si para las nueve no está, tendré que llamarle a alguien. ¿A quién? Tal vez a alguna de sus amigas, no sé si tenemos el número de teléfono del tal Daniel con el que sale a veces. Voy a tener que hablarle seriamente porque no tengo tiempo realmente de andar con estas cosas, especialmente hoy que tengo que terminar de preparar este informe; ya me falta poco y el diagrama ya lo tengo hecho. Me salió bien. Esta nueva computadora es fenomenal, hasta a colores puede sacar los cuadros. Espero convencerlos con estas estadísticas; si deciden asociarse con la compañía, podremos ampliar la producción y así aumentar las ventas para el próximo año, como quiere el jefe. Estos nuevos programas van a revolucionar la industria de las computadoras y nosotros los vamos a producir. Bueno, yo no, claro, sino la compañía. Increíble pensar que ya comienzo a pensar como "company man" o mejor dicho, "woman" —como si no me explotaran bien a bien; me sacan el jugo pero tampoco me pagan mal, por lo menos desde que les armé el gran lío. Ya pensaban que los iba a demandar por discriminación. Y ¿por qué no?, si me tenían allí de asistente cuando la que hacía todo el trabajo del jefe era yo. Y después de la reunión de mañana, habrá que presentarles el plan a los mero-meros. ¿Me habrán hecho la reservación del cuarto en Nueva York? Bueno todavía hay tiempo; mañana se lo pregunto a Cheryl. Lo que son las cosas. Ahora es cosa de llamar y hacer la reservación y le tienen a una todo listo cuando llegue. No saben que la que llega toda vestida con su portafolio y todo es la misma que pizcó algodón y durmió con sus padres en el suelo. Recuerdo que una vez tuvimos que pasar la noche en la orilla del camino, durmiendo en el carro, porque no teníamos con qué pagarnos un cuarto en un motel. Sí, la noche misma que me gradué y salimos tarde, tuvimos que pararnos en las afueras de Austin. Amá quería ir a visitar a la tía de paso, pero cómo íbamos a llegar a medianoche sin avisar. Tampoco podíamos volver a San Angel. Y allí estuvimos toda la noche, incómodos, de mal humor, peleándonos unos con los otros hasta que amaneció y pudimos llegar a San Antonio para ver a la tía, que a fin de cuentas nos recibió de mala gana. No, no saben quién les presenta el informe. La que lo sabe soy yo, la que no lo olvida soy yo. No, el sueldo de ahora no borra nada. No borra las miraditas que me dan en las reuniones de Marketing cuando soy yo la que hago la presentación. No borra el ninguneo que siempre padecimos. No borra el que, a pesar de todo el entrenamiento en teneduría de libros, mecanografía y dactilografía en secundaria, no pudiera yo conseguir trabajo después de graduarme, más que como operadora de ascensor. Por eso me decidí y me fui a a la universidad, con préstamo del gobierno claro.

Como me sabía mal vestida, no iba nunca a ninguna parte; me dedicaba a estudiar. Hasta que en mi primer trabajo después de graduarme de la universidad conocí a Ricardo; parecía interesado en mí y yo estaba feliz, feliz de la vida, y por eso cuando me comenzó a invitar a salir, acepté, lo acepté todo, pensando que era mi futuro, mi compañero del alma. ¡Qué estúpida fui! A él le interesaba sólo una cosa. Y ya después . . . ni para qué estar pensando en eso.

—Amá, Amá, ven para que me cuentes. Ahora que han salido los muchachos con Apá, quiero que me cuentes lo que le pasó a Antonia.

—Mira, hija, cuando Antonia se enteró de que su marido andaba quedando con Elodia, decidió hacer lo que podía para no perder al marido. Ya tenían cuatro niñas y estaba de nuevo encinta. La vecina venía a darle la mano, como estaba viuda recién y no tenía más que hacer, y en una de ésas le voló el marido. Te acuerdas que andaban los tres de aquí para allá y de allá para acá. Pues un día Antonia los agarró juntos en la cocina y la mandó a volar a la Elodia; hasta acá oí yo los gritos, donde le decía que se fuera mucho a la tiznada. Después, una mañana, días después, vino corriendo una de las niñas para pedirme que fuera a ver a su mamá, que se estaba desangrando. Corrí a la casa y cuando vi que se estaba vaciando, llamé pronto a la ambulancia. Ya sabes cómo tarda la ambulancia para llegar al barrio. Para cuando llegó, ya estaba pálida, color de cera. Duró sólo unas horas en el hospital y allí murió. ¡Lo que son capaces de hacer las mujeres por no perder a un hombre! Sí, al verse de nuevo embarazada y sin tener a quien acudir, se metió un gancho de la ropa, para que se le viniera. Ah, hija de mi alma, no vayas a hacer nunca una locura semejante. Si alguna vez te ves en tales aprietos, tenlo nomás. Ya encontraríamos cómo cuidarlo. Aunque, sí, tienes razón, tu papá se moriría de vergüenza. Mejor no te metas en tales líos, hija.

Le pedí que me lo contara cuando vine de San Antonio para el funeral de Antonia; fue al verla allí en la casa mortuoria que decidí tener el bebé, no importaba lo que pasara. Cuando lo supo Ricardo se enfadó conmigo y me dijo que él no quería casarse. Le dije que estaba bien, que lo tendría yo sola, pero parece que su mamá le dijo que debía casarse, para darle el apellido a la criatura , y así fue. Hicimos las paces, nos casamos; se vino a vivir a mi departamento y un año después, me pidió el divorcio. En mi familia nunca había habido un divorcio. Así que eso también fue doloroso para mi papá, tanto o más que el "sietemesino" que tratamos de hacerle creer. Aunque ... después fui la primera de varias primas que se divorciaron. La nueva generación. Después, cuando me ofrecieron trabajo en California, con esta compañía de software para las computadoras, me vine con la niña que ya para entonces tenía cinco años. Aquí me ningunearon lo que quisieron por muchos años hasta que me sentí segura y comencé a exigir lo que hacía años me debían. Cambiaron el personal dirigente y por fin pude lograr el ascenso en Marketing. Con ello vinieron más presiones y tensiones y los viajes constantes. Y la niña ha ido creciendo, casi sin darme cuenta. Allí va llegando. A esa Mari tengo que hablarle; es una desconsiderada, no aprecia lo que hago por ella. Por ella y por mí. Porque me he ido llenando la vida de trabajo, de trabajo y a veces de Alfredo. A lo mejor me llama de San Francisco.

—¡Mari! ¡Mari! Ven acá un momento. ¿Dónde has estado?

Por fin llegó la Mari; viene como endrogada. Pero me alegro que esté aquí Hilda, para que la vea, para que se entere, porque cuando yo trato de decirle algo, como que no me escucha, como que no quiere oír lo que no le conviene. Esta vida moderna, ¡quién la entiende! Ya son las nueve. Me haré un taco yo también de las fajitas que le calenté a Hilda y me iré a ver el Canal 34. Aquí ya casi ni se cocina, ¿para qué? Cualquier cosa para hacerse una un taco. Ni modo que cocine para mí sola, porque ni Hilda ni Mari acostumbran cenar aquí. A ver qué dice el horario de televisión. Recuerdo que antes lo único que había eran los programas por radio que agarrábamos de noche de México. Manolín y Chilinski. Palillo. Las novelas, "El derecho de nacer". El programa del Doctor I.Q. No sé cómo le hacíamos; no había alcantarillado, no había pavimentación, no había mas que pizca de algodón. Y ahora, todo tan moderno, todo tan grande, pero todos tan desunidos, toda la familia regada por todas partes. Los muchachos en Maryland y en Minnesota y yo en California. Ahora como que ya los hijos y los padres ni se hablan; los vecinos no se visitan. Aquí ni conocemos a los vecinos de al lado siquiera. Sólo a la gente de la iglesia, y eso porque tengo carro y puedo ir hasta la iglesia mexicana los domingos, porque si no, ni eso. Aunque tengo que ir sola, porque aquí ya nadie quiere saber nada de iglesia ni de nada. M'hija creo que hasta se ha hecho atea. Pero por lo menos yo sigo yendo y allí veo a mi gente mexicana. No, si es como le digo a mi comadre Pepa cuando me llama de Texas, la ciudad es muy diferente; aquí constantemente estoy oyendo la sirena de la ambulancia o de la policía. Enfrentito mismo de la iglesia balacearon el otro día, dizque por error, al vecino de doña Chona. Que cosa de "gangas", de pandillas, de muchachones que no tienen ni adónde ir, ni dónde trabajar, ni más que hacer que andar en la calle sin que los padres tengan idea de dónde andan. Así como nosotras, que no sabemos ni adónde va la Mari, ni con quién, ni qué hace. Me temo que ande con esas mugres, que se inyectan o fuman, y uno aquí como si nada. ¡Como si nada! ¡Y ni modo de meterme! Yo aquí ni papel pinto. ¿Qué se le va a hacer? No hay más que distraerse un poco, porque yo también tengo mi droga, la tele. Ya es hora de ver "El maleficio". Y después viene "Trampa para un soñador." Sólo en las telenovelas se resuelven todos los problemas, en seis meses o en un año; será porque todas las historias son de ricos y con dinero lo arreglan todo. Pero en la vida real, en la vida de los barrios, en la vida de los que duermen en la calle, las cosas parece que sólo van de mal en peor. Por este camino no sé adónde vamos a llegar.

Sandra María Esteves

Amor negro

in our wagon oysters are treasured
their hard shells clacking against each other
words that crash into our ears
we cushion them
cut them gently in our hands
we kiss and suck the delicate juice
and sculpture flowers from the stone skin
we wash them in the river by moonlight
with offerings of songs
and after the meal we wear them in our hair
and in our eyes

Portraits for Shamsul Alam

Every morning when the sun rises
We stand in the light, capture
The warm heat to begin
The day with power, stirred with energy
We path a golden way, full of lifehood
Spirit laying seed for each
Man woman child encircling
The purpose of each progression of hours

Why are we here? A question
Unfathomable because the reasons keep changing
And we, stumbling the road
Feel for miscellaneous vegetation
to strengthen our stand

And after we greet the yellow king star
We salute ourselves, revel
In our existence, marvel at our nakedness
Possessed in independent power
Challenge the king sun itself
Side by side to see which light shines brighter
Together plotting the renovation of this world
The evolution of harmonic revolution
Octaves as great as galaxies.

Today I will create a small dent
Which the atmosphere will hardly notice
If I could just, If I could just not
Contribute to the mess
If I could this day build a great mansion
Seeded from pyramids
And the ancient accumulated abundance
Offer the challenge
How great can communities
Rise and revive what is true

When will knowledge cease to be child?
Mature to realization, our great merging

Sustaining the captured morning throughout
The cycle of daynight
Not color, but texture
Not prisoner, yet participant

Now open our eyes and tell me how
We know it is possible to realize our dreams

Now open wider, imagine
The water is clear and the Sun
Is standing next to us.

Transference

Don't come to me with expectations
Of who you think I should be
From some past when
You were going through changes

I'm not your mother who didn't hold you all day long
Or kiss away the rough cuts when you fell
I'm not your sister who wouldn't play with you
Mashing up your favorite toys on purpose
I'm not the lady upstairs who keeps you up all night
Playing Lawrence Welk Muzac
And I'm not your girlfriend who left you flat
The one who promised forever never to go
For whom you would never love another
Or the one who used you for sex
And forgot your first name
I'm not the one who beat you
For ten dollars and dinner
Or ate up your cookies and milk
Or gave you the wrong kind of presents
I'm not your neighbor who hates you
'Cause you have more roaches than them
Or the landlord who steals your rent
And leaves you out in the cold
I'm not the meter maid who gave you $300 in parking tickets
Or the kid who plugged your tires just for fun
Or the psycho who smashed your front windshield
Or the truck that hit your rear bumper and ran
I'm not the traffic court judge who insists you're the liar
Or the junkie who popped your trunk lock
And tried to steal your spare tire
I didn't take your virginity with empty promise
Or con you with a job for sex
And I'm definitely not the one who ripped off your mind
And did not allow you to speak your own tongue
Or tried to turn you slave or dog
No, I'm not the bitch who denies you your true history
Or tries to hide the beauty of yourself

I am not the colonizer or the oppressor
Or the sum total of your problems, I am not the enemy
I am not the one who never called you
To invite you to coffee and dinner
Nor the friend who never gave you friendship
Or the lover who did not know how to love

So when you come to me, don't assume
That you know me so well as that
Don't come with preconceptions
Or expect me to fit the mold you have created
Because we fit no molds
We have no limitations
And when you do come, bring me your hopes
Describe for me your visions, your dreams
Bring me your support and your inspiration
Your guidance and your faith
Your belief in our possibilities
Bring me the best that you can

Give me the chance to be
Myself and create symphonies like
The pastel dawn or the empty canvas
Before the first stroke of color is released

Come in a dialogue of we
You and me reacting, responding
Being, something new
Discovering.

Ángela de Hoyos

Ten Dry Summers Ago

you could've planted Bermuda grass,
your neighbor to the right says.
But no, you didn't
    ... and yes it's true, your life
    never depended upon it ...

So now I have to landscape
this bare and godless ground
that keeps eroding
  into flyaway dust
    changing hands
      as easily as identity

have to dance, pivoting
—as a Chicano would say
              "en un daimito"—
        watering this wasteland

have to keep it moist
  until it grows
  until there's room enough
            to hold
    your god and mine

How to Eat Crow on a Cold Sunday Morning

you start on the wings
niggling, apologetic-like
because, after all
   it was you who held the gun
and fired pointblank
the minute you saw the whites of their eyes
just like the army sergeant
   always instructed you.

—Damn it, this thing's
gonna make me sick!

—No it won't. Go on. Eat the
blasted thing (for practice)

because you'll be sicker later on
when your friends
start giving you
an iceberg for a shoulder.

. . . So the giblets are dry and tough.
But you can digest them.

It's the gall bladder
—that green bag of biliousness—
that wants to gag your throat
in righteous retribution
refuses to budge
won't go up or down, just
      sticks there

makes you wish that long ago
you'd learned how to eat
a pound of prudence
      instead.

Ramillete para Elena Poniatowska

... esta necesidad mía
de tocar a la gente
    manos amigas
    abrazo hermano
    beso fraterno

sentir que todos somos uno
que salimos del mar
para mezclarnos
con el barro
de la madretierra

somos
    tronco fruto semilla
    ojos carne hueso
    agua luna flores
    llanto felicidad

mas algún día
apagaremos el sol de noche

y nosotras
ovejas soñolientas
nos dormiremos todas

cada una a su vez
para renacer reina-diosa
como Jesusa Palancares
por allá ... en la Vía Láctea
y se repetirá la historia

mientras tanto
... este sempiterno
ramillete fleur-de-lis
para Elena ...

When Conventional Methods Fail

... bat your eyelashes!

ain't nothing wrong
with using wile

:Eve used an apple
:Cleopatra used a rug
:La Malinche? oh she

    used Cortez
    to create
    La Nueva Raza

there's something
to be said for a
gal who understands
humanity, and thereby
the secret to success

feminists,
take heed:

    no se compliquen
    la vida!!

you're going at it
the hard way.

Judith Ortiz Cofer

La fe

The bells peal in octaves in my head
at Vespers,
I fight an urge to genuflect
before marble statues,
to light candles in dark rooms.
I chant to saints as I breathe,
to save the day.
Each night as I kiss a crucifix, I pray
to be released from rituals.

El olvido

(según las madres)

It is a dangerous thing
to forget the climate of
your birthplace; to choke out
the voices of dead relatives when
in dreams they call you by
your secret name; dangerous
to spurn the clothes you were
born to wear for the sake of fashion;
to use weapons and sharp instruments you
are not familiar with; dangerous
to disdain the plaster saints before
which your mother kneels praying for you with
embarassing fervor that you survive in
the place you have chosen to live; a costly,
bare and elegant room with no pictures
on the walls: a forgetting place where
she fears you might die of exposure.
Jesús, María y José.
El olvido is a dangerous thing.

So Much for Mañana

After twenty years in the mainland
Mother's gone back to the Island
to let her skin
melt from her bones
under her native sun.
She no longer wears stockings,
girdles or tight clothing.
Brown as a coconut,
she takes siestas in a hammock,
and writes me letters that say:
"Stop chasing your own shadow, niña,
come down here and taste the piña,
put away those heavy books,
don't you worry about your shape,
here on the Island men look
for women who can carry a little weight.
On every holy day,
I burn candles and I pray
that your brain won't split
like an avocado pit
from all that studying.
What do you say?
Abrazos from your Mamá and a blessing
from that saint, Don Antonio, el cura."
I write back: "Someday I will go back
to your Island and get fat,

The Latin Deli

Presiding over a formica counter,
plastic Mother and Child magnetized
to the top of an ancient register,
the heady mix of smells from the open bins
of dried codfish, the green plantains
hanging in stalks like votive offerings,
she is the Patroness of Exiles,
a woman of no-age who was never pretty,
who spends her days selling canned memories
while listening to the Puerto Ricans complain
that it would be cheaper to fly to San Juan
than to buy a pound of Bustelo coffee here,
and to Cubans perfecting their speech
of a "glorious return" to Havana—where no one
has been allowed to die and nothing to change until then;
to Mexicans who pass through, talking lyrically
of *dólares* to be made in El Norte—
                              all wanting the comfort
of spoken Spanish, to gaze upon the family portrait
of her plain wide face, her ample bosom
resting on her plump arms, her look of maternal interest
as they speak to her and each other
of their dreams and their disillusions—
how she smiles understanding,
when they walk down the narrow aisles of her store
reading the labels of packages aloud, as if
they were the names of lost lovers: *Suspiros*,
Merengues, the stale candy of everyone's childhood.

                              She spends her days
slicing *jamón y queso* and wrapping it in wax paper
tied with string: plain ham and cheese
that would cost less at the A&P, but it would not satisfy
the hunger of the fragile old man lost in the folds
of his winter coat, who brings her lists of items
that he reads to her like poetry, or the others,
whose needs she must divine, conjuring up products

from places that now exist only in their hearts—
closed ports she must trade with.

Achy Obejas

Kimberle

on the stone like white shadows indistinguishable
from the marble the heat the white shadows
the heat of young woman a woman white woman with
cavernous cheeks in a perfect face and the cheeks
are the flaw the error the pain the mistake imperfection
the cheeks with white shadows the stone and the
grain of the stone burning to the touch the white
heat of the stone indistinguishable.

kimberle says no to the gods to the marble the
stones to the white heat that coarses her veins
the system the muscular arms that hand low with
no purpose (an exile) perfect face imperfect
face kimberle is friends with a spectre a black
coat hands that mechanically tease at her neck
at her sex at the holes in her cheeks the sick
yellow dog eyes that respond with enchanted disease
to the shadows and the heat from the stones that
burn to the touch start again start again kimberle

Sugarcane

can't cut
cut the cane
azuca' in chicago
dig it down to the
roots sprouting spray paint on the
walls on the hard cold
stone of the great gritty city
slums in chicago
with the mansions in the hole
in the head of
the old old rich left behind
from other times lopsided
gangster walls overgrown taken
over by the dark
and poor overgrown with no
sugarcane but you
can't can't cut
cut the water
bro'
from the flow and
you can't can't cut
cut the blood
lines from this island
train one by one throwing off
the chains siguaraya
no no
no se pue'e cortar
pan con ajo quisqueya
cuba y borinquen no
se pue'en parar

I saw it
saw black a-frica down in the city
walking in chicago y
la cuba cuba
gritando en el solar
I saw it
say quisqueya

brown
uptown in the city
cryin' in chicago
y borinquen
bro'
sin un
chavo igual but
you can't can't cut
cut the water
bro'
from the flow and
you can't can't cut
cut the blood
lines from this island
train one by one throwing off
the chains siguaraya
no no
no se pue'e cortar
pan con ajo quisqueya
cuba y borinquen no
se pue'en parar

¡azuca'!

Evangelina Vigil-Piñón

The Bridge People

in the mornings you can see them
crawling out of their natural environs
yawning, stretching, slithering out of their foxholes
along the bayou
where they find refuge and protection
when the city lights go out and day begins to break
but right now they are rising
it's time to scrounge for empty beer cans
take in some sun
maybe quench that thirst that's constant

in the mornings you can see them
crawling out of the bayou
like grotesque marsh creatures, man-made
they adopt the camouflaging colors
of mud and slime and water stagnant green
their clothes are the color of crude
as in the oil that pollutes
the once clean and vibrant waters
of the Buffalo Bayou

they ascend and descend as they please
amid the busy urban streets they wander
at once isolated and intermingled
with the higher forms of life
"bridge people," downtowners call them
"transcients" on their way to nowhere
"the scum of the earth" they are
creatures that fell from grace with life

against the majestic futuristic buildings
and hustle and bustle of downtown Houston
the winos, the hobos and bums

and other down-trodden beings
are stark reminders
of human vulnerability
and of time that must advance and waits on no one:
surely along the way
the weak, the susceptible, the damned
must meet their fate
for as spectacular as man's accomplishments have been
in this age of boundless future
wherein the limits of the intellect remain a mystery
that continues tugging at the soul for more
modern man has not yet succeeded
in altering that basic constitution
of the human animal

the society that we create
is like a laboratory zoo worthy of continued scientific study
here, creatures of all sorts co-exist:
precarious is the balance.

Dumb Broad!

dumb broad!
I'm believing it as I'm seeing it!
dumb broad!
keep you eyes on the road, stupid!
a passenger sits next to her
motionless
oblivious
or just doesn't care
why don't you comb your hair at home, you stupid broad!
hey!
I mean, I've seen women yank off their steam rollers at stop lights
brandish brush
and then drive, one-handed
while expertly arranging their hair
with a few quick precision strokes—
I've done it myself
you have to in order to get to work on time
but, oh! this is too much!
I cannot believe this!
look! now she's teasing her hair!
both of her hands are off the steering wheel!
stupid broad!
you'd better keep your eyes on the road!
I'd hate to be in the car in front of her
she can't see the traffic behind her
for she's got the rearview mirror in a perpendicular position
while she fixes her eye makeup
at first with quick casual glances
but now very intently
peering into hazard
I mean, I know one gets distracted sometimes
you know, you look into the mirror to fix your lipstick
and you end up re-doing your eyeshadow!
god! you know you should've worn hyacinth instead of celery!
it looks so different in the daylight!

look at her!
I can't believe she's teasing her hair!
and with both hands off the steering wheel
now I can't get over that!
and in fast moving bumper-to-bumper 8 a.m. traffic
at a five-point intersection
and at a school zone at that! now you tell me if this is not a
    dumb broad!

my god!
and the passive passenger sits!
doesn't nudge!
involuntary purposeless conjecturing:
he's probably her husband who has simply given up on her
his bitching was of no use
or rather, he's probably one of those passive husbands
who doesn't give a shit
but then, maybe he's a carpooler with no choice in the matter
or simply unaware that his life is in danger

now wait a minute!
hey! I'm believing this as I'm seeing it!
she is now spraying her hair generously
in round swooping motions
utilizing both the rearview and sideview mirrors
which she has expertly adjusted
the traffic is of no concern to her
and the passenger remains a mannequin
except for one slow motion glance over and back
as she squirts the spray
on her mass of teased hair and his bald head
it's not four blocks later
there she drives ahead of me
sporting a splendid hair-do
she brakes on and off sporadically
as she shifts her weight around in her seat
finding a position of comfort
while tuning the radio
and flicking her bic at a cigarette that's stuck in her mouth
then she looks over

and puffs smoke into the face of her motionless passenger
who, obeyingly, hands her a cup of steaming coffee

dumb broad!

Telephone Line

there are two lines of post-noontime customers
waiting to pick up phones
they are displeased because:
it is storming outside
their umbrellas and legs and shoes are drenched
this damn line is gonna make them late back to work
and, worse, it doesn't seem to be going anywhere!

a young Black girl waits on customers at one counter
she is very very slow
at the other counter is another line of waiting customers
and no one waits on them
but the sign says: "Form two lines here"
and they oblige

at the head of the line
stand a pair of Mexicanos
they're short of stature
with a boyish innocence about them
they're here like the rest of us
to pick up a telephone
for, as a voice informed me through the wires
"Ma Bell don't delive' no mo"

"What color, style of phone and length of cord would you like?"
the girl asks mechanically
looking off into the distance
as if to find the answer there
you can tell she asks this question countless times a day
"¿Qué?" they respond simultaneously
from my perspective at the end of the line
their short-haired heads and skinny necks
look like two human question marks looking at each other
"What color do you want, blue ... white ... yellow ... white?"
the girl repeats disinterestedly
they begin to comprehend as she points to the different color
    phones
repeating the question and rolling her eyes

they pause in thoughtful consideration
exchanging opinions in Spanish
while assorted pairs of legs shift their weight impatiently
from right foot to left foot
from left foot to right foot
and perturbed expressions
and a side step over to the left to check and see
what's taking so damn long!
and a side step over back in line
and frustration and impatient sighs
and feet tapping to the tick of clocks
tip tap-tap-tap-tap tip tap-tap-tap-tap
that refuse to wait on unexpected delays
while the two Mexicanos make up their mind several times
as to what style, what color of phone, what length of cord they
    want

¡ah, qué vida en los Estados Unidos!
¡tierra de pura ventaja!
no more waiting in line at the Stop-n-Go phone booths
no more quarters lost
no more standing for hours at the Seven-Eleven pay phones
waiting for that call from San Francisco del Rincón:
"¡ah, qué la Juana!
me prometió que me llamaba a las meras tres, ¡hombre!
¡Ya son después de las seis!
Bueno, pues . . . vámonos ya. ¡Ni modo!"

most likely they live in a multi-unit apartment building
along with a number of other undocumented residents
most likely the style and color of phone
little matters to the habitat's decor
although important is
the length of cord

wearing smiles of satisfaction on their faces
they walk off into the storm with no umbrellas
but phone, cord and directories held securely under their arms:
yes, indeed!
why, if they all pitch in for the monthly bill
it's all very worth it!

what a bargain from Ma Bell!
"Sí, costea! Sí, costea!"

Yvonne Sapia

Del medio del sueño

My mother's face blushing
above me like a lung
checks my eyes to be assured
I am trapped somewhere
in the walls of my dream.
She glides in quietness to my dresser,
shifts the intimate fabrics around
like fresh evidence.
Del medio del sueño,
I am not so far that I cannot come back
to watch her wear down in purpose.

She thinks I have her food.
She thinks I listen at the bathroom door
when she washes what the doctors cut.
Sometimes she forgets who I am,
asks for the keys to the house.
Sometimes she forgets who she is,
asks to be walked to the ocean.

My father yearns to be patient,
then bites his fingernails
and sorrowfully turns to the television.
I pretend to go to sleep
and wait in the insomnia dark
for my mother and her suspicions
to verify the passing of nights
which permit few easy exits.

La Mujer, Her Back to the Spectator

Aloof, you are deep in thought.
Undoubtedly your head is turned intently.

And you are a young woman whose dress
Is inscribed with vividly
Colored flowers.

The blur of your extended arm,
Your right leg frozen in the foreground,

You look out and upward,
Held to the barest minimum
Of the road ahead.

Your full body does not pivot
To look back at your pursuers
Who move closer.

Attempting to dispell
Their headlong intensity,
Mistrusting the value of words,

Your mouth may open,
The emblems of power
On the rouged blossoms
Of your cheeks.

La desconocida

These clues to my identity are unmistakable.
Only the light portrays itself.
I am unable to recall
the street which turns out
to be my old neighborhood.
The familiar substance is the landscape
receiving a difficult winter.

When I turn around,
I am a contradiction.
I am not the one walking the dog,
I am not the one who lives the same life.
I am the one trying to avoid
stepping on the seams in the sidewalk.
I am the one searching for unreasonable things.

I have seen the angel of death
and thought of inadequacy.
I have studied the duration of sin
while lost in the long skirt of the night.
I am the one who has
a monster under my bed.

In the sequence of events,
mine is the name I have not memorized,
mine is the conscience I do not have.

Defining the Grateful Gesture

According to our mother,
when she was a child
what was placed before her
for dinner was not a feast,
but she would eat it
to gain back the strength
taken from her by long hot days
of working in her mother's house
and helping her father make
candy in the family kitchen.
No idle passenger
Traveling through life was she.

And that's why she resolved
to tell stories about
the appreciation for satisfied hunger.
When we would sit down
for our evening meal
of arroz con pollo
or frijoles negros con plátanos
she would expect us
to be reverent to the sources
of our undeserved nourishment,
and to strike a thankful pose
before each lift of the fork
or swirl of the spoon.

For the dishes she prepared,
we were ungrateful,
she would say, and repeat
her archetypal tale about the Pérez
brothers who stumbled over themselves
with health in her girlhood town
of Ponce, looking like ripe mangoes,
their cheeks rosed despite poverty.

My mother would then tell us about the day
she saw Mrs. Pérez searching

the neighborhood garbage,
picking out with a missionary's care
the edible potato peels, the plantain skins,
the shafts of old celery to take
home to her muchachos
who required more food
than she could afford.

Although my brothers and I
never quite mastered the ritual
of obedience our mother craved,
and as supplicants failed
to feed her with our worthiness,
we'd sit like solemn loaves of bread,
sighing over the white plates
with a sense of realization, or relief,
guilty about possessing appetite.

Aquí

A place like nowhere else.
A single point in space,
not agreed upon by astronomers
as stationary, but experienced
by the figure as the only location
existing at the time.

Here, the figure is freed of its contour.
Here, it satisfies an inordinate hunger
for asymmetricity.
The restrictions are its own.
The patterns it tries to deceive
fold into the flesh
with no plan for direction.

Here, interrupted only by earth
and the quiet constellations,
the drift of time decelerates
leaving the figure
when the moment has given way
to the emotional state of
a place like nowhere else.

Bailando

I will remember you dancing,
spinning round and round
a young girl in Mexico,
your long, black hair free in the wind,
spinning round and round
a young woman at village dances
your long, blue dress swaying
to the beat of *La Varsoviana*,
smiling into the yes of your partners,
years later smiling into your eyes
when I'd reach up to dance with you,
my dear aunt, who years later
danced with my children,
you, white-haired but still young
waltzing on your ninetieth birthday,
more beautiful than the orchid
pinned on your shoulder,
tottering now when you walk
but saying to me, *"Estoy bailando,"*
and laughing.

Elena

My Spanish isn't enough.
I remember how I'd smile
listening to my little ones,
understanding every word they'd say,
their jokes, their songs, their plots.
   Vamos a pedirle dulces a mamá. Vamos.
But that was in Mexico.
Now my children go to American high schools.
They speak English. At night they sit around
the kitchen table, laugh with one another.
I stand by the stove and feel dumb, alone.
I bought a book to learn English.
My husband frowned, drank more beer.
My oldest said, "*Mamá*, he doesn't want you
to be smarter than he is." I'm forty,
embarrassed at mispronouncing words,
embarrassed at the laughter of my children,
the grocer, the mailman. Sometimes I take
my English book and lock myself in the bathroom,
say the thick words softly,
for if I stop trying, I will be deaf
when my children need my help.

Martín Espada

David Leaves the Saints for Paterson

Primo David's arm hung near-paralyzed
after the stabbing,
and there was no work in the coffee
of Barrio Hills Brothers,
so he learned to smoke with the other hand
and plotted to leave Puerto Rico.

His mother sponge-washed the wooden santos
every week, draped statues crowded
with white flowers. Then Tata, la abuela,
would nod with ceremony, foretelling money
and sickness, mouth quavering ajar with the dialects
of the many dead. In spite of prophecy
of Jardines Del Paraíso housing project,
no one could stop drinking.

David left the saints for Paterson:
bad civil service exam, the boot factory,
then a hospital job wheeling carts of delicate bottles
through light-bleached corridors on late shift.

Together with his father at the Paterson hospital,
the gallo-man who learned to box in prison,
who also pushed the medicine carts to impatient doctors
and cannot stop drinking.

Colibrí

—for Katherine, one year later

In Jayuya,
the lizards scatter
like a fleet of green canoes
before the invader.
The Spanish conquered
with iron and words:
"Indio Taíno" for the people
who took life
from the rain
that rushed through trees
like evaporating arrows,
who left the rock carvings
of eyes and mouths
in perfect circles of amazement.

So the hummingbird
was christened "colibrí."
Now the colibrí
darts and bangs
between the white walls
of the hacienda,
a racing Taíno heart
frantic as if hearing
the bellowing god of gunpowder
for the first time.

The colibrí
becomes pure stillness,
seized in the paralysis
of the prey,
when your hands
cup the bird
and lift him
through the red shutters
of the window,
where he disappears
into a paradise of sky,
a nightfall of singing frogs.

If only history
were like your hands.

The Words of the Mute Are Like Silver Dollars

—Prince George's County, Maryland, 1976

Scrubbing cars for the factory showroom:
back pressed against the cool oily floor,
stink of the turpentine sponge,
radio sizzle, Maryland afternoon
cement-pale as the ceiling,
Ed the boss
leaning his cowboy face
over me.

"When I was in the Air Force,"
he said, "how come you Spanish greasers
always cut the lunch line?"
A picture of jostling metal trays,
brown soldiers accused
and paraded to the toilets
for the discipline of labor.

And so we are sprinkled with grease
and christened greaser: named
not for our hair and skin, as Ed
brave on beer would say,
but for the hours
we drag ourselves obediently
along his warehouse floor,
or whitening the urinals
in the barracks
with words for Ed
imprisoned in a cage of teeth, always
mute and stained as the sponge.

The words accumulate, stacked
like silver dollars in a box.
Brought from hiding,
they flash.

"Ed," I said, "how else
you get seconds
in America?"

Shaking Hands with Mongo

—For Mongo Santamaría

Mongo's open hands:
huge soft palms
that drop the hard seeds
of conga with a thump,
shaken by the god of hurricanes,
raining mambo coconuts
that do not split
even when they hit the sidewalk,
rumbling incantation
in the astonished dancehall
of a city in winter,
sweating in a rush of A-train night,
so that Chano Pozo,
maestro of the drumming Yoruba heart,
howling Manteca in a distant coro,
hears Mongo and yes,
begins to bop
a slow knocking bolero of forgiveness
to the nameless man
who shot his life away
for a bag of tecata
in a Harlem bar
forty years ago.

Alberto Ríos

Five Indiscretions, or

The Unfortunate Story of the Unmarried Flora Carrillo
And the Man Who Loved Her Before He Died his Famous Death,
From Whose Single Liaison a Daughter Was Born
And the Advice, Rather the Explanation,
Both of Them Left for Her, And the Story Also
Of What She Became, and That She Was Happy

1.
Three did not count.
A fourth was forgiven by the Father Torres
In exchange for reasonable payment,
Two full days of the Hail Mary.
Bigger than priests, the fifth
Indiscretion was born on a Thursday, early
Evening in a November not too cold.
No rain had fallen
And the birds had not yet gone.
She chose a black dress, this Flora, Florita

+ here evoke the names of saints +

Underneath which she carried tonight
An old blade, but of fine Toledo forging
Long as the member of this man
In love with this woman standing at his door.
Her head was filled with the vines of the jungle
The noises of a lion, the feel of ten birds
Trying with their beaks to get out.
All anger: that she had hoped he would
Come to her bedroom.
And that he had.
Faster than that she took from him his rolled tongue
Hanging there between his thin legs, his two-fingers,

182

This girl's wrist and fist of his
Its central tendon and skin that moved on itself,
This small and second body of his
Which had found its way to her second mouth,
This part of himself which he had given her
Then taken back on this same day, earlier
His ugly afternoon of loving her too much.
He would scream as she had
When she had taken him in first as a leg-bone
And held him there too long, too much
Until he had become a pinky-finger

+ here evoke the holy names +

Which she took now and put in the dowry
She would make for her new daughter.
With it she would write a note,

Nothing else was left to do:
 Daughter, you will be an only child.
 The story of your birth will smell on you.
 Do this: take baths filled with rosemary
 With leaves, with pinched orange peels.
 Keep secret the fact of yourself
 Be happy enough, happy with this much life.
 Ask for nothing. Do not live for a long time.

2.
He sang to her the oldest song
That he was a piccolo flute in the small of her heart
Or, if that were not convincing, too much filled with flowers,
A small noise, then, a smart, a cut which is healing
Its face feeling good to be scratched
The way even wild cats like;
A piccolo flute in the small of her heart
Nothing more, and nothing more necessary
A noise different from all the rest
Louder and more shrill, a good sound of haunting
The voice of a Muslim caller at dawn
A bird, a Saturday, four directions and a need.
He sang this and did not sing

In that manner of speech afforded the heart:
That he was a man
Came to her not from any words, not like that
  But from the measure of his breathing
  From the five-ladder depth of his left eye
  The one that did not move, his one eye which
  While his right eye could move through the every day
  Could only stay looking at her.
When she looked at this eye at first
The sight of it made a noise in her, a start,
A note somewhere at the top of the piano scales
Fear, almost; a grasped breath; a glass dropped.
In the moment was the music of being wanted.
  Or of wanting, but she could not think it.
Certainly she could only say no
The way anyone would after a glass falls
No and Jesus. And as an afterthought, that he should go away.
  Many years later she read a book and it took
  Her breath: how neatly the glasses for champagne
  Thrown by the fine heroes
  Broke against the walls holding fire.
  That this was a celebration.
  That this was the continental, the European.
No, she said, to this thick railroad tie of a man
Who sang to her the oldest song, the one
Of being young, that he was a piccolo flute
In the small of her heart. No
She said, but said it with her mouth, not with her heart
Making no a spoken word, like all other words
So that he did not hear, so that he kept singing
Until one day it was enough, but not for her, not now:
Now, instead, the afternoon, which was kind
Which is what she was earlier, had only pretended for him
I am her, whispered it to him, let him be strong
In its arms one more time before it took him,
Holding tighter than a grandmother.
  This was not at all what he wanted
  But what he wanted he could not have.
  No, she said, and he could not get close enough
  Could not put the ear of his song heart
  Against her chest

To know what the word meant, no.

3.
He had written no note for his daughter.
It had not been necessary.
She knew now what it would have been,
What the word no means
When it is pronounced, when the last half of it lingers, *o*
Imagined that the *o* was like this

    Together as if it were now nude in the afternoon
    They must have danced the wild Apache
    Without lunch, into the hours
    Imagining themselves French, striped shirt and berets
    Two carp on a rug in the ocean of the room
    Two june beetles, two bees
    Beings with impossible wings, pulleys from the roof
    Pulling the two of them up like birthday piñatas
    Two of them, then four: hands and legs
    Tied more expertly than the best dream of an old salt sailor
    Bread dough wound round and again into afternoon cakes,
    Two, four, then six of them: all the parts of the face
    Then twelve of them: their two faces together
    Twenty-four then and thirty-six and words and breaths
    Inside each other their tongues
    Like the wings of hummingbirds in flight
    Like bees, his fingers, faster than possible

That it was like this exactly.

4.
Her fame was as a maker of oval mats many years later
Mats for placement behind photographs,
How the old ones were, sometimes in colors
Sometimes to highlight, sometimes for support simply,
Always making the best faces.
But what she loved most, what was true for her
Was her firm putting of the tongues and most heavy parts
Of several men of the town, each on a different night
Sundays being specially reserved for the troubled boy
On a rancho several kilometers out of town,
Putting them slowly into her mouth, this best of all
And sucking there at them better

Than if she were drawing out the juice of an orange
Small hole made in it, the way children do
Squeezing out the everything.
It was, better described, this *deliverance* of her men
This taking out from their baby-arms
What it was that troubled them
So much all at once, so much like the stories
She had heard of the ghost being delivered,
Being let go, from the mouth
Exactly at the point of death.
She would trade nothing for this
For being able to say yes where others had said no.
To say yes, and watch her men die.
Die and then be brought back, to be strong at this
This was her power, this is what made her laugh
Being happy for them all
Never once making love to a man.

On January 5, 1984,
El Santo the Wrestler Died, Possibly

The thing was, he could never be trusted.
He wore the silver mask even when he slept.
At his funeral as reported by all the Mexican news services
The pall bearers also put on their faces
Sequined masks to honor him, or so it was said.
The men in truth wore masks as much to hide from him
That he would not see who was putting him into the ground
And so get angry, get up, and come back after them
That way for which he was famous.
His partner el atomico pretended to think
There was no funeral at all.
He would have had to help el santo be angry
Come like the Samson running against the pillars
These men were, holding up the box
In which el santo was trapped;
Would have had to angle his head down, come at them
Mount them three men to a shoulder
As he ran through the middle, ducking under the casket
Bowling them down like all the other times
Giving el santo just a moment to breathe, get strong.

He will be missed
But one must say this in a whisper, and quickly.
One knows of the dead, of their polite habit of listening
Too much, believing what they hear, and then of their caring.
One knows of the dead, how it all builds up
So that finally something must be said.
One knows of the year in which the town of Guaymas
Had its first demonstration of a tape recorder.
It confirmed only what was already known:
That people speak. And that the voice of the wind
Captured finally, played back slowly
Given its moment to say something of lasting importance
Made only a complaint.
If el santo were to hear of his being missed
He might get hold of the wind, this voice of the dead,

And say too much, the way the best wrestlers do
With all the yelling.
So one will always be responsible enough only to whisper
The best things about el santo
Out of concern for the crops and the sapling trees.
This much was decided at the funeral.

The decision to whisper was not too much.
One had to be suspicious of this man with a mask
Even as he reached out to shake your hand,
That you might be flung and bent around
Knocked on the head and forced to say
How glad you are to meet him, and his uncle;
How suspicious that hand, which he always raised
More slowly than a weightlifter's last possible push
As if he too were suspicious of you
That you might at the last second
Be the Blue Demon after all—*el demonio azul*: ¡aha!
He recognizes you, *but too late!* that you might
In this last moment avoid his hand raised to shake
Hook the crook of your arm into his
And flip him with a slam to a cement canvas.
No, he could not be trusted
And he could not trust you.

In his last years very far from 1942
The year he gave his first bruise to another man
One received as a greeting no hand from him any longer.
A raised eyebrow, perhaps, *good morning to you,* Just visible
        through the mask on his morning walk.
This was his greeting, one man to another, now.
But even then he could not be trusted
Had not slipped with age even an ich:
As he moved the hairy arm of his brow up and down
Like a villain taking possession of the widow's house,
If one quickly did not get out of his way—
Well, then, he kept it moving up and down, had gotten you
Had made you imagine his eyebrow like that
Making the sound of a referee's hand
Slam beating the canvas ten times
Telling you that you have lost.

Jimmy-Santiago Baca

Martín III

Driving across country
I thought back to my boyhood.
Those I'd known in New Mexico
came back to me again.

In Arkansas, on a fallen oak trunk,
half its limbs in the pond,
sat old one-armed Pepín.
"Martín, your father and I
were in the El Fidel cantina
with unas viejas one afternoon.
Tú sabes, nos pusimos bien chatos.
And then Sheri, your mamá, walks in.
I don't remember what she asked Danny,
but la vieja that was with your father said,
I thought your wife was a cripple.
Sheri started crying and sin una palabra,
she turned and went out."

In September Estella Gómez appeared.
She stood mid-air in a gust of wind,
blind, dressed in black, and with a religious voice, said,
"92 years, m'ijito. ¿Qué pasó? There was no more
beans to pick, no beans to load
on trains. Pinos Wells dried up, como mis manos.
Everyone moved away to work.
I went to Estancia, con mi hijo, Refugio.
Gavachos de Tejas, we worked for them. Loading
alfalfa, picking cotton for fifty cents a row.
¿Y Danny? La borrachera. ¿Y Sheri? La envidia.
That's what happened, Martín, to your familia."

In Ohio, December 14th, great pines

189

crackled icicles to the forest floor,
jarring the air with explosions of sparkling flakes.
Wrapped in my serape, snow up to my knees,
at a bend in a dirt road.
When I reached the bend, Antonia Sánchez,
La Bruja de Torreón, said to me,
"¿Dónde está tu mamá? Safe from that madman.
Se casó otra vez y tiene dos niños.
No, no te puedo decir dónde viven."

Four or five months later I moved
to North Carolina
in a red brick house at the edge of Piedmont Woods.
Narrow red mud roads marked with tractor treads,
sultry air droning with insects and steamy
with harvest crops—
day after day in green dark shade I walked,
bending under briar riggings, my pole
with a blue rubber worm bait
dangling from 30 pound line, down deer trails,
skipping creek rocks, climbing over sagging
barbwire fences, until I found a secluded pond,
shores choked with bullrush I thrashed down,
as I tossed my line out into the sunset burning water,
big-mouth bass puckered, sending water rings
rippling through towering pines leaning over the water.
I fished until I could no longer see my bait
plop, until the far shore disappeared and the moon
bobbed in the black water
like a candle flame in a window against the night darkness.

One evening as I walked back
up a hill to the house,
I could hear all their voices
drifting through the trees—
I said aloud to myself
and the memories they lived in,
I am leaving in the morning.

Passing back through Tennessee
on the way to Albuquerque,

deep down a mountain dirt road bend,
walking barefoot on pebbles,
I see a woman talking with two men,
in the dark silence of the forest,
Señora Martínez walked toward me,
wavering like smoke in the cold air,
"Sheri was scared to go home for her purse.
So she sent me. Dios mío,
I'll never forget that day, mijo.
When I opened the closet door, there was Danny,
standing with a butcher knife raised high,
ready to kill."

April in Tennessee
Merlinda Griego appeared to me—she sat
on a rock, skirt raised to her knees, her bare toes
playing with petals floating in the creek.
"You cried a lot, Martín. Dios mío cómo llorabas.
A veces your jefito brought you to Las Flores Cantina
where I worked. He came to see me. You played on the floor
with empty whiskey bottles.
One day I was at El Parke, sitting like now, on a rock, my
feet in the water.
Your mother came up to me and started yelling
that I gave you mal de ojo, and she dipped you
in the freezing water. I thought she was going to drown you
because of Danny seeing me. Quién sabe, m'ijo,
all I remember is that she was jealous."

A week after I saw Merlinda, I was looking
through an old tobacco barn in a field.
In a corner with moldy gunney sacks
and rusting field tools, peeling an apple with his knife,
Pancho Garza sat, the retired manager of Piggly Wiggly
in Santa Fe.
"I gave her bruised fruit, old bread
and pastries. Once a week I gave her a sack of flour.
Danny drank up her pay check,
so I let her have a few things.
Besides she was a good checker."

It was June in Virginia.
One evening walking through the woods
I could see someone waiting for me
her infant straddling her hip.
I thought of my boyhood in the South Valley
where women took summer evening walks,
their children fluttering like rose leaves
at their skirts.

Through the Texas panhandle
I remembered Estancia
where harvest dust smolders and insects whiff
empty crates and vegetable boxes
stacked against the produce stands.
Transparent wings of bees
wedge board bins, cracks sticky with chili mash.
Gorged flies buzz in tin pails and paper sacks
dropped on the saw-dusted earthen floor,
their feet glazed with potato guck. And parked alongside
the stands at evening, rugged eight wheelers
simmer hot rubber and grease odors, their side board racks
oozing with crushed fruits.

Finally driving over the Sandía Mountains,
on the outskirts of Albuquerque,
I thought of you, mother—long ago
your departure uprooted me,
checked the green growing day,
hollowed out the core of my childhood—
whittled down
to keep me
in your rib crib
clothed in webs—
a doll in a cradle
in a barn loft in Willard.

Your absence
is a small burned area in my memory,
where I was cleared away
like prairie grass,
my identity smoldering under the blue sand of my soul—

my appearance dimmed to smoke,
in the glowing light somewhere
beyond your house each dusk.

Night now as I come into Albuquerque,
moon's rusty rings pass through one another
around me—
broken chain of events
decaying in black sand and ash
of the empty dark past
I dig through.

An embering stick
I call the past,
my dream of a mother existed in,
I breathed on to keep light
from extinguishing
like a star at dawn.
I come to inspect the old world,
those green years burned silvery with time,
by silence in the mind.

Luis Omar Salinas

What Is My Name?

In this yellow and green
presence of light shooting
through the kitchen window,
in the forgotten asylums
of awkward gesturing ...
I've forgotten my name.
Solitary, poor, lonely,
what is my name?
In the geography
of the afternoon I've
named rocks, rivers, mountains,
women.
Is it Carlos the playboy?
Or perhaps Paco the schizophrenic?
No need to fear, I'll remember.
It will come to me suddenly
While I'm frying an egg and the yolk
bursts, when I am sincere, amiable,
friendly.
In this carefree light
I invoke gently voices,
ones that have guided cranes
through the hardship of dunes.
And I've stopped praying to saints.

Nights in Fresno

It is pleasant in October
where the nights lie lovely
driving away the valley heat.
This evening I drive
through the sad part of town
and see the streets
huddled in the shadows—
I stop the car and walk.
I catch the murmur or breathing
and long silences
and a drink from a bottle
of wine, passing slow as a cloud among
faces Van Gogh would have been
familiar with,
faces that wake
to the same dismantled vision.
Hands shaking
with the cold milieu of twigs,
itching their bones.
I say a prayer.
and I'm off
to a warm kitchen,
and hot coffee,
an air of solitude
growing around me
ripe with darkness.

When the Evening Is Quiet

When the evening is quiet and the moon
gazes down like a God I surrender
to the Muse. Silence is God and I am
tightlipped. I salute a woman
who is near insanity and I hurt.
The creatures of the afterlife
prowl and bring messages of pain.
How sad to touch the insane
and feel useless. Today I picked
flowers and put them in a vase.
Silence kneels, it is time for prayer.
Between loved ones silence
is a flower, a beautiful silence.
When the evening is quiet and the moon
gazes down like a God I surrender
what is mine and give hope
a chance to breathe. Hope
beaten and dragging it's torso
like a cripple.

Middle Age

I converse with my uncle
here, where the day begins
early like a hen in the cold
seeking higher ground.
My dreams come here
like a beaten toenail.
And I feel as if
I've been incarcerated
for the better part of my life

I raise my beer to my uncle
toasting him on his third marriage.
He tells me, "No man need be alone
especially with October
in the trees, fruit ripening
and the abundance of sunlight."
I am caught speechless.
I have no wisdom
to speak of—unlike
my father who ages gracefully.

My uncle says "Espera la
suerte, wait for luck,
and do what you can with it."

I leave his house
and step outside
to the fresh smell
of autumn
walking through the thinning
olive groves
the sky fearful
half empty of birds.

Sweet Drama

On a night like this ...
with rain in the distant mountains
soup steaming in the kitchen
my father reads the newspaper
polite, gentle, and at peace
with himself nearing his 80th birthday
There is little in the news
that disturbs him now.
He is happy God has
given him a long life
a woman to love and a son
who knows enough
to walk outside and praise
the olive groves and figs
to whistle along with the sunlight
as they both saunter along
the quiet farming roads ...

My mother sleeps the sleep of angels
the blue sleep of gardenias touched
by moonlight. Today
she poured orange juice
on her cereal by mistake
she smiled and shook her head—
old age here has the makings
of a sweet drama ...

Poem for Ernesto Trejo

In Memory

Gone to that place
where your dreams
did not carry you,
my friend, we are sad
as the stray dogs of winter
without you.

Cheerful troubadour—
death forlorn, death detested,
too soon taken,
too soon lost to this world.

Yet your voice rises
to the mountains, still
poetic there among the sequoias
and the young evening stars
stop to listen, bemused
by your conversations.

With the exuberance,
the courage of the bullfighter
you took your place and fought.
Finally a night came down,
a black cape, a sweeping
Veronica and you were gone.
I direct my voice
to the dust still hovering
somewhere above the arena—
good night now, sweet amigo.

Ray González

Walk

for John Brandi

Here is the trail to the mountain.
May your feet kiss it
with intent laughter,
the taste of your travels,
the courage of your hands
that released those inmates
that listened to you.

Here are the cliffs of the soul.
May you fall off knowing
the carpet of snow is
no explanation, no cushion,
but the canvas waiting
for the impact of your body,
the drawing to unfold.

Here are your words at dusk.
May the night recite
what it learned upon
giving up the red horizon,
your line toward the other side,
where flame etches
whatever you transcribe.

Two Wolf Poems

You can look at a gray wolf standing in the snow in winter twilight and not see him at all. You may think I'm pulling your leg. I'm not. Sometimes, even the Eskimos can't see them, which causes the Eskimo to smile.

Barry López, *Of Wolves and Men*

1

The invisible stance is how it survives
the vision of blood and snow.
What it hides is what remains,
season after season.
What it guards is the trail of its den,
the patch where the will to deliver
the shadow before its victim is marked.

The invisible presence grows in strength
as tomorrow's cold light becomes tomorrow's
howling dance of animal reason,
the cry to the pack to gather
around the things that vanish,
to surround the source that makes
all breathing things disappear.

The invisible face is the stare of
the surviving heart that will not move
until the blood has dried in the snow,
until the need to be seen explodes before
the oncoming boundaries of the wilderness,
the hard border where the four paws break
the ice without leaving a single track.

> *The wolf exerts a powerful influence on the human imagination. It takes your stare and turns it back on you. Bella Coola Indians believed that somone once tried to change all the animals into men but succeeded in making human only the eyes of the wolf.*

> Barry López, *Of Wolves and Men*

2

To see how the human stumbles
in the snow because the end is near.
To knaw at the bone of the sun
when it blinds the hunter
from its prey.
To stare at the approaching figures
without fear.
To return the look of discovery
when the rifle shot
shatters the stillness.

To watch the ceremony of the fires
from the black distance of the night.
To spot the way out of the forest
without disturbing the unseen eye,
the motion that brings it
closer to its own death,
its defiance of what must
be seen in the snow, what moves
when recognized as a vision.

Tato Laviera

Latero Story

i am a twentieth-century welfare recipient
moonlighting in the sun as a latero
a job invented by national state laws
designed to re-cycle aluminum cans
returned to consumer's acid laden
gastric inflammation pituitary glands
coca diet rites low cal godsons
of artificially flavored malignant
indigestions somewhere down the line
of a cancerous cell

i collect garbage cans in outdoor facilities
congested with putrid residues
my hands shelving themselves
opening plastic bags never knowing
what they'll encounter

several times a day i touch evil rituals
cut throats of chickens
tongues of poisoned rats
salivating my index finger
smells of month old rotten foods
next to pamper's diarrhea
    dry blood infectious diseases
hypodermic needles tissued with
heroin water drops pilfered in
slimy greases hazardous waste materials
but i cannot use rubber gloves
they undermine my daily profits

i am a twentieth-century welfare recipient
moonlighting in the day as a latero
that is the only opportunity i have
to make it big in america

some day i might become experienced enough
to offer technical assistance
to other lateros
i am thinking of publishing
my own guide to latero's collection
and a latero's union offering
medical dental benefits

i am a twentieth-century welfare recipient
moonlighting in the night as a latero
i am considered some kind of expert
at collecting cans during fifth avenue parades
i can now hire workers at twenty
five cents an hour guaranteed salary
and fifty per cent two and one half cents
profit on each can collected

i am a twentieth-century welfare recipient
moonlighting in midnight as a latero
i am becoming an entrepreneur
an american success story
i have hired bag ladies to keep peddlers
from my territories
i have read in some guide to success
that in order to get rich
to make it big
i have to sacrifice myself
moonlighting until dawn by digging
deeper into the extra can
margin of profit
i am on my way up the opportunistic
ladder of success
in ten years i will quit welfare
to become a legitimate businessman
i'll soon become a latero executive
with corporate conglomerate intents
god bless america

Viejo

sí, yes, es verdad, we cannot
run too fast anymore,
but we know that if a thief
overtakes us,
on any street corner,
we will not allow ourselves
to be touched.
we will talk mildly
to the assailant.
we will hand over to
the sinvergüenza
everything in our possession,
and, if we're walking with a lady,
we will calm all our emotions,
bien tranquilito, "take it all,
you can have it, just don't hurt the lady,
do anything you want to me,
we will turn our backs,
walk in the middle of the street,
without any trouble, go in peace,
take it all."

good. he took it all,
but he left me intact,
but i know he lives in the neighborhood,
i will not call the police,
the network of our bodega, barbería
bakeries will identify el canalla,
my grandson fights karate,
he went out looking for his heart,
to deliver it to his mother,
and i told him it was my business,
so everybody,
can rest assured,
that any moment, now,
his groins
will be ground
as basement

appetizers
for
alley
cat's
milk— verdad
socio?

Melao

Melao was nineteen years old
when he arrived from Santurce
speaking spanish streets

Melao is thirty nine years old
in New York still speaking
Santurce spanish streets
en español

Melaíto his son now answered
in black american soul english
talk with native plena sounds
and primitive urban salsa beats

somehow Melao was not concerned
at the neighborly criticisms
of his son's disparate sounding talk

Melao remembered he was criticized
back in Puerto Rico for speaking
arrabal black spanish in the
required english class

Melao knew that if anybody
called his son american
they would shout puertorro
in english and spanish
meaning i am Puerto Rican
coming from
yo soy boricua
jíbaro dual mixtures
of Melao and Melaíto's
spanglish speaking son
así es la cosa papá

Bochinche Bilingüe

los únicos que tienen
problemas con el vernáculo
lingüístico diario de nuestra gente
cuando hablan oralmente
las experiencias de su cultura popular
son los que estudian solamente
a través de los libros
porque no tienen tiempo para
hablarle a nadie ya que se pasan
analizando y categorizando
la lengua exclusivamente
sin practicar el lenguaje.

el resto de estos
boring people
son extemistas aburridos,
educadores perfumados,
consumidores intelectuales
de la lengua clásica castellana
al nivel del siglo dieciocho,
monolingües racistas en inglés,
monolingües comemierdas en español,
filósofos nihilistas,
y revolucionarios mal entendidos,
todos comparten
una gran pendeja
minoría.

Lucha Corpi

Invernario

En los ojos que observaron
la tormenta avecinarse
había calles empedradas
y trigales todavía húmedos
por la lluvia de la noche,
un triángulo de sombra
entre dos casas blancas,
un viejo campesino con su violín
envuelto en periódico
en camino a la feria del pueblo.

Me observé en esos ojos
como quien mira en el mar
su imagen fragmentada,
por la corriente indómita
y la ve convertirse
en coral
y sombra
y pez
en roca
y mineral fosforescente.

Desde entonces
aprisionado
entre el demiángulo del ojo
y el origen del cantar
como un suicida impenitente
me acecha mi deseo
por sus brazos.

Fuga

Cansada de llevar en los ojos
resplandor, muro y silencio
y al oído
un rumor de alas y lluvia,
entre adiós y puerta inesperada
me decidí por el fuego
y en su promesa de agostos oportunos
mi corazón ardió
una noche de invierno.

Crucé la insolente geometría
que tus manos construyeran
en las agrestes latitudes de febrero.

Tu milagrería de tigres al acecho lancé
a la insubordinada ecología del viento.

Lavé el sabor temible de tu piel
de mis labios.

Cautericé motivo, causa y sentimiento.

Borré tu mirada de mi cuerpo.

Y clausuré las puertas de la historia
para no recordar más tu nombre ni mi nombre.

Afuera
en el invierno de los dioses
con mano temblorosa destapé el silencio.

Conjuré las semillas del fuego.

Las sentí palpitar en mis sienes, en mis pechos.
En el espacio abierto de mis dedos eran

    sangre

trigo

y luz de junio.

Eran la noche y sus mil ojos

crepúsculo

dolor

y canto

y la espiga tendida en el campo

acantilado

delta

y pez dorado

secretos de estrellas en la arena

escama

espuma

y sal

y el lamento melancólico de la ballena
anunciando la amplitud ecuánime
de un equinoccio boreal.

212 / *Lucha Corpi*

Canción de invierno

A *Magdalena Mora*
(*1952–1981*)

En un abrir
y cerrar de ojos
lleno de
magia
relojes
y sueños viejos
llega el invierno:

El viento rumora melancólico
como el todoencalma del sereno
que velaba la casa de mis padres
—ahí vuelvo cada invierno
para no olvidar quién soy
ni de dónde vengo.

Cantando baja la lluvia
a su destino de mineral y semilla.

Entre el hueco del ala que se extiende
y el entrecerrar de la mirada que descansa
aprendemos a amar en instantes y entregas
y entre la pregunta íntima de la noche
y la respuesta dulciobscura de la madrugada
gestamos dolorosamente una nueva vida.

Nada hay fijo ni perenne
ni la lluvia
ni la semilla
ni tú
ni yo
ni nuestro dolor
en este mundo que sangra
porque vamos siempre tirando senda,
abriendo brecha por caminos desconocidos,
venciendo la furia del olvido verso a verso.

Ricardo Sánchez

En-ojitos: canto a Piñero

recuerdos dejan huellas
en las humosas palabras
El Paso—10 Nov. 88

we joked once, Piñero,
on nuyorican streets
while visions fused
a world of biting sounds
weaving chicano-boricua
tales of survival
through steel-cement barbarities,

short-eyed enojos unfurled
legacies yet to be understood,
in those ojitos
an "enojo" burnished
nuyorican reality and served it
with a dry-witted feeling

as hungered denizens
careened through loisaida avenues,
each pair of eyes
not able to match
the intensity of Mikey
spiking madness
into another day of survival,

words swirled upon
the asphalt, each
a universe of streets'
survival training
as you lurched through
a nation
which only saw the surface

while the inner pain
embroiled a borinquen sensibility
breaking through
layers of amerikan plastique,
unraveling an island's mystique
through the bars and barbarity
of our isolation,
simón que yes, carnal
of the fiery pen
and pensive eyes
which bore into our consciousness,

your words pierce and uncover
the film within
the mindsoul, the poems & sketches
gouge as they caress,
the truths hurt, but the pain
is one of growth & knowing . . .
    adiós, Mikey, adiós . . .

Notas a Federico García Lorca
(con disculpas y festejos)

infechable / el sentimiento
recorre mundos solitarios
San Anto

I.

plateadas eran las noches
en la jungla nuevayorquina,
chillantes fueron los gritos
en la mayateada esquina,

la cuchara de polvo excitante
brillaba en los ojos del mono,
brindaba expresión inconstante
matándonos con abandono;

el gitano llegó angustiado
labrando poemas dorados,
con un canto enajenado
compartió con los malvados,

ay, reyes de pieles morenas,
cocodrilos y azucenas,
chillantes fueron los gritos,
sangrientos asfaltos y arenas;

se oyeron los pasos nocturnos
por las barriadas norteñas,
buscando mundos y turnos
de hombres perdidos sin señas,

dentro lo gris de las sombras,
poemas mordieron la luna,
de caras hizo alfombras
del todo hizo su tuna,

ay, Lorca, poeta y mago,
tu voz nuestra golondrina,

en cosas de amor fuiste vago,
maestro de palabra fina ...

II.

years have died, young poets have lived,
and reptilian images have danced
upon Harlem Streets
within spoonfuls of dreams
harpooned into arms and legs,
leaving humpedback dreams
riding simian hopelessness
on the El overlooking hungered/mean street
monologues haranguing the self
on veins dried and pillaged,
feeling dies
on teeming avenues,
eyes desiccate
while crocodile fangs
slash through the creeping silence,

Lorca, the word,

the poet,

the nuance
dwells in hidden causeways
burrowing through
Queens, Brooklyn,
Bedford-Sty, Long Island Sound,
Lower Eastside poetics café,
sojourning in all minds seeking reason,
within the respite and the mania,
nimbly evading ultrarealistic imagery
within the daemon words
cascading on brownstone laden streets,
as dilated yeska-pupils dance upon
wives—unchastized—swirling
on asphalt-cement-jungle floors,
twirling gitana earrings glisten

as pride rides on the trigger
while mad-eyed believers
deliver a poet's dreams
unto the mud-encased ravine,
all the while
nocturne melodies
play at your five o'clock songfest
the same holy requiem oft requested
    when three friends dined
    on verdant lizard pastries,
    drinking the fairy blood
    of festooned hopes and boys,
then as now, now as then

when the Bronx was jelling its outcry
and the cracks in heated sidewalks
gave you shoots of weeded verses
and bent reeds of despair,
black hands saluted
King H of Harlem dejection,
silver harpoons shot whale powder
into veins of despair and rejection,

ay, Lorca,

anguished and self-assailed,
stoker of insight into the nether madness
of humankind, your eyes gouged
the barren humanscapes of New York City
corridors of alienation, your eyes cut
through the fabric of distortion
while caressing Daliesque grotesqueries
on the gypsy canvas of a Spain
lurching through Republican, Fascist,
Nazi, communist, anarchist, Christian
xenophobic Iberian strains, robed
and mad-hatted, processional phantasms
plumed mind theatrically hurling out
barbed incantations,
the utterings churning/burning,
embossing imagery, fulminating metaphors

processional

incessant marching, chanting
phantasms, ay, Lorca, siren poet
to cloistered/fearful voices
seeking in you the key, the outlet
in every hermitage, in every human zoo,

Lorca of the biting lover in green,
green in the passion of self, drawn
within a gleam
in Dalí's song to himself,
drawn within whispers
and nocturnal caresses,
furtive and unfaithful
within a wife's fear and hope
of being found out, verses, oh,
verses cut the deserving
while appeasing
the also deserving,
awaiting only
the penetration of a slug,
a fine, furious lead point,
the heated metal gnashing
through the word, slashing
metaphor and pirouetting
upon the fine-limned image
of a Lorquian dialectic
when there were no guards
who were civil, and
later Bernarda found many homes
as the world you anointed
with the pulsing-blooded-heart-beats
your anguish sibilated
now pays homage
to a vagabond, wounded poet
singing blue-grey notes of incomprehension
to a swarming multitude
still stumbling
toward the life giving spoon
harpooning

black-armed-shrinking-blue-ridged-veins,
oh, green of ambuscaded promise & poesies,

drinks and racks shore up
vengeful robes riding through Spanish plains,
h(a)unting coasts and portal cities,
gnashing their way through layers
of Iberian lisping plaintive wails,
gladhanding touring critics,
each an explosive expletive—
a ready rifle seeking a creative mind
to explode into legendary words and myths,
the taurian poet bellows
and paws the sands,
poetry sings its challenge
as virgin song wails
through brassy notes—

   "Olé," the plaza cries

as the sun drenches an España
awaiting a gitano's cante jondo
to ululate a blood-spawn poem
on the granulated earth,

I walked the cement-steel jungle
of Soledad, clutching
verses hurling New York
at toilet-grey-colored-bars,
resonant and chaotic words
woven into images of discovery,
feeling the slug
lead-pointing its poison
on a ravine bank of a ravenous Iberia,

ay, Lorca,

blooded poems and weddings
again await a gitano's cante jondo
to dig deep into ritual and tribulation,
caressively exploring nuance and sensibility

only to unravel the deprecations
of centuries-old incantations

that

green verses and verbs might flow
and inundate the senses, Lorca ...

III.

cáscaras de naranja,
miel de la humanidad,
castaños pensamientos
y verde la moralidad;

crujías de seres inertos,
castillo de grandes promesas,
vanguardia de imágen y canto,
fusiles y muecas en fresas ...

IV.

te encontré, Lorca,
a la orilla
de un barranco de acero,
en una celda
donde se moldeaban
almas de azufre y cobre,
vi tu sonrisa gitana
culebrear por una fila de rejas,
las sombras bailaban
enloquecientes rimas
en lo infinito de un mundo sin sueños,

abrí tus páginas, Lorca,
con la locura de un duende,
buscando en tu canto a Whitman
una cáscara de vida-frutal,
la noria daba aguas

y mi sed brindaba

al océano de imágen y canto
inundando lo solitario
del cimento y acero
de mis ensueños ...

V.

ante los fusiles
un poema lloró
lo grande de su expresión,
el plomo voló
con fuerza torquemeante,
los crédulos festejaron
lo vacío de sus antojos ...

VI.

there is only music now
    at five in our afternoon,
there is the green of our hopes
    at five in our afternoon,
there is the peace of our dreams
    at five in our afternoon,
there is romance in our hopes
    at five in our afternoon,
and
from harshness our eyes turn away
    at five in our afternoons ...

VII.

de tres amigos
quedó uno,
loco en su traje de duende,
    festivo y malicioso,
duende distorsionado
por la fantasía mundial
distorsionando
una verdad ilusiva,
de tres amigos
vivió uno

entumbado
en el corazón del mundo,
    Don Federico García Lorca,
poeta dorado de sangre ...

Dear Tía

I do not write.
The years have frightened me away.
My life in a land so familiarly foreign,
a denial of your presence.
Your name is mine.
One black and white photograph of your youth,
all I hold on to.
One story of your past.

The pain comes not from nostalgia.
I do not miss your voice urging me in play,
your smiles,
or your pride when others called you my mother.
I cannot close my eyes and feel your soft skin;
listen to your laughter;
smell the sweetness of your bath.
I write because I cannot remember at all.

Papa

The two sat on the shoreline
under a piercing sun
ignoring the calls of their children
begging them to join them in play.

Both shared moments never lived
as wrinkled bodies crossed them
offering advice.

Without a glance they continued
almost whispering about a sacred man,
an outcast of their past,
an omen in their future.

Diana Rivera

Learning to Speak

On a cold, rainy day,
we walked to the fishermen's village,
shacks sealed by dry palm leaves,
but if they have walls they usually have
no roof,
and the wooden boats lap over waves baptized
"Goddess," "Our Faith,"
"La Chaconzita,"
and we gathered conch shells, corals
carved by sea breezes and warm shallow waters,
and we walked toward the unknown fish that gasped over sand,
her last breath
was our frail misunderstanding
that it could be her first
cry of living hope—
and we returned it to the sea
but she was soon washed ashore again
near where her dear ones glittered, danced translucent
fat like small tender breasts
silver and striped and humming their underwater
joy of life,
and we walked to where the black
baby snails quivered
in masses under the thin
layer of refracting water;
how they stretched their wormy
vulnerable selves
coiling, uncoiling
away from our path of footsteps
where, even the conch shells
bruised by the sea,
travelled and glittered,
their splendor within.

Time
creaks,
the chango lands on the grape branch,
the one tree
in a multitude of others
shedding flames of orange leaves,
toll two notes—
joy, pain,
land inside our balcony, shudder
in fear, feed on our coffee crumbs.
Sand travels between wind-chimes
and carries something
in-between her hands.

All at once
on a wet edge of sand, a wave unfurls,
sand is licked dry by wisps of air,
the wave slides back into the sea
in the trance of the unfinished;

nearby, fifty sandpipers edge the ocean line,
their tiny cross-legged feet
marking the newly dry sand.
They avoid crossing the wet edge
leading into the throbbing rush,
the ending crash,
the sulphuric splash—

and then, another wave comes
to dissolve
the old one.

We wait patiently
for the black, coagulated clouds
to move away from over our heads—
dark, ominous, treacherous haloes and diadems—
with the help of this wind which is our salvation
but also makes us cold,
we wait
for the 'blue' to filter through like a worthy, shining sword,
and strike us

living—

Passing
passive elements
we dream through—

Instead,
the change,
entering into the realm of selfhood
comes when we remove
the dark veil of the bruised and buried
feelings we hide.
We rip this veil
and tear it away with words
(For godly lips we have
for a more divine, mysterious purpose
than singing,
or practical speech.
Not even the poet's written tongue can save us,
this old purgation, sepulchre of distillation,
this odd catharsis, opening chasms
to veer and understand
what flickers, stiff or alive.)
In the eternal interim much is changed, disguised,
made lovely,
and somehow, the lips of the poetic heart
remain sealed
from those we live with.

All that is ugly
throbs to be freed.

Wind-tilted trees, palm strands
speak of stroking blue space
like the slender fingers of a far-away pianist.
Children carry little plastic cups of water for their
castles,
small dreamy footsteps in the sand
which the light rain
fossilizes—indentations
which mark a lifetime in the furrows of heels and toes.

Oh, raindrops, please don't come again
to wash away our wholly reverent
footsteps in the sand

but somehow, in the distance,
a hairline-cracked
storm begins to form.
Dense and confused clouds shade the ocean olive green
and from the tips of crashing waves a steady mist
rises to suffuse us.

Seagulls, angels and vampires,
glide majestically over us,
the glittered dome pours open.

Learning to speak,
which can bring love,
bursts our welled hearts.
At once the coolness
glares to warmth.
The hooks of the mast ropes uncoil
clanging against the mast
of the boat settled on grass
facing the sea.

Our black, leathery birds
sing of their pain,
their flesh
and feathers burn.
The sky jerks tearing
her gloom, easing
the ache,
starlings strewn to every tree.

Fluid, in our own fluids,
gushed in moon-liquids,
moon-gulls above,
milk-gulls our eyes,
we learn to speak
like any child would.

Pablo Medina

Madame America

I.
Privy

Midnight he entered
the dream shore where oceans pounded
and fish puckered for the kiss of maidens.

Midnight and his bladder sang.
Finished, too
tired to revel in relief,
he pushed the lever, saw Hades' mouth
fill quicker than it could swallow,
dribble over icy lips
down stony chin to toes:
islands, minnows in tidal waste,
stunned amphibians.

2.
Poker

She lay on a crimson recliner
languorous, fully dressed. Her caftan
swelled with every breath. The candle
flickered and he thought of Jewish Alps,
Shoshone burial mounds . . .
Outside hyacinths were blooming,
peonies were up.

His last card was the ace of clubs.
Her white feet arched, the night
was hers. She wagered all: her clothes,
the fillets on her hair, her crescent
custom pin. He stiffened. She yawned.
The room was still. A scent of lilac

and musk tarnished the air.

"Do you call me or raise?"
She mocked his scant mannering.

When the moon broke
and the eel's fast ended she showed her hand.

Landscape, bare yourself!

3.
Spanish Lesson

"Ven" he said, accented
but impervious. "Dame lo que das."

Water she,
sluicing water,
sent him headlong to despair
where he wallowed till he woke.

She went home
with wallet and watch.
Day's work for day's wages.

Joseph the last of his names
he made his choice:
clean teeth and the radiance of failure.
"Death will wear me smiling."

4.
Next-to-Last Supper

He cooked horizons.
Star tongues slapped
the roof of night.

He lived insouciant to the end
and listened to the neighbor's dogs
yelping at the heels of time.

The pan of his thought lay idle,

lard of memory popping,
insomnia the flame.

The breeze was tar, the evening
on its steel bed sighed
for the mothers of dawn.

He closed his eyes and his hunger died
and he sank to where the fish sleep
and the earth cries.

5.
Deluge

    Under the pillow was sand,
splinters from an ancient tree,

centuries of syntax,
syllables of land, pruned mind,
heart in brine.

Words fell apart
turned Babel babe hell
tongue slither grunt
Calliope.

The angels of Freedom
gathered pieces with the up
side down
and let the punctuation loose

touch me
rub my knee
one
last
blessed
time

Après moi

232 / Pablo Medina

The Apostate

To breathe fire
in this land is a conspiracy
of wrong.

The moon outside
wanes over yellowing fields.

Only the teeth of barking dogs
give light.

There is coffee
and phones ringing
and funereal smoke.

Na na, na na sings a girl
on the road into autumn.
She stops, she turns, she goes.

Far away behind the hills—
birth, red earth.

Behind that
God's face receding.

The land is full of innocence
and comfortable slumber.
Na na, na na.
Few birds remain. The grass
is dying. The earth turns hard.

Lorna Dee Cervantes

The Poet Is Served Her Papers

So tell me about fever dreams,
about the bad checks
we scrawl with our mouths,
about destiny missing
last bus to oblivion.
I want to tell lies
to the world and believe it.
Speak easy, speak
spoken to, speak lips
opening on a bed of nails.
Hear the creaking of cardboard
in these telling shoes?
The mint of my mind
gaping far out of style?
Hear the milling
of angels on the head
of a flea? My broke blood
is sorrel, is a lone
mare, is cashing in
her buffalo chips.
As we come to the cul-de-sac
of our heart's slow division
tell me again about true
love's bouquet, paint hummingbird
hearts taped to my page.
Sign me over
with xxx's and "passion."
Seal on the lick
of a phone—
my life. And pay.
And pay. And pay.

Blue Full Moon in Witch

I come to you on an angel's moon,
when heat off foam rises to a crest,
on sheets of stainless sea, on
shallowed ice on shattered diamond leis,
where above it all an arctic cauldron lies
and covers us in woven halo gems.
Spring still forms and shudders crystals.
Since before the hail there is this ring.
Before the rest there is this missing
fractured light in the captioned
reruns of our dreams. I want you
and my heart still licks
its heaven. I want you
and heaven pulls its ring.

From the Cables of Genocide

Who gave you permission to detonate
this neutron bomb in my heart?
My imploding senses reel
in the left over scent of you,
squirrel, plural wrecker, acorn
masher. My laurel leaves
whither to ash, the clot
of my rose, a dirt devil
in the branches of my veins.
Proven destination, where are you
now? Does the blood still flow
camellias like a slap when I see you
crossing my backyards, the alleys
where we met, where we kissed
red stars? Moon of my moon,
let me wish you. Let April
catch in the throat of our beating
white flags. Let me not be
the only fool standing.
The only gas breathed
is you.

On Love and Hunger

You can want to do nothing and then decide instead to do this: make leek soup, I mean. Between the will to do something and the will to do nothing is a thin, unchanging line: suicide.

—Marguerite Duras, *Leek Soup*

I feed you
as you hunger.
I hunger
as you feed
and refuse
the food I give.

Hunger is the first sense.
Imagination is the last.
You are my sixth sense,
imaginary lover,
missed meal.

Food is the first choice,
first flaw, fatal
in its accessibility,
fearless on the tongue
of mean denial.

First word,
first sight.

Food is love
in trust.

The Captive's Verses

after Neruda

There is another side to you
un lago where the huesos
border in ripples of hot
and cold water. A mammal

breath upon the hair of your
chest. Chrysanthemums
in your ears, your pods,
stellular. I would tell

of another isle, another gill
upon the shark's fin of you,
an infestation of expectations.
Espíritus. Adelante. Bury

it all. Gold upon break.
You are Captain of it all.
And me, the ship's booty.
You are brave. Decay.

I'm left my cunning. My
country ruined. My nation,
wasted. My wash of it,
left wringing in the mud.

My bloodmeal seals the crop.
There is this side to you:
He who doesn't give her
any pleasure but triggers it,

cocksure by doubt. By love
I swear by it.
Bite by it.
Swear.

Leo Romero

I Bring Twins Over to Meet Pito

I bring twins over to meet
Pito, I thought they'd go
for him because they're short
But not as short as Pito
At 4'10" they tower over him
They look at each other
and give each other identical
looks, I wonder what their looks
mean, The same old stuff, I think
You're ready to go? I ask
They look at each other and
give each other those same
identical looks, What do you
make of it? I whisper to Pito
I think they like me, he says
Both of them? I ask, Sure
says Pito, what's not to like
doubly, That was a fun night
They stayed for hours, Not
saying much but looking beautiful
And that pleased Pito, But
they didn't spend the night
with him, I don't know any woman
who's ever done that, And when
I drove them home, I wondered
which one of them I'd kiss
Perhaps both I thought, And when
I parked, I said, Well, fun night
And they looked at each other
giving each other those identical
looks and then they burst out
laughing, It was that much fun?
I said, They laughed all the way

to their door, You ever tried
to kiss someone who was laughing?

How Did I Land Up in this City

How did I land up in this city
How did I land up in this room
Pito wonders, A coffin room
he thinks, Hardly enough room
to turn around, that's how he feels
most of the time, It's been twenty
years he's been stuck in this city
Born in Mexico, he never found anything
better than this city, this room
How did I land up in this life
He thinks in this dwarf's body, Not
my body, he thinks, A real mistake
that he's been paying for all
his life, I never bargained for this
he thinks, and wonders how it could
have been different, Where in time
it could have been avoided, His
parents meeting, that's it, he thinks
Why did they do what they did do
Pito is perplexed, If he could have
stopped the doing, but how, How
indeed, he wonders, and gone is youth
and all the avenues are leading
to the old city, Old city building
Old city room, Old city Pito, growing
old before he can figure it all out
And what good would it do, anyway
he thinks, Late as it all is
It was too late to begin with
he thinks, That's Pito for you
sitting back and thinking hard.

Pito Had a Dream That

Pito had a dream that
Diane Arbus came
to his door, I had been
showing him her photographs
and talking about her
the day before
She says, says Pito,
that she had seen me walking
in the park, And she
follows me and she's got
all these cameras hanging
from her neck, and she says
Can I come in, I want
to get to know you
and I want to photograph you
and I say, You'll have
to go to bed with me
And she says, Sure
as if it was something
she was expecting to do
That stunned me, says Pito
I never had a woman say yes
before, But first, she says
let's talk, and I say
about what, and she says
tell me about everything
in this place, and while
I'm talking, she's rummaging
through my dresser drawers
poking her nose into everything
She even finds the porno
magazines I had hidden
And she says, Do these
do anything for you, they
don't do anything for me
She flips through them
You should see the photos
of genitalia I have, she says

I'll bring them over sometime
she says, I'm stunned
I'm too stunned to tell her
to stop poking her nose
into everything, finally
I tell her to leave, Get
out of here, I tell her
But we haven't had sex
yet, she says, I have to
throw her out practically
And then I notice all
of her cameras are on the floor
and she's banging on the door
Yelling for her cameras
Calling me every obscene name
I can't believe it, I say
to Pito, even in your dreams
you can't make it
with a woman, and after
all the lusting you do
Pito seems ashamed
that he mentioned the dream
When I woke up, he says,
I was sweating, it seemed
so real, I looked all over
for her cameras, and I
listened at the door
wondering if she was out there
I really blew it, I
thought to myself, this
normal woman wants to go
to bed with me, and I
kick her out, but she was
getting too deep,
And I could tell, if we
got into bed, she'd see
me for all that I was
It was embarrassing
and then I
couldn't believe how angry
I was getting

It was just a dream
I say to Pito, in real
life I bet you would have
gone to bed with her
You think so, Pito says
sounding relieved
You better believe it, I say
Let's look at those pictures
again, he says, And I start
showing him the Diane
Arbus book again
That photo, people
Would spit at it when it
it was at the Museum of Modern Art,
I can believe it
says Pito, Let's get to
the picture where she's
in my room,
What? I say, there isn't
any such picture, Remember
It was just a dream
That's right, says Pito
I was forgetting
And you say she's dead
Yeah, she killed herself,
She didn't have any friends?
Sure, I say,
I don't know why
she killed herself
If I ever see her in a dream
again, says Pito, I'll
be nicer to her.

Diane's Knocking

Diane's knocking
on the doors of his dreams
all night, Pito, let
me in, he hears her far
away fading voice
But the knocking is louder
each time, mountains
of knocking, and he's afraid
to answer, because he
knows Diane is dead, and
what can he do about that
and what does she want
from him, Take his picture
is all she wants, she says
through the cracks of the
door, she whispers it
seductively, more seductively
coming as it does
from death, Open up, Pito
she says, I will do anything
she says, to take your picture
And Pito is terrified of this
voice and of his dream room
and the dream doors that
resound louder and louder
with deathly demands, and
when he wakes up he never
wants to go back to sleep
Not like in the beginning
In the beginning of his
love affair with Diane, he
could accept that she was
dead, but dreams, he had thought
they should be safe, safe
to love the dead in dreams
Now he knows there's no safe
place, and dreams worst of all.

When Pito Tried to Kill

When Pito tried to kill
me with his knife, long
switchblade that slit
my side, but not bad just
cut the flesh, bled worse
than it was, I knew it was
because he was crazed with
Diane and the wine of a
long night gone to the dogs
And when I promised to
kill him in return, I thought
I could do it, but then I
thought, what would I do
Cradle him in my arms
with the life out of him
or the life seeping out of
him and no scotch tape
or any glue to hold it in
I could kill him, I know
But then where would I be
But I promised him, and
all because of Diane, we
both love her too much
And all for a dead woman
When Pito came at me, I
could see myself dying
and Pito yelling at me
as my slippery blood poured
out on the floor like
the flowing blood of slaughter
houses, Him yelling at me
You're going to her, aren't
you, You son of a bitch, you
pushed me to kill you, so you'd
be with her, Pito, I'd say
I love her, You don't know
love, I'd say to Pito, as
I was dying, You never loved

no one, I'd say to Pito, not
even a dog much less a woman
I saw all that coming as
he lunged at me with his
brilliant knife, But it was
only a flesh wound, You got
yours coming I yelled
tripping him to the floor
and getting out the door
And I heard him yelling
drunkenly after me, You
don't go talking about her
no more, and I yelling back
I can talk of anyone I love
You're dead, he yelled, and
I could hear him sobbing
We're all dead, I yelled back
And so I left that place
And I dreamed a dream of Diane
And she said to me, You two
were fighting for me, weren't
you, and I said, we were
And she placed her hand on
my bleeding wound that was
still flowing like a river
and she placed her hand in
and I couldn't believe how deep
that wound was, Her arm
went all the way in, and then
all of her had disappeared
into my wound, Diane, I yelled
Get out of there, that's my
wound, I yelled, not yours
But she was not hearing me
She had gone into the hurting
that had become unbearable
So unbearable that I could
have killed myself to end
the pain, And there was a knocking
in that dream, and it was Pito
I know she's in there, he yelled

Let me in, he yelled, And
I looked frightened at my
wound, but there was no trace
of Diane, And I wouldn't open
the door for Pito or say a word
And the knocking grew louder
on the dream door, in my dream
life, and anyway there is no
difference between walking and
sleeping, and the only thing
is hurting, Diane I whisper to
the deep inside of me, I know
you're there, Come out, I
whisper, How can I love you
inside of me, I whisper, Diane
I hear Pito yell from beyond the
door What you've done with Diane
And then I smile a little
But I don't answer, I'm at peace
Even with all this hurting, I'm
at peace.

Rane Arroyo

Blonde as a Bat

Me, I'm Ricardo and I was born blonde as a bat.

Sometimes you have to improvise—it's like being stoned and you know the saxophone inside your head is going to hit one perfect note that you know is going to just shatter your wisdom teeth—but it doesn't happen.

Then out of nowhere, a surprise.

Night gives you something else.

A moan.

A whisper.

A moon saying nothing, nothing at all but still somehow the sound it doesn't make hurts your ears.

I figure bleaching my hair is not a very big deal in such a big universe.

It's just that simple.

Why I don't have blue contacts for my eyes, that's another story and it's not that simple.

Maybe one day I'll bring pictures in of me as a kid.

There is one of me at Lincoln Zoo where I look like a runaway penguin.

I always knew I looked good in black—black pants, black leather coat, a black eye.

At school I use to pretend I couldn't pick out the state of Illinois from the other 50 states but I always knew which one it was—it's the only state that looks like a top that is about to stop spinning.

Once I used to cry whenever my top stopped spinning.

I wanted it to spin forever because I figured, even then, that forever must be longer than two or three minutes.

Yeah, my heart gets broken all the time.

I'm used to it.

I'm a romantic and I have to play any jukebox that I happen to see.

And I think about Sal Mineo a lot.

I wonder what he was feeling after *Rebel Without A Cause*?

Did he walk around the movie set thinking of ways he could spend all the money he was making now that he was a movie star?

The funny bastard is dead, right?

I mean in the movie, not in life—well he is dead in life but NOT to me.

Sal Mineo lives.

He's flesh and blood to me.

And I don't care if he had to taste James Dean.

None of my business.

A hero is a hero and you take your hero in whatever shape the hero shows up in.

Finding a hero is tough business.

There were the fat Mexicans in the movies.

They could never be my heroes though they did dress in black.

They looked like my father.

Fatter.

You knew they were going to be killed.

Heroes never die in front of your eyes—it's a kind of universal law.

The rule says there can't be a camera in sight when heroes bite bullets.

Ricky Ricardo?

The human Cuban cigar?

He could have been a hero.

He had the looks and I bet he owned his own tuxedo too.

That's something.

But he married a redhead, a very famous red-head instead of a blonde.

She never taught little Ricky to talk Spanish and you know my name is Ricky and I knew she would have been a terrible mother if I had been her son which I wasn't and that's one thing I'm grateful for.

If little Ricky ever got lost in the streets of Havana, how the hell would he take care of himself?

What kind of mother is that?

What kind of hero lets his son get raised like that?

No—it was Sal Mineo, all the way.

He was dark.

You knew that he would have to fry his hair for hours just to get those smooth long waves.

He had eyes that were black as a blind man's moon.

He always looked up so slowly and he always turned away so quickly and that's because he had the kind of eyes that you could see through.

I don't have those eyes, but I do see things.

Sometimes when I ride a bus I can tell when a girl just got pregnant and maybe she doesn't even know it yet—but I do.

I hear the baby just knocking at the door to this world and I'm not talking about the world you see in the movies.

It's crying "Are there heroes out there?" And you better tell me the truth because I'll find you somehow and someday.

It stretches its little bat wings.

It thinks it'll be the one to finally put out the sun with its wings.
I tell you baby that my friend Sal Mineo tried putting out the sun.
I've tried it too.
Chase the sun and it'll just lead you to another sunrise, kid.
I'm blond as a bat and see how I'm on fire with every day I've ever lived.

Columbus's Children

I have stood at the corner of Broadway and Clark—what the poets in Chicago call *The Crotch of the Midwest*—and I like that because I have a crotch too—and on that corner I once had a fight with another Spanish man—tattooed on his knuckles was the world F A T E —I was dressed in clean clothes—invisible in a crowd of so many other people—Americans I call them—they call me Johnny because in Chicago that's short for Juan—I was lost among Americans—and then out of nowhere he bumped into me— and I said excuse me—and he said that my mother had to rape my father to make me—and I said that his mother made food that gave nuns gas—and he raised his fists at me—and I raised mine—and I could just feel our mothers fall to their knees—suddenly filled with the need to scrub all the places their children have contaminated with their shadows—and a police car drove by and we both stopped fighting—and then raised our fists again—and I said Rico why are we fighting—then he punched me in the mouth because words were his weakest muscles—I saw blue cars drive right through flashing red lights—and I could see the neon light in the dentist's office across the street— and I felt the pain of my first punch when I was ten years old—Georgie from across the way—he was a white boy in a Green Beret suit he would grow into—Georgie would spit at me—you stupid sixth grader—and I was in the sixth grade—and so was Georgie but he had been a sixth grader twice— and at that moment I suddenly realized who had been smearing mud on our windows—my beautiful mother couldn't see outside to look at my father's garden—we were trapped in that house—and Rico hit me again because I wasn't hitting back—so I hit him—and the dance of angry atoms began— my friend I was with tried pulling us apart—think of the shame you give your fathers—fight them —not each other—but Rico, bleeding from where my fist pronounced itself, said where is your accent, where is your fucking accent—you talk American you are American—and then he jumped at me again—and the Great Ace guard looked out through a window and threw a dime at us—we could hear him laughing—how to stop—how to stop—I jumped at Rico—he jumped out of the way—we were really sweat dancing but then he pretended to twist his ankle—hey he said—you sure lucky your mother ate Mexican jumping beans when she had you—and then he ran across the street because the light had turned green and the Clark Street bus was coming down—I was breathing hard—the man turned around—grabbed his crotch with one hand and raised his fist with the other—I grabbed my crotch and became his mirror—then the bus left—and the fight was over— my friend who had tried breaking up the fight said to me—Ah hijo—hijo—I

252 / *Rane Arroyo*

hadn't been anyone's son in a long time—not in Chicago, not in Boston, not in New York, not in San Juan, not in Salt Lake City, not in San Diego—I hadn't been anyone's son—I hid the tears in my eyes—Where shall we go Johnny and get coffee—I think my adrenaline glands are shot to hell—I said to my friend—and he hit me on the back—saying a man is a man—and I looked into a closed clothing store's windows—my eyes were still brown—no one had slipped blue contacts into them while I was fighting—I had already lost my accent—I wasn't going to lose my eyes—we are all Columbus' Children I said—Yeah he said, Columbus just followed the direction his crotch led him to and look at the women he ended up with—America—and we laughed and we tried hiding the dance of our bones the best we could—we headed home, what we call home—and the crowd swept our footsteps clean—we had never been there, at the corner of the Clark and Broadway—never— never—never—

Gustavo Pérez Firmat

Lime Cure

I'm filling my house with limes
to keep away the evil spirits.
I'm filling my house with limes
to help me cope.
I have limes on the counters, under the sink,
inside the wash basin.
My refrigerator is stuffed with limes
(there's no longer any space for meat and potatoes).
Faking onionship, they hang from the walls.
Like golf balls, they have the run of the carpet
(but I would not drive them away).

I stash them in flowerpots.
I put them on bookshelves.
I keep them on my desk, cuddling with my computer.
I have two limes in every drawer of every chest
of every room.
I don't bathe, I marinade.

At night, I think of their cores, plump and wet.
I imagine myself taking off the peel and squeezing
until they burst in my hands.
I taste the tart juice dripping on my tongue.
I shudder.
Then I sleep peacefully inside green dreams of lime
and when I wake, I bask in the morning's lime light.

Were it not for limes, I would not know
what to do with myself.
I could not bear this loneliness.
I would burst. But there is a wisdom in limes, an uneventfulness
that soothes my seething, and whispers to me:
think, be still, and think some more,
and when the night arrives, dream of juice.

The Poet's Mother Gives Him a Birthday Present

Thirty masses is what I got
for my birthday. Thirty masses
and a bottle of Paco Rabanne.

> *Gustavo Pérez Firmat*
> *will share in the following*
> *spiritual benefits for one year:*
> *Thirty Masses*
> *Two Novenas of Masses*
> *Requested by Mrs. Gustavo Pérez*
> *Signed: Father Edward.*
> *Salesian Missions.*

It must be I'm tottering on the brink.
It must be I'm in perilous condition.
It must be I'm losing my soul.
Surely these are critical masses.
Jump start my soul, ma.
Pile mass on mass till I stop fibrillating.
Drip cool hosannas into the IV.
Pump me with 42 cc's of saintliness,
one for each of my errant years.
Slip that catholic catheter into my prick
and bring my peccant prostate to its knees.
Have me break out in ejaculations, ma.

Do it.
Make me holy.
Put an end to this wanton life.
I shall sin no more.
And all for you, ma.
All for you.

> *May the joy of this your birthday*
> *Continue all year through*
> *And make each day that comes your way*
> *A happy day for you!*

Amalio Madueño

Alambristas*

Alambristas curl in their sleep,
Turning their hips on the bushy hill.
Dreams come dashing across the brush,
Laughing, becoming an evening party,
Saying everything with street style,
Continually conversing, continually providing
What they want to know.

On the dark hill the dreamsmile
Twirls in the leaves, repeating itself
Like the leaves all around,
Smiling in each root and vein.
Delivering streets smart advice.

Turning in their sleep they dream
With city smiles expecting, approaching
The streets in a sauntering dream,
Turning in their corners on the quiet hill.

On the secluded hill the backstreets beckon,
Filling each man's dream with dread.
Each dreams the city's dream.
Each turns his corner. Each makes his scene.

Asleep on the hill they dream.
They see how the TVs glow in each window.
They feel the city dreaming them into the day.

---

*A border term for illegal aliens in the U.S.

The Bato Prepares for Winter

I

I cross Pennsylvania and
The desert speaks to me.
From the stare of monument stone
From the traffic's rage—
Speaks to me as my elders,
Each face a frosted shrub.

Cactus needles pierce my ears
As cold morning whispers.
Sand spills from my mouth
As I come home at night.

Blue Deer fetches me at sunrise
And my dream snakes
Down the alley to the river,
Settling in its black sludge.

Staked out to dry, waiting
For the weather, his dream expects
The right day to feel
Humming winter.

II

Day clouds scud the billboards.
Coyote descends to the house,
Cutting through yards and hedge.
Massachusetts sets its signals.
The house fills with underbrush.
Diamondback warms on the hearth.

A skull of ice pinned to the brick pile
Shivers with my reflection
As I feel the winter bite.